Fighting and Victimhood in International Criminal Law

The act of fighting or being a fighter has certain consequences in international law. The most obvious example can be found in international humanitarian law, where a distinction is drawn between fighters and civilians, with fighters being military objectives and civilians being protected from attack. Another example is from international human rights law, where it has been held that the particular characteristics of military life have to be taken into account when interpreting the human rights of members of state armed forces. This volume focuses on the field of international criminal law and asks the question: what relevance does fighting have to victimhood in international criminal law?

Among the topics that are explored are: how have international criminal courts and tribunals untangled lawful casualties of war from victims of war crimes? How have they determined who is a member of an organised armed group and who is not? What crimes can those who fight be victims of during hostilities? When does it become relevant in international criminal law that an alleged victim of a crime was a person *hors de combat* rather than a civilian? Can war crimes be committed against members of non-opposing forces? Can persons *hors de combat* be victims of crimes against humanity and genocide? What special considerations surround peacekeepers and child soldiers as victims of international crimes?

The author carries out an in-depth exploration of case law from international criminal courts and tribunals to assess how they have dealt with these questions. She concludes that the import of fighting upon victimhood in the context of international criminal law has not always been appreciated to the extent that it should have been.

Joanna Nicholson is a postdoctoral researcher at PluriCourts: Centre for the Study of the Legitimate Roles of the Judiciary in the Global Order, at the Faculty of Law, University of Oslo, Norway.

Routledge Research in International Law

For a full list of titles in this series, visit www.routledge.com/Routledge-Research-in-International-Law/book-series/INTNLLAW

Available:

Fighting and Victimhood in International Criminal Law
Joanna Nicholson

Human Security Discourse and International Law
A Principled Approach
Shireen Daft

Prosecuting Juvenile Piracy Suspects
The International Legal Framework
Milena Sterio

Nationalization, Natural Resources and International Investment Law
Contractual Relationship as a Dynamic Bargaining Process
Junji Nakagawa

Queering International Law
Possibilities, Alliances, Complicities, Risks
Edited by Dianne Otto

Sovereignty Conflicts and International Law and Politics
A Distributive Justice Issue
Jorge E. Núñez

The Rule of Law in the United Nations Security Council Decision-Making Process
Turning the Focus Inwards
Sherif Elgebeily

Universal Jurisdiction in International Criminal Law
The Debate and the Battle for Hegemony
Aisling O'Sullivan

Fighting and Victimhood in International Criminal Law

Joanna Nicholson

Routledge
Taylor & Francis Group
LONDON AND NEW YORK

First published 2018 by Routledge

2 Park Square, Milton Park, Abingdon, Oxfordshire OX14 4RN
52 Vanderbilt Avenue, New York, NY 10017

Routledge is an imprint of the Taylor & Francis Group, an informa business

First issued in paperback 2019

British Library Cataloguing in Publication Data
A catalogue record for this book is available from the British Library

Library of Congress Cataloging in Publication Data
Names: Nicholson, Joanna, (Lawyer), author.
Title: Fighting and victimhood in international criminal law /
Joanna Nicholson.
Description: New York, NY : Routledge, 2017. | Series: Routledge research in international law | Includes bibliographical references.
Identifiers: LCCN 2017022162 | ISBN 9781138669062 (hardback) |
ISBN 9781317210559 (Adobe Reader) | ISBN 9781317210542 (epub) |
ISBN 9781317210535 (Mobipocket)
Subjects: LCSH: Combatants and noncombatants (International law) | War (International law)–Protection of civilians. | International criminal law. |
Humanitarian law. | War victims–Legal status, laws, etc.
Classification: LCC KZ6515 .N53 2017 | DDC 345/.0238–dc23
LC record available at https://lccn.loc.gov/2017022162

ISBN: 978-1-138-66906-2 (hbk)
ISBN: 978-0-367-87777-4 (pbk)

Typeset in Galliard
by Taylor & Francis Books

To Dave, Poppy and Dougal

Contents

Acknowledgments

In its previous incarnation, this work was my doctoral thesis, written at the Norwegian Centre for Human Rights at the Faculty of Law, University of Oslo. I owe a huge debt of gratitude to my supervisors, Nobuo Hayashi and Jo Stigen, for their generous help throughout the writing process and beyond. My thanks to the academic and administrative staff at the Centre and at the Faculty of Law for their collegiality and support through the years. I also wish to thank Jann Kleffner, who commented at the mid-way examination for my thesis, and Kjetil Mujezinović Larsen, Robert Cryer and Paola Gaeta, who formed the committee for my defence, and gave me some excellent feedback and suggestions.

The thesis was transformed into its current form while I was sitting at PluriCourts, Centre for the Study of the Legitimate Roles of the Judiciary in the Global Order, University of Oslo. I am supremely grateful to PluriCourts' directors, Geir Ulfstein and Andreas Føllesdal, for giving me the time, space and opportunity to write the book, and to Cecilia Bailliet for her unfailing support and advice.

Many colleagues and friends have taken time to read and reflect on my work and discuss ideas with me. They are simply too many to mention individually, but I particularly wish to thank Anna Andersson, Isabel Mota Borges, Rozemarijn van der Hilst, Carola Lingaas and Gentian Zyberi. Thanks also to the staff of Routledge for their patience and help.

I am indebted to my family and friends who have accompanied me on this long journey: Ann, Trevor, Heidi, Mairi, Nick, Charlie, Morag, Joy, Kevin and Emma. Above all, thanks to my ever supportive, patient and loving husband, Dave, and my children, Poppy and Dougal, who for half their lives or more have had to endure a mother who has been preoccupied with the contents of this book.

Abbreviations

AbiH	Army of the Republic of Bosnia and Herzegovina
AC	Appeals Chamber
AFRC	Armed Forces Revolutionary Council
AMIS	African Union Mission in Sudan
APH	active participation in hostilities
CCW	Convention on Prohibitions or Restrictions on the Use of Certain Conventional Weapons
CDF	Civil Defence Forces
DPH	direct participation in hostilities
ECCC	Extraordinary Chambers in the Courts of Cambodia
ECHR	European Convention on Human Rights
ECMM	European Community Monitoring Mission
ECtHR	European Court of Human Rights
FN	footnote
HVO	Croatian Defence Council
IAC	international armed conflict
ICC	International Criminal Court
ICL	international criminal law
ICRC	International Committee of the Red Cross
ICT	international criminal tribunal
ICTR	International Criminal Tribunal for Rwanda
ICTY	International Criminal Tribunal for the former Yugoslavia
IHL	international humanitarian law
ILC	International Law Commission
ILO	International Labour Organization
JEM	Justice and Equality Movement
JNA	Yugoslav People's Army
NATO	North Atlantic Treaty Organization
NGO	non-governmental organisation
NIAC	non-international armed conflict
NLA	National Liberation Army of Macedonia
POW	prisoner of war
RUF	Revolutionary United Front

SCSL	Special Court for Sierra Leone
SFRY	Socialist Federal Republic of Yugoslavia
SLA	Sudan Liberation Army
SRK	Sarajevo Romanija Corps
TC	Trial Chamber
TO	Territorial Defence
UN	United Nations
UNAMIR	United Nations Assistance Mission in Rwanda
UNAMSIL	United Nations Mission in Sierra Leone
VCLT	Vienna Convention on the Law of Treaties

Table of cases and treaties

1863 Instructions for the Government of Armies of the United States in the Field (Lieber Code)
1864 Convention for the Amelioration of the Condition of Wounded in Armies in the Field (Geneva Convention 1864)
1868 Declaration Renouncing the Use, in Time of War, of Explosive Projectiles Under 400 Grammes Weight, Saint Petersburg (St Petersburg Declaration)
1874 Project of an International Declaration concerning the Laws and Customs of War (Brussels Declaration 1874)
1880 The Laws of War on Land, Oxford (Oxford Manual)
1899 Convention (II) with Respect to the Laws and Customs of War on Land and its annex: Regulations concerning the Laws and Customs of War on Land (Hague Regulations 1899)
Declaration (IV, 2) concerning Asphyxiating Gases
1906 Convention for the Amelioration of the Condition of the Wounded and Sick in Armies in the Field (Geneva Convention 1906)
1907 Convention (IV) Respecting the Laws and Customs of War on Land with its Annex, Regulations concerning the Laws and Customs of War on Land (Hague Regulations 1907)
1925 Protocol for the Prohibition of the Use of Asphyxiating, Poisonous or Other Gases, and of Bacteriological Methods of Warfare (1925 Gas Protocol)
1929 Convention for the Amelioration of Conditions of the Wounded and Sick in Armies in the Field
1945 Charter of the International Military Tribunal, annexed to the London Agreement for the Prosecution and Punishment of the Major War Criminals of the European Axis (London Charter)
Control Council Law No 10, Punishment of Persons Guilty of War Crimes, Crimes against Peace and against Humanity (Control Council Law No 10)
1948 Convention on the Prevention and Punishment of the Crime of Genocide (Genocide Convention)
Universal Declaration of Human Rights

1949 Geneva Convention for the Amelioration of the Condition of the Wounded and Sick in Armed Forces of the Field (Geneva Convention I)

Geneva Convention for the Amelioration of the Condition of Wounded, Sick and Shipwrecked Members of Armed Forces at Sea (Geneva Convention II)

Geneva Convention Relative to the Treatment of Prisoners of War (Geneva Convention III)

Geneva Convention Relative to the Protection of Civilian Persons in Time of War (Geneva Convention IV)

1950 Convention for the Protection of Human Rights and Fundamental Freedoms (ECHR)

1969 Vienna Convention on the Law of Treaties (VCLT)

1972 Convention on the Prohibition of the Development, Production and Stockpiling of Bacteriological (Biological) and Toxin Weapons and on their Destruction (Biological Weapons Convention)

1977 Protocol Additional to the Geneva Conventions of 12 August 1949, and relating to the Protection of Victims of International Armed Conflicts (Protocol I)

Protocol Additional to the Geneva Conventions of 12 August 1949 and relating to the Protection of Victims of Non-international Armed Conflicts (Protocol II)

1980 Convention on Prohibitions or Restrictions on the Use of Certain Conventional Weapons Which May be Deemed to be Excessively Injurious or to have Indiscriminate Effects (CCCW)

Protocol on Non-Detectable Fragments (Protocol I) (CCCW Protocol I)

Protocol on Prohibitions or Restrictions on the Use of Mines, Booby-Traps and Other Devices (Protocol II) (CCCW Protocol II)

Protocol on Prohibitions or Restrictions on the Use of Incendiary Weapons (Protocol III) (CCCW Protocol III)

1984 Convention against Torture and Other Cruel, Inhuman or Degrading Treatment or Punishment (Torture Convention)

1989 Convention on the Rights of the Child

1990 African Charter on the Rights and Welfare of the Child

1993 Convention on the Prohibition of the Development, Production, Stockpiling and Use of Chemical Weapons and on their Destruction (Chemical Weapons Convention)

Statute of the International Criminal Tribunal for the Prosecution of Persons responsible for Serious Violations of International Humanitarian Law Committed in the Territory of the Former Yugoslavia since 1991 (ICTY Statute)

1994 Convention on the Safety of United Nations and Associated Personnel (Safety Convention)

Statute of the International Criminal Tribunal for Rwanda (ICTR Statute)

1995 Protocol on Blinding Laser Weapons (Protocol IV) (CCCW Protocol IV)
1996 Amended Protocol on Prohibitions or Restrictions on the Use of Mines, Booby-Traps and Other Devices (Amended Protocol II) (CCCW Amended Protocol II)
1997 Convention on the Prohibition of the Use, Stockpiling, Production and Transfer of Anti-Personnel Mines and on their Destruction (Ottawa Convention)
1998 Statute of the International Criminal Court (ICC Statute)
1999 International Labour Organization (ILO) Convention 182, Concerning the Prohibition and Immediate Action for the Elimination of the Worst Forms of Child Labour
2000 Optional Protocol to the Convention on the Rights of the Child on the Involvement of Children in Armed Conflict
2002 Statute of the Special Court for Sierra Leone (SCSL Statute)
2004 Law on the Establishment of the Extraordinary Chambers in the Courts of Cambodia for the Prosecution of Crimes Committed During the Period of Democratic Kampuchea, as amended (ECCC Law)
2005 Optional Protocol to the Convention on the Safety of United Nations and Associated Personnel

Table of cases

International case law

Abu Garda

Prosecutor v Bahar Idriss Abu Garda, Decision on the Confirmation of Charges, ICC-02/05-02/09, 8 February 2010 (*Abu Garda* Decision)

AFRC case

Prosecutor v Alex Tamba Brima, Brima Bazzy Kamara and Santigie Borbor Kanu, SCSL-04-16-T, Trial Judgment, 20 June 2007 (*AFRC* case TC)

Akayesu

Prosecutor v Jean-Paul Akayesu, ICTR-96-4-T, Trial Judgment, 2 September 1998 (*Akayesu* TC)

Prosecutor v Jean-Paul Akayesu, ICTR-96-4-T, Sentencing Judgment, 2 October 1998 (*Akayesu* Sentencing Judgment)

Akbulut v Turkey

ECtHR Application No 45624/99, Admissibility Decision, 6 February 2003

Aleksovski

Prosecutor v Zlatko Aleksovski, ICTY, IT-95-14/1-A, Appeal Judgment, 24 March 2000 (*Aleksovski* AC)

Bagosora *et al*

Prosecutor v Bagosora et al, ICTR-98-41-T, Trial Judgment, 18 December 2008 (*Bagosora* TC)

Banda

Prosecutor v Abdallah Banda Abakaer Nourain and Saleh Mohammed Jerbo Jamus, Corrigendum of the Decision on the Confirmation of Charges, ICC-02/05-03/09, 7 March 2011 (*Banda* Decision)

Bemba

Prosecutor v Jean-Pierre Bemba Gombo, Decision on Confirmation of Charges, Case no ICC-01/05-01/08, Pre-Trial Chamber II, 15 June 2009 (*Bemba* Decision)

Bisengimana

Prosecutor v Paul Bisengimana, ICTR-00-60-T, Trial Judgment, 13 April 2006 (*Bisengimana* TC)

Blagojević and Jokić

Prosecutor v Vidoje Blagojević and Dragan Jokić, ICTY, IT-02-60-T, Trial Judgment, 17 January 2005 (*Blagojević* TC)

Blaškić

Prosecutor v Tihomir Blaškić, ICTY, IT-95-14-T, Trial Judgment, 3 March 2000 (*Blaškić* TC)

Prosecutor v Tihomir Blaškić, ICTY, IT-95-14-A, Appeals Judgment, 29 July 2004 (*Blaškić* AC)

Boškoski and Tarčulovski

Prosecutor v Ljube Boškoski and Johan Tarčulovski, ICTY, IT-04-82-T, Trial Judgment, 10 July 2008 (*Boškoski and Tarčulovski* TC)

Prosecutor v Ljube Boškoski and Johan Tarčulovski, ICTY, IT-04-82-A, Appeal Judgment, 19 May 2010 (*Boškoski and Tarčulovski* AC)

Brđanin

Prosecutor v Radoslav Brđanin, IT-99-36-T, Trial Judgment, 1 September 2004

CDF case

Prosecutor v Moinina Fofana and Allieu Kondewa, SCSL-04-14-T, Trial Judgment, 2 August 2007 (*CDF* case, TC)

Prosecutor v Moinina Fofana and Allieu Kondewa, SCSL-04-14-A, Appeal Judgment, 28 May 2008 (*CDF* case, AC)

Čelebići

Prosecutor v Zejnil Delalić et al, ICTY, IT-96-21-I, Indictment, 19 March 1996 (*Čelebići* Indictment)

Prosecutor v Zejnil Delalić et al, ICTY, IT-96-21-T, Trial Judgment, 16 November 1998 (*Čelebići* TC)

Prosecutor v Zejnil Delalić et al, ICTY, IT-96-21-A, Appeal Judgment, 20 February 2001 (*Čelebići* AC)

Đorđević

Prosecutor v Vlastimir Đorđević, ICTY, IT-05-87/1-T, Trial Judgment, 23 February 2011 (*Đorđević* TC)

Engel

Engel v The Netherlands (No 1) (1976) 1 ECtHR 647.

Erdemović

Prosecutor v Dražen Erdemović, ICTY, IT-96-22-A, Appeal Judgment, 7 October 1997

Separate and Dissenting Opinion of Judge Cassese (*Erdemović*, Judge Cassese)

Separate and Dissenting Opinion of Judge Li (*Erdemović*, Judge Li)

Joint Separate Opinion of Judge McDonald and Vohrah (*Erdemović*, Judges McDonald and Vohrah)

Prosecutor v Erdemović, Sentencing Judgment, IT-96-22-T, 29 November 1996 (*Erdemović* Sentencing Judgment)

Galić

Prosecutor v Stanislav Galić, ICTY, IT-98-29-I, Indictment, 26 March 1999 (*Galić* Indictment)

Prosecutor v Stanislav Galić, ICTY, IT-98-29-T, Trial Judgment, 5 December 2003 (*Galić* TC)

Prosecutor v Stanislav Galić, ICTY, IT-98-29-A, Appeal Judgment, 30 November 2006 (*Galić* AC)

Gotovina

Prosecutor v Ante Gotovina et al, ICTY, IT-06-90-T, Trial Chamber, 15 April 2011 (*Gotovina* TC)

Halilović

Prosecutor v Sefer Halilović, ICTY, IT-01-48-T, Trial Judgment, 16 November 2005 (*Halilović* TC)

Jelisić

Prosecutor v Goran Jelisić, ICTY, IT-95-10-T, Trial Judgment, 14 December 1999 (*Jelisić* TC)

Prosecutor v Goran Jelisić, ICTY, IT-95-10-A, Appeal Judgment, 5 July 2001 (*Jelisić* AC)

Kajelijeli

Prosecutor v Juvénal Kajelijeli, ICTR-98-44A-T, Trial Judgment, 1 December 2003 (*Kajelijeli* TC)

Kamuhanda

Prosecutor v Jean de Dieu Kamuhanda, ICTR-95-54A-T, Trial Judgment, 22 January 2004 (*Kamuhanda* TC)

Karadžić

Prosecutor v Radovan Karadžić, Case no IT-95-5/18-AR72.5, Decision on Appeal of Trial Chambers Decision on Preliminary Motion to Dismiss Count 11 of the Indictment, 9 July 2009

Prosecutor v Radovan Karadžić, Case no IT-95-5/18-AR73.9, Appeal from Denial of Judgment for Acquittal for Hostage-Taking, 25 July 2012

Prosecutor v Radovan Karadžić, Case no IT-95-5/18-AR73.9, Decision on Appeal from Denial of Judgment of Acquittal for Hostage-Taking, 11 December 2012

Prosecutor v Radovan Karadžić, IT-95-5/18-T, Trial Judgment, 24 March 2016 (*Karadžić* TC)

Katanga

Prosecutor v Germain Katanga, Warrant of Arrest, Case no ICC-01/04-01/07, Pre-Trial Chamber I, 2 July 2007 (*Katanga*, Warrant of Arrest)

Prosecutor v Germain Katanga and Mathieu Ngudjolo Chui, Decision on Confirmation of Charges, Case no ICC-01/04-01/07, Pre-Trial Chamber I, 30 September 2008 (*Katanga* Decision)

Prosecutor v Germain Katanga, Judgment pursuant to article 74 of the Statute, Case no ICC-01/04-01/07, 7 March 2014 (*Katanga* TC)

Kayishema

Prosecutor v Clément Kayishema and Obed Ruzindana, ICTR-95-1-T, Trial Judgment, 21 May 1999 (*Kayishema* TC)

Prosecutor v Clément Kayishema and Obed Ruzindana, ICTR-95-1-A, Appeals Judgment, 1 June 2001 (*Kayishema* AC)

Kordić and Čerkez

Prosecutor v Dario Kordić and Mario Čerkez, ICTY, IT-95-14/2-T, Trial Judgment, 26 February 2001 (*Kordić and Čerkez* TC)

Prosecutor v Dario Kordić and Mario Čerkez, ICTY, IT-95-14/2-A, Appeal Judgment, 17 December 2004 (*Kordić and Čerkez* AC)

Krnojelac

Prosecutor v Milorad Krnojelac, ICTY, Motion to Withdraw Article 2 Counts, 27 October 2000

Prosecutor v Milorad Krnojelac, ICTY, IT-97-24-T, Trial Judgment, 15 March 2002 (*Krnojelac* TC)

Krstić

Prosecutor v Radislav Krstić, ICTY, IT-98-33-T, Trial Judgment, 2 August 2001 (*Krstić* TC)

Prosecutor v Radislav Krstić, ICTY, IT-98-33-A, Appeal Judgment, 19 April 2004 (*Krstić* AC)

Kunarac

Prosecutor v Milorad Kunarac et al, ICTY, IT-96-23-T, Trial Judgment, 22 February 2001 (*Kunarac* TC)

Prosecutor v Milorad Kunarac et al, ICTY, IT-96-23 and IT-96-23/1-A, Appeal Judgment, 12 June 2002 (*Kunarac* AC)

Kupreškić

Prosecutor v Zoran Kupreškić et al, ICTY, IT-95-16-T, Trial Judgment, 14 January 2000 (*Kupreškić* TC)

Kvočka

Prosecutor v Miroslav Kvočka et al, ICTY, IT-98-30/1, Trial Judgment, 2 November 2001 (*Kvočka* TC)

Lubanga

Prosecutor v Thomas Lubanga Dyilo, Pre-Trial Chamber I, Decision on the Confirmation of Charges, ICC-01/04-01/06, 29 January 2007 (*Lubanga* Decision)

Prosecutor v Thomas Lubanga Dyilo, Trial Chamber I, Judgment pursuant to Article 74 of the Statute, ICC-01/04-01/06, 14 March 2012 (*Lubanga* TC)

Prosecutor v Lubanga, Decision on Sentence pursuant to Article 76 of the Statute, ICC-01/04-01/06, 10 July 2012 (*Lubanga* Sentencing Decision)

Prosecutor v Thomas Lubanga Dyilo, Appeals Chamber ICC-01/04-01/06, 1 December 2014 (*Lubanga* AC)

Martić

Prosecutor v Milan Martić, ICTY, IT-95-11-T, Rule 61 Hearing Decision, 8 March 1996 (*Martić* Rule 61 Decision)

Prosecutor v Milan Martić, ICTY, IT-95-11-T, Trial Judgment, 12 June 2007 (*Martić* TC)

Prosecutor v Milan Martić, ICTY, IT-95-11-A, Appeal Judgment, 8 October 2008 (*Martić* AC)

Milošević

Prosecutor v Dragomir Milošević, IT-98-29/1-T, Trial Judgment, 12 December 2007 (*Milošević* TC)

Prosecutor v Dragomir Milošević, ICTY, IT-98-29-A, Appeal Judgment, 12 November 2009 (*Milošević* AC)

Mladić

Prosecutor v Ratko Mladić, ICTY, Fourth Amended Indictment, IT-09-92-PT, 16 December 2011 (*Mladić* Indictment)

Mrškić

Prosecutor v Mile Mrškić et al, ICTY, IT-95-13/1-T, Trial Judgment, 27 September 2007 (*Mrškić* TC)

Prosecutor v Mile Mrškić et al, ICTY, IT-95-13/1-A, Appeal Judgment, 5 May 2009 (*Mrškić* AC)

Musema

Prosecutor v Alfred Musema, ICTR-96-13-A, Trial Judgment, 27 January 2006 (*Musema* TC)

Naletilić and Martinović

Prosecutor v Mladen Naletilić and Vinko Martinović, ICTY, IT-98-34-T, Trial Judgment, 31 March 2003 (*Naletilić* TC)

Prosecutor v Mladen Naletilić and Vinko Martinović, ICTY, IT-98-34-A, Appeal Judgment, 3 May 2006 (*Naletilić* AC)

Nicaragua

Certain Military and Paramilitary Activities in and against Nicaragua (*Nicaragua v United States of America*) Judgment (Merits), International Court of Justice, 27 June 1986

Niyitegeka

Prosecutor v Eliézer Niyitegeka, Case no ICTR-96-14-A, Appeal Judgment, 9 July 2004

Norman

Prosecutor v Sam Hinga Norman, SCSL-2004-14-AR72(E), Appeal Decision on Preliminary Motion Based on Lack of Jurisdiction (Child Recruitment), 31 May 2004 (*Norman* Decision)

Ntaganda

Prosecutor v Bosco Ntaganda, ICC-01/04-02/06, Document Containing the Charges, 10 January 2014 (*Ntaganda*, Document Containing the Charges)

Prosecutor v Bosco Ntaganda, ICC-01/04-02/06, Decision on the Confirmation of Charges, 9 June 2014 (*Ntaganda* Decision)

Prosecutor v Bosco Ntaganda, ICC-01/04-02/06, Second Decision on the Defences challenge to the jurisdiction of the Court in respect of Counts 6 and 9, 4 January 2017 (*Ntaganda* Second Decision)

Nuclear Weapons Advisory Opinion

Legality of the Threat or Use of Nuclear Weapons, ICJ Advisory Opinion, 8 July 1996 (Nuclear Weapons)

Popović *et al*

Prosecutor v Vujadin Popović et al, IT-05-88-T, Trial Judgment, 10 June 2010 (*Popović* TC)

Prosecutor v Vujadin Popović et al, IT-05-88-A, Appeal Judgment, 30 January 2015 (*Popović* AC)

Prlić *et al*

Prosecutor v Jadranko Prlić et al, ICTY, IT-04-74-T, Trial Chamber, 29 May 2013 (*Prlić* TC)

RUF case

Prosecutor v Issa Hassan Sesay, Morris Kallon and Augustine Gbao, SCSL-2004-15-PT, Corrected Amended Consolidated Indictment, 2 August 2006 (*RUF* case Indictment)

Prosecutor v Issa Hassan Sesay, Morris Kallon and Augustine Gbao, SCSL-2004-15-T, Trial Judgment, 2 March 2009 (*RUF* case TC)

Rutaganda

Prosecutor v George Anderson Nderubumwe Rutaganda, ICTR-96-3-T, Trial Judgment, 6 December 1999 (*Rutaganda* TC)

Semanza

Prosecutor v Semanza, ICTR-97-20T, Trial Judgment, 15 May 2003 (*Semanza* TC)

Seromba

Prosecutor v Athanase Seromba, ICTR-2001-66-I, Trial Judgment, 13 December 2006 (*Seromba* TC)

Simić

Prosecutor v Blagoje Simić et al, ICTY, IT-95-9-T, Trial Judgment, 17 October 2003 (*Simić* TC)

Šljivančanin

Prosecutor v Šljivančanin, Review Judgment IT-95-13/1-R.1, 8 December 2010

Stakić

Prosecutor v Milomir Stakić, ICTY, IT-97-24-A, Appeal Judgment, 22 March 2006 (*Stakić* AC)

Strugar

Prosecutor v Pavle Strugar, IT-01-42-AR72, Decision on Interlocutory Appeal, 22 November 2002 (*Strugar* Decision)

Prosecutor v Pavle Strugar, ICTY, IT-01-42-T, Trial Judgment, 31 January 2005 (*Strugar* TC)

Prosecutor v Pavle Strugar, ICTY, IT-01-42-A, Appeals Judgment, 17 July 2008 (*Strugar* AC)

Tadić

Prosecutor v Duško Tadić, ICTY, IT-94-1-AR72, Decision on the Defence Motion for Interlocutory Appeal on Jurisdiction, 2 October 1995 (*Tadić* Decision)

Prosecutor v Duško Tadić, ICTY, IT-94-1-T, Trial Judgment, 7 May 1997 (*Tadić* TC)

Prosecutor v Duško Tadić, ICTY, IT-94-1-A, Appeals Judgment, 15 July 1999 (*Tadić* AC)

Prosecutor v Duško Tadić, ICTY, IT-94-1-T *bis*-R117, Sentencing Judgment, 11 November 1999 (*Tadić* Trial Chamber Sentencing Judgment)

Prosecutor v Duško Tadić, ICTY, IT-94-1-A and IT-94.1-A *bis*, Judgment in Sentencing Appeals, 26 January 2000 (*Tadić* Appeals Chamber Sentencing Judgment)

Taylor case

Prosecutor v Charles Ghankay Taylor, SCSL-03-01-T, Trial Judgment, 18 May 2012 (*Taylor* TC)

Van Araat v The Netherlands, ECtHR Application no 65389/09, 6 July 2010

Vasiljević

Prosecutor v Mitar Vasiljević, ICTY, IT-98-32-T, Trial Judgment, 29 November 2002 (*Vasiljević* TC)

National case law

France

Barbie: Fédération Nationale des Déportés et Internés Résistants et Patriotes and Others v Barbie, Court of Cassation (Criminal Chamber), 20 December 1985, reported in 78 ILR 125 (*Barbie*)

Touvier, Court of Cassation (Criminal Chamber), 27 November 1992, reported at 100 ILR 338 (*Touvier*)

Germany

Heynen, Karl Supreme Court at Leipzig, 26 May 1921, *Verhandlungen*, 2543-7, English translation available in 16 *American Journal of International Law* 674-84 (1922)

Llandovery Castle, German Supreme Court of Leipzig 26 *American Journal of International Law* (1922) Supp. 708–723

Iraq

Al Anfal, Iraqi High Tribunal, Case No 1/CSecond/2006, 24 June 2007. Available at: www.asser.nl/upload/documents/DomCLIC/Docs/NLP/Iraq/Anfal_verdict.pdf (last accessed 1 May 2017)

Israel

The Public Committee against Torture in Israel v Government of Israel, HCJ 769/02 Supreme Court Sitting as High Court of Justice, 11 December 2005 (*Targeted Killings Judgment*)

Netherlands

Pilz, Dutch Special Court of Cassation, 5 July 1950, NederJ (1950), No 681, 17 ILR 391–392 (1950)

United States

United States of America v Otto Ohlendorf et al, IV Trials of War Criminals before Nuernberg Military Tribunals under Control Council Law No 10, US Govt Printing Office, Washington DC, 1951 (Einsatzgruppen case)

United States v Wilhelm List et al, XI Trials of War Criminals Before the Nuernberg Military Tribunals under Control Council Law No 10, US Govt Printing Office, Washington DC, 1947–1951 (Hostages case)

USA v Carl Krauch et al, VIII Trials of War Criminals Before the Nuernberg Military Tribunals under Control Council Law No 10, US Govt Printing Office, Washington DC, 1947–1951 (I.G. Farben case)

United States of America v Erhard Milch, II Trials of War Criminals Before the Nuremberg Military Tribunals under Control Council Law No 10, US Govt Printing Office, Washington DC, 1947–1951 (Milch)

United States of America v Ulrich Greifelt et al, 10 March 1948, V Trials of War Criminals Before the Nuremberg Military Tribunals under Control Council Law No 10, US Govt Printing Office, Washington DC, 1950 (RuSHA Trial)

UK

Eck case (*The Peleus Trial*), British Military Court at Hamburg, 20 October 1945

H., 18 October 1949; Entscheidungen des Obersten Gerichtshofes für die Britische Zone in Strafsachen, St S 309/49

P and Others, 7 December 1948, Entscheidungen des Obersten Gerichtshofes für die Britische Zone in Strafsachen, St S 111/48

Von Ruchteschell, British Military Court at Hamburg, 21 May 1947

Wickman, British Military Court at Hamburg, 26 November 1947

1 Introduction

'Soldiers are not as other men.'[1] A divide has existed between those who fight and the rest of us since time immemorial,[2] and while the nature of this divide may change with the times, it endures nonetheless.[3] During peacetime, this separation between military personnel and civilians manifests itself in various ways,[4] but it is in times of conflict that the distinction becomes most apparent.

Differences between fighters and civilians emerge in a number of fields of international law. The most obvious example occurs in international humanitarian law (IHL), the foundations of which rest upon the premise that there is a distinction between combatants and civilians, with the former being liable to attack (unless *hors de combat*) and the latter being protected (unless directly participating in hostilities – DPH).[5] However, differences exist in other areas too: in the field of human rights, for example, the European Court of Human Rights (ECtHR) has held that the interpretation and application of the European Convention on Human Rights (ECHR) can be different when being applied to members of state armed forces than when being applied to civilians;[6] while in international criminal law (ICL), military personnel have been held to different standards of behaviour than their civilian counterparts. In the case of *Erdemović*, the Appeals Chamber of the International Criminal Tribunal for the former Yugoslavia (ICTY) was required to consider whether the defence of duress was available to a soldier who had been forced to take part in a firing squad and kill innocent people. The

1 John Keegan, *A History of Warfare* (Pimlico Military Classics, 2004) p. xvi.
2 Colm McKeogh, *Innocent Civilians, The Morality of Killing in War* (Palgrave, 2002).
3 For example, there is presently a trend towards greater 'civilianisation' of the military within some Western state armed forces which are making greater use of external civilian contractors to carry out tasks that would previously have been performed internally. For a discussion of the legal consequences of this, see Michael N. Schmitt, 'Humanitarian Law and Direct Participation in Hostilities by Private Contractors or Civilian Employees', 5 *Chicago Journal of International Law* 511 (2005).
4 For example, members of the armed forces are often subject to a separate and distinct body of law.
5 See Article 48, Protocol Additional to the Geneva Conventions of 12 August 1949 and relating to the Protection of Victims of International Armed Conflicts, 1977 (Protocol I).
6 *Engel v The Netherlands (No 1)* (1976) 1 ECtHR 647, para. 54; and *Akbulut v Turkey*, ECtHR Application No 45624/99, Admissibility Decision, 6 February 2003.

soldier's superior officer had threatened to shoot him if he refused to comply with the order to fire.[7] Majority Judges McDonald and Vohrah stated:

> we are of the view that soldiers or combatants are expected to exercise fortitude and a greater degree of resistance to a threat than civilians, at least when it is their own lives which are being threatened. Soldiers, by the very nature of their occupation, must have envisaged the possibility of violent death in pursuance of the cause for which they fight. The relevant question must therefore be framed in terms of what may be expected from the ordinary soldier in the situation of the Appellant.[8]

The majority held that 'soldiers or combatants' could not plead the defence of duress when innocents had been killed, leaving open the possibility that a civilian acting under similar conditions could rely on the defence.[9] That an individual has been involved in the fighting, therefore has consequences in international law.

This book explores the nature of the divide between those involved in fighting and those who are not in a specific context, that of ICL. It asks what difference the act of fighting has to victimhood in ICL. When, and in what way, should an international criminal tribunal (ICT) take cognisance of the fact that an alleged victim had been involved in fighting? What consequences arise in ICL if an alleged victim had been fighting? Of what crimes can they and can they not be victims? These questions are analysed by reference to treaty law and decisions from ICTs, with particular emphasis upon cases from the International Criminal Court (ICC), the ICTY, the International Criminal Tribunal for Rwanda (ICTR) and the Special Court for Sierra Leone (SCSL). It is not the intention of this book to provide a list of every international crime that can be committed against those involved in fighting, but rather to explore some of the more intriguing legal issues that can arise.

Atrocities against those who fight do not feature as prominently before ICTs today as they have done in the past. The majority of atrocities in contemporary armed conflicts are committed against civilians.[10] Civilians are protected under international treaties and customary law, and international bodies and non-governmental organisations (NGOs) work tirelessly to promote their protection.[11]

7 *Prosecutor v Erdemović*, Sentencing Judgment, IT-96-22-T, 29 November 1996, paras 78–80.

8 *Prosecutor v Dražen Erdemović*, ICTY, IT-96-22-A, Appeal Judgment, 7 October 1997, Joint Separate Opinion of Judges McDonald and Vohrah, para. 84.

9 Ibid., paras 73–78. However, see Judge Cassese's dissenting opinion: *Erdemović*, Separate and Dissenting Opinion of Judge Cassese; and see Valerie Epps, 'The Soldier's Obligation to Die when Ordered to Shoot Civilians or Face Death Himself', 37 (4) *New England Law Review* 987 (2002); and Luis E. Chiesa, 'Duress Demanding Heroism and Proportionality', 41 *Vanderbilt Journal of Transnational Law* 741 (2008).

10 Adam Roberts, 'Lives and Statistics: Are 90% of War Victims Civilians?' *Survival: Global Politics and Strategy*, 52(3), 115 (2010).

11 For example see www.securitycouncilreport.org/protection-of-civilians/.

This emphasis is reflected in the cases appearing before ICTs, the majority of which concern civilian victims.[12] This is a relatively new development: the Leipzig trials held in the wake of the First World War predominately considered cases where combatants had been victims,[13] reflecting the fact that most of the casualties in the war had been military rather than civilian. Military personnel were also prominent as victims in the trials held in the post-Second World War period, primarily as prisoners of war (POWs).

While relatively few contemporary ICL cases have considered crimes committed against those who fight, this does not mean that such incidents have not fallen under the jurisdiction of an ICT. In the *Katanga* case from the ICC, for example, there was credible evidence that atrocities had been committed against persons *hors de combat*,[14] but no charges were brought concerning these potential crimes.[15] Clearly, prosecutors must take many factors into account when determining which particular incidents to prosecute,[16] and there were probably sound prosecutorial reasons for focusing on the civilian victims in that particular case. Nevertheless, one cannot help having the overall feeling that military personnel tend to be perceived as being the perpetrators of atrocities, rather than the victims of them.[17]

12 For a study of the number of civilian victims as compared to the number of military victims in cases before the ICTY, see Claire Garbett, 'The Legal Representation of the Civilian and Military Casualties of Contemporary Conflicts: Unlawful Victimisation, its Victims and their Visibility at the ICTY', 16(7) *The International Journal of Human Rights* 1059 (2012).

13 For a contemporary account of the trials see Claud Mullins and E.M. Pollock, *The Leipzig Trials: An Account of the War Criminals' Trials and a Study of German Mentality* (London, H.F. & G. Witherby, 1921).

14 The case concerned an attack on the village of Bogoro in the Democratic Republic of the Congo. In its Decision on the Confirmation of Charges the Pre-Trial Chamber noted that the Prosecution were not including the deaths of soldiers who had been killed after surrendering, despite evidence given in at least one testimony that those soldiers who were found by the attacking forces who were unable to defend themselves, were killed with a machete in order not to waste ammunition, and that no prisoners were taken during the attack. See *Prosecutor v Germain Katanga and Mathieu Ngudjolo Chui*, Decision on Confirmation of Charges, Case no ICC-01/04-01/07, Pre-Trial Chamber I, 30 September 2008, para. 288 and FN 395.

15 See *Prosecutor v Germain Katanga*, Warrant of Arrest, Case no ICC-01/04-01/07, Pre-Trial Chamber I, 2 July 2007.

16 For example, see Robert Cryer, *Prosecuting International Crimes, Selectivity and the International Criminal Law Regime* (Cambridge University Press, 2005), chapter 5; Carla del Ponte, 'Investigation and Prosecution of Large-scale Crimes at the International Level: The Experience of the ICTY', 4 *Journal of International Criminal Justice* 539 (2006); and Luc Reydams, Jan Wouters and Cedric Ryngaert, *International Prosecutors* (Oxford Scholarship Online, 2012).

17 'Many analysts have a general bias against members of armed forces, viewing them as merely thugs or perpetrators of violence.' Lara J. Nettelfield, 'From the Battlefield to the Barracks: The ICTY and the Armed Forces of Bosnia and Herzegovina', 4(1) *International Journal of Transnational Justice* 87–109 (2010), p. 90.

1.1 A note on terminology

Different categories of people can be involved in fighting during an armed conflict: members of state armed forces; members of organised armed groups; and civilians who DPH. For the purposes of this book, it has proved challenging to find a suitable uncontroversial collective term to encompass those who are involved in fighting.

One option is the term 'combatant'. Combatant status is defined in treaty law and carries an entitlement to certain rights and privileges;[18] yet the word 'combatant' is also frequently used in a generic sense to mean those who are involved in fighting, regardless of their legal status. Until the middle of the twentieth century, 'combatant' tended to be used to describe the conduct of a person, while the word 'belligerent' was used to describe status.[19] From the 1950s onward, the term 'belligerent' fell out of favour as a means of describing status, and 'combatant' began to be used in its place. It is the sense of having a particular status that is currently used in IHL treaty law. Nevertheless, the term 'combatant' continues to be used in both senses: colloquially as a means to describe conduct, and legally as a means to describe status.[20] The tendency to use the term 'combatant' when referring to those who fight in general permeates legal literature and case law, yet, due to its specific meaning in treaty law, its use in a generic sense in a legal context can cause unnecessary confusion.[21]

Another possibility would be to distinguish between 'lawful combatants', i.e. those who have combatant status, and 'unlawful combatants', i.e. those who fight without having combatant status. This terminology came into vogue in the years following the attacks on the United States on 11 September 2001.[22] The terms are unsatisfactory for several reasons: the term 'lawful combatant' is a tautology, as

18 Article 43(2), Protocol I and see subsequent discussion.

19 For example, Chapter I of the Hague Regulations is headed 'The Qualifications of Belligerents', and see Charles Garraway, 'Combatants. Substance or Semantics' in Schmitt *et al*, *International Law and Armed Conflict: Exploring the Faultlines: Essays in Honour of Yoram Dinstein* (Martinus Nijhoff, 2007), pp. 318–327.

20 The UK Manual explains: 'The expression "combatant" has in the past been used in two senses. Sometimes it has been used to describe any person who actually engages in hostile acts in an armed conflict on behalf of a party to the conflict, whether or not he is permitted to do so. It has also been used to describe only those persons with a right to take a direct part in hostilities. For this reason it has often been qualified by the use of the adjectives "lawful" or "unlawful"'. UK Ministry of Defence, *The Manual of the Law of Armed Conflict* (Oxford University Press, 2004), para. 4.2.1.

21 For an example of where it is made clear as to in what sense the term is being used, see Commentary to Rule 3 of Jean-Marie Henckaerts and Louise Doswald-Beck (eds), *Customary International Humanitarian Law, Vol. 1: Rules* (Cambridge University Press, 2009) available at: https://ihl-databases.icrc.org/customary-ihl/eng/docs/home (ICRC Study).

22 However, Dörmann explains that the terms 'unlawful combatant' and 'unprivileged combatant/belligerent', 'have ... frequently been used at least since the beginning of the last century of legal literature, military manuals and case law'. Knut Dörmann, 'The Legal Situation of "Unlawful/Unprivileged Combatants"', 85(849) *International Review of the Red Cross* 45–74 (2003), p. 46.

to be a combatant is to be a lawful fighter under IHL, in that only combatants have the right to DPH.[23] Furthermore, the terms are particularly confusing if used in the context of a non-international armed conflict (NIAC), where the concept of combatant status does not apply.[24] Indeed, one could potentially describe all of those who fight in a NIAC as 'unlawful combatants', but this too is unsatisfactory, as most states would not regard members of their own armed forces as being 'unlawful combatants'.[25]

A further choice would be to use the term 'fighter'. Precedent exists for using the term in a legal context as a means of avoiding reference to the term 'combatant', with its corresponding legal implications. Most notably, the San Remo Manual makes use of 'fighter' in the context of NIACs,[26] but there are also increasing examples of ICTs using 'fighter' as an alternative to 'combatant' in their judgments.[27] Although the term has generally been used in the context of NIACs, it is also useful in the context of international armed conflicts (IACs), as not all of those who are fighting necessarily have combatant status. The term is not without its disadvantages, however. It is vague. Its use has been discounted by those involved in the drafting of IHL documents, as 'fighter' would be translated into 'combatant' in a number of other languages in any event.[28] In addition, including civilians who DPH on an intermittent basis within the term 'fighters' is not a particularly satisfactory solution.

The choice of a suitable term has therefore not been easy. Throughout the book, the term 'combatant' is principally used to describe those who qualify for combatant status under IHL. In the event that it is used in a generic sense, this will be made clear. Otherwise, the book refers to 'those who fight' or to 'fighters'

23 Article 43(2), Protocol I.
24 At least according to most commentators. See subsequent discussion.
25 See subsequent discussion.
26 The Manual defines fighters for its purposes as follows: 'fighters are members of armed forces and dissident armed forces or other organized armed groups, or taking an active (direct) part in hostilities'. See International Institute of Humanitarian Law, *The Manual of Non-International Armed Conflict* (San Remo, 2006), available at www.iihl.org/iihl/Documents/The%20Manual%20on%20the%20Law%20of%20NIAC.pdf, para. 1.1.2.
27 For example, see *Prosecutor v Issa Hassan Sesay*, Morris Kallon and Augustine Gbao, SCSL-2004-15-T, Trial Judgment, 2 March 2009 (*RUF* case TC), p. 307 at FN 1901, where the Trial Chamber opts to use the term 'fighters' to refer to those who directly participate in hostilities in a NIAC. Also see *Prosecutor v Mile Mrškić et al*, ICTY, IT-95-13/1-T, Trial Judgment, 27 September 2007, para. 457, where the Trial Chamber states: 'the term "fighter" now seems to be the appropriate term to be used as the equivalent for "combatants" in non-international armed conflict.' See *Prosecutor v Vlastimir Đorđević*, ICTY, IT-05-87/1-T, Trial Judgment, 23 February 2011, for example at paras 860, 886, 943 and 1583.
28 Jean-Marie Henckaerts, 'The Conduct of Hostilities: Target Selection, Proportionality and Precautionary Measures under International Humanitarian Law' in The Netherlands Red Cross, *Protecting Civilians in 21st-Century Warfare, Target Selection, Proportionality and Precautionary Measures in Law and Practice* (8 December 2000) p. 13, FN 6.

to encompass anyone who is involved in the fighting, including members of state armed forces, members of dissident armed forces or other armed groups, and civilians who DPH. If only one type of fighter is being discussed, for example members of state armed forces, this will be made clear in the text.

1.2 Outline of the book

The book begins by exploring how ICTs have untangled victims of war crimes from lawful casualties of war. Chapter 2 explains that war crimes involving persons can be divided into two categories: one where the primary focus is on the status of the alleged victim as a civilian; and the other where the primary focus is on the victim's conduct as not actively/directly participating in hostilities (APH/DPH). The chapter argues that this distinction between status and conduct has not always been fully appreciated or understood in ICL. It analyses how ICTs have addressed issues in relation to these two categories of crimes, and explores how ICTs have identified who was a victim of a war crime rather than a legitimate military target.

IHL prohibits certain means and methods of warfare from being used during armed conflicts and violation of these prohibitions are war crimes. Although combatants and other fighters are legitimate military targets unless *hors de combat*, they are also protected by some of these IHL provisions during hostilities. Chapter 3 discusses these war crimes and explores when the fact that an alleged victim had been involved in the fighting becomes relevant.

As soon as fighters become *hors de combat* they can be victims of many of the same crimes as civilians; however, some crucial differences remain. These differences are investigated in Chapter 4. The chapter analyses how ICTs have established entitlement to POW status and asks to what extent POW status, which is traditionally prized by states, is important in ICL.

During times of armed conflict, atrocities can be committed not only against members of enemy forces, but also against members of non-opposing forces. In the past, the majority view has been that these crimes cannot constitute war crimes, as IHL does not proffer protection to a party to the conflict's own forces. Chapter 5 challenges this view. It analyses IHL treaty provisions and case law from ICTs to argue that IHL does indeed protect members of non-opposing forces and, accordingly, that violating these provisions constitutes a war crime.

The next two chapters concern two particular groups who can be involved in fighting. Child soldiers and the war crimes of conscripting, enlisting and using children under 15 years of age to participate actively in hostilities are the subject of Chapter 6. These crimes have been interpreted and clarified in recent years by the SCLS and the ICC. The chapter examines the challenges that these courts have had in defining and interpreting these offences.

Chapter 7 addresses crimes against peacekeepers. Although peacekeepers are civilians, their particular situation means that they can become drawn into the fighting, whether through the peacekeeping mission becoming a party to the conflict or by individual peacekeepers who APH/DPH. The chapter explores difficulties that ICTs have had in differentiating between status and conduct in relation to peacekeepers. It discusses the war crime of attacking peacekeeping personnel, as well as peacekeepers as victims of other international crimes.

Chapter 8 explores issues surrounding those who fight as victims of crimes against humanity or genocide. The issue of whether persons *hors de combat* can be victims of crimes against humanity has been a matter of contention at the ICTY, whereas other ICTs have not experienced the same difficulties. The chapter explains why this is so, and analyses the merits of the different approaches that have been taken on this issue. It also asks whether persons *hors de combat* should be able to qualify as victims of these crimes. The complicating factors that can arise when those who fight are alleged to be victims of genocide are also discussed.

Finally, Chapter 9 draws some overarching conclusions.

The final part of this introductory chapter briefly considers some aspects of IHL that are of specific relevance to the discussions which follow.

1.3 International humanitarian law as it pertains to persons

Violations of IHL against persons can broadly be divided into two categories: first, those committed by a party to a conflict against protected persons who are under its control, such as POWs or other detainees. Second, violations committed by a party to the conflict against protected persons not under its control, including violations of the principle of distinction, and violations by using prohibited means and methods of warfare during the conduct of hostilities. In order to understand some of the issues discussed in the following chapters, it is necessary to have a grasp of certain fundamental aspects of IHL, including the principle of distinction; combatant status and civilian status and their consequences; the application of the principle of distinction in NIACs; and the concept of APH/DPH.

1.3.1 The rule of distinction

The principle of distinction lies at the heart of IHL.[29] It requires that during armed conflict parties must distinguish between civilians and civilian objects on the one hand, and military persons and objectives on the other, and that only the latter be made the object of attack. The rules regarding distinction were formulated in the nineteenth century, when the dividing line between combatants and civilians was clearer than it is today. At that time, most armed conflicts

29 Article 48, Protocol I; Rule 1, ICRC Study and *Nuclear Weapons Advisory Opinion*, paras 78 and 79. Watkin describes distinction as 'the primary vehicle for the humanising of war'. Kenneth Watkin, 'Warriors without Rights? Combatants, Unprivileged Belligerents and the Struggle over Legitimacy', *Program on Humanitarian Policy and Conflict Research, Harvard University, Occasional Paper Series*, Winter 2005, Vol. 2, p. 9. Dinstein writes that distinction is 'the hallmark of IHL: remove the principle of distinction and the entire IHL system collapses'. Yoram Dinstein, 'The System of Status Groups in International Humanitarian Law', in Wolff Heintschel von Heinegg and Volker Epping (eds), *International Humanitarian Law Facing New Challenges: Symposium in the Honour of Knut Ipsen* (Springer, 2007), p. 145.

involved large-scale military attacks by one state army against another, on battlefields situated apart from civilian populations. Today, the majority of armed conflicts involve at least one non-state actor, using fighters who may not be equipped, trained or disciplined to the same degree as a state armed force and who are fighting within urban settings intermingled with the civilian population. This makes it far harder to draw a clear dividing line between civilians and non-civilians for the purposes of distinguishing between legitimate and non-legitimate targets.

How the principle of distinction is applied varies to a degree according to whether the armed conflict is classified as an IAC[30] or a NIAC.[31] In IACs, IHL treaty law provides for combatant status and civilian status, whereas in NIACs, the principle of distinction becomes more difficult to apply.

1.3.2 International armed conflicts: combatants and POW status

The notion of a 'combatant' is often used in a generic sense to mean someone who has lost their civilian protection under IHL.[32] This is different from the legal notion of combatant status. Combatant status applies only in IACs,[33] and is defined in Article 43(2) of Protocol I:

> Members of the armed forces of a Party to the conflict (other than medical personnel and chaplains covered by Article 33 of the Third Geneva Convention) are combatants, that is to say they have the right to directly participate in hostilities.[34]

30 See Common Article 2, Geneva Convention for the Amelioration of the Condition of the Wounded and Sick in Armed Forces in the Field, 1949 (Geneva Convention I); Geneva Convention for the Amelioration of the Condition of Wounded, Sick and Shipwrecked Members of Armed Forces at Sea, 1949 (Geneva Convention II); Geneva Convention Relative to the Treatment of Prisoners of War, 1949 (Geneva Convention III); and Geneva Convention Relative to the Protection of Civilian Persons in Time of War, 1949 (Geneva Convention IV); and Article 1(3) and (4), Protocol I.

31 Common Article 3, Geneva Conventions and Article 1, Protocol Additional to the Geneva Conventions of 12 August 1949 and relating to the Protection of Victims of Non-International Armed Conflicts, 1977 (Protocol II).

32 See summary to Rule 1, ICRC Study.

33 However, see Henderson who argues that '[i]t makes legal sense for the law to be that government forces enjoy a form of combatant privilege' in a NIAC. Ian Henderson, 'Civilian Intelligence Agencies and the Use of Armed Drones', in M.N. Schmitt *et al* (eds), 13 *Yearbook of International Humanitarian Law* (2010), pp. 149–150. Also see Jens David Ohlin, 'The Combatants' Privilege in Asymmetric and Covert Conflicts', 40 *Yale Journal of International Law* (2015) pp. 337–393.

34 The armed forces of a Party to a conflict are defined as consisting: 'of all organized armed forces, groups and units which are under a command responsible to that Party for the conduct of its subordinates, even if that Party is represented by a government or an authority not recognized by an adverse Party. Such armed forces shall be subject to an internal disciplinary system which, *inter alia*, shall enforce compliance with the rules of international law applicable in armed conflict.' Article 43(1), Protocol I.

The right of combatants to DPH,[35] also known as the 'combatant's privilege',[36] has been described as being 'in essence a licence to kill or wound enemy combatants and destroy other enemy military objectives. A privileged combatant may also cause civilian casualties'.[37] It permits combatants to use violence against people and property without fear of punishment,[38] providing that they act in accordance with IHL.[39] The flip-side of the combatant's right to DPH is that they themselves constitute lawful targets for enemy combatants at all times, unless *hors de combat*.[40] Solis explains that combatants: 'May be targeted wherever found,

35 Baxter questions whether there is a 'right' to participate directly in hostilities: 'The propriety of statements that international law confers a "right" ... to exercise "belligerent rights" is highly questionable, and it is probably more accurate to assert that international law has dealt with war as a state of fact which it has hitherto been powerless to prevent.' Major Richard R. Baxter, 'So Called "Unprivileged Belligerency", Spies, Guerrillas and Saboteurs', 28 *British Yearbook of International Law* 323 (1951), pp. 323–324.

36 The terminology surrounding the term 'combatant privilege' can be confused. The Inter-American Commission refer to the combatant's privilege as being a separate thing from their right to POW status. See Inter-American Commission on Human Rights, *Report on Terrorism and Human Rights*, OEA/Ser.L/-V/II.116.Doc.5-rev.1corr, 22 October 2002, para. 67. Other commentators refer to the combatant's privilege as including both the right to kill or injure without fear of punishment and the right to POW status upon capture, for example see Baxter, ibid., pp. 326–327.

37 Inter-American Commission on Human Rights, ibid., para. 68.

38 'Those who are entitled to the juridical status of "privileged combatants" are immune from criminal prosecution for those warlike acts that do not violate the laws and customs of war but that might otherwise be common crimes under municipal law.' W.A. Solf, 'The Status of Combatants in Non-international Armed Conflicts under Domestic Law and Transnational Practice', 33 *American University Law Review* (1983), p. 57.

39 'War consists largely of acts that would be criminal if performed in times of peace ... Such conduct is not regarded as criminal if it takes place in the course of war, because the state of war lays a blanket of immunity over the warriors. But the area of immunity is not unlimited, and its boundaries are marked by the laws of war.' Telford Taylor, *Nuremberg and Vietnam: An American Tragedy* (Quadrangle Books, 1970), pp. 19–20.

40 Some debate whether a duty exists under international law obliging combatants to use the minimum force necessary to accomplish a military purpose when engaging with members of opposing forces. See Interpretive Guidance on the Notion of Direct Participation in Hostilities under International Humanitarian Law, adopted by the Assembly of the International Committee of the Red Cross on 26 February 2009 (ICRC Guidance), pp. 77–82. For a critique, see W. Hays Parks, 'Part IX of the ICRC "Direct Participation in Hostilities" Study: No Mandate, No Expertise, and Legally Incorrect', 42 *New York University Journal of International Law and Politics* 769 (2009–2010); Michael Schmitt, 'The Interpretive Guidance on the Notion of Direct Participation in Hostilities – A Critical Analysis', 1 *Harvard National Security Journal* 5 (2010), pp. 39–43; Jann K. Kleffner, 'Section IX of the ICRC Guidance on Direct Participation in Hostilities: The End of *Jus in Bello* Proportionality As We Know It?', 45(1) *Israel Law Review* 35–52 (2012); Jens D. Ohlin, 'The Duty to Capture', 97 *Minnesota Law Review* 1268 (2013); and Ryan Goodman, 'The Power to Kill or Capture Enemy Combatants', 24(3) *European Journal of International Law* 819–853 (2013).

armed or unarmed, awake or asleep, on a front line or a mile or a hundred miles behind the lines.'[41]

Combatants also have the right to POW status upon capture.[42] POWs are entitled to certain agreed standards of treatment during their incarceration,[43] and must be released at the end of hostilities.[44] The categories of those who are entitled to combatant status and those who are entitled to POW status are not identical:[45] most of those who qualify for combatant status are entitled to POW status upon capture,[46] whereas not all those who are entitled to POW status are combatants. For example, while persons accompanying the armed forces are entitled to POW status when captured, they are not combatants.[47]

1.3.3 Civilians and the civilian population

Article 50(1) of Protocol I defines a civilian as:

> any person who does not fall into one of the categories referred to in Article 4A(1), (2), (3) and (6) of Geneva Convention III and Article 43 of Additional Protocol I. In case of doubt whether a person is a civilian, that person shall be considered to be a civilian.

Civilians are therefore negatively defined as persons who are not members of the armed forces. This has been found to be a rule of customary law applying in both IACs and NIACs.[48] The 'civilian population' is defined as comprising 'all persons who are civilians'.[49] The presence within the civilian population of individuals who are not civilians does not deprive the population of its civilian character.[50]

41 G. Solis, 'Targeted Killing and the Law of Armed Conflict', 60 *Naval War College Review* (2007), p. 127.
42 Article 3, Hague Regulations 1907; Article 4A(1)–(3) and (6), Geneva Convention III and Article 44(1), Protocol I.
43 For example, Geneva Convention III details how POWs should be treated from the beginning of their captivity; their conditions of internment; labour conditions; the relations between POWs and the exterior; and penal and disciplinary sanctions.
44 Articles 118 and 119, Geneva Convention III.
45 Article 4A(1) and (2) is often referred to when defining who is entitled to combatant status; however, strictly speaking the provision defines entitlement to POW status only. Nils Melzer, 'The Principle of Distinction between Civilians and Combatants', in Andrew Clapham and Paola Gaeta (eds), *The Oxford Handbook of International Law in Armed Conflict* (Oxford University Press, 2014), p. 301.
46 Unless they are engaged in espionage, Article 46(1), Protocol I. Combatants also forfeit their right to POW status if they fail to distinguish themselves in an attack or in a military operation preparatory to an attack. Article 44(3) and (4), Protocol I and Rule 106, ICRC Study.
47 Articles 4A(4) and (5), Geneva Convention III.
48 Rule 5, ICRC Study.
49 Article 50(2), Protocol I.
50 Article 50(3), Protocol I.

Civilians enjoy general protection from military operations[51] and must not be made the object of attack.[52] Parties to the conflict must take constant care in the conduct of military operations to spare the civilian population, civilians and civilian objects.[53] Indiscriminate attacks are prohibited,[54] as are attacks against the civilian population or attacks by way of reprisals.[55] Civilians lose their civilian protection for such time as they DPH.[56]

1.3.4 Direct participation in hostilities

Civilians are protected from attack 'unless and for such time as they directly participate in hostilities'.[57] The phrase to 'directly participate in hostilities' is undefined in treaty law and has been the subject of much debate. In 2009, the International Committee of the Red Cross (ICRC) issued Interpretative Guidance on the Notion of Direct Participation in Hostilities (ICRC Guidance). It recommended that in order to qualify as DPH, an act must fulfil three cumulative criteria:

1 The act must be likely to adversely affect the military operations or military capacity of a party to an armed conflict or, alternatively, to inflict death, injury, or destruction on persons or objects protected against direct attack (threshold of harm).
2 There must be a direct causal link between the act and the harm likely to result either from that act, or from a coordinated military operation of which that act constitutes an integral part (direct causation); and
3 The act must be specifically designed to directly cause the required threshold of harm in support of a party to the conflict and to the detriment of another (belligerent nexus).[58]

Civilians performing acts that meet these three conditions lose their civilian protection and can be attacked as if they were combatants. They regain civilian protection once they cease to carry out each specific act of DPH.[59] The Guidance argues that '[t]he "revolving door" of civilian protection is an integral part, not a malfunction of IHL'.[60] Thus, according to the ICRC Guidance, civilians who

51 Articles 48 and 51(1), Protocol I and Article 13(1), Protocol II.
52 Articles 48 and 51(2), Protocol I and Article 13(2), Protocol II.
53 Article 57 and 58, Protocol I.
54 Article 51(4) and (5), Protocol I.
55 Article 51(6), Protocol I.
56 Article 51(3), Protocol I and Article 13(3), Protocol II.
57 Article 51(3), Protocol I; Article 13(3), Protocol II and Rule 6, ICRC Study.
58 Ibid., p. 46, and see pp. 46–64.
59 ICRC Guidance, pp. 70–71.
60 ICRC Guidance, p. 70. However, see Kenneth Watkin, 'Opportunity Lost: Organised Armed Groups and the ICRC "Direct Participation in Hostilities" Interpretive Guidance', 42 *New York University Journal of International Law & Politics* 641 (2010), pp. 682–690.

regularly or repeatedly DPH nevertheless regain their civilian protection once they cease so doing.[61]

1.3.5 Distinction in non-international armed conflicts

Despite the sparsity of treaty law governing NIACs,[62] a substantial body of customary law means that the same fundamental categories of persons are protected in NIACs as in IACs, including civilians,[63] persons *hors de combat*,[64] and medical and religious personnel.[65] One of the most significant differences between the two types of conflict is that the notion of combatant status, and its accordant right to POW status, does not exist in NIACs. In order for the principle of distinction to function effectively, some means is needed to distinguish between those who are protected against attack and those who are not. This has been a significant challenge which IHL has had to address in recent decades.

The ICRC Guidance contains recommendations concerning how the principle of distinction can operate effectively in NIACs. Aspects of the Guidance have been controversial and are not universally accepted, but nevertheless they provide an important reference point.[66] The Guidance distinguishes between members of state armed forces and members of organised armed groups.

(i) Members of state armed forces

Members of state armed forces, including regular armed forces and other armed groups or units organised under a command responsible to the state, are not civilians.[67] Membership in state armed forces is based on a formal approach to

61 However, see Schmitt *supra* FN 40, p. 38; Watkin, ibid., pp. 686–690; Bill Boothby, '"And for Such Time as": The Time Dimension to Direct Participation in Hostilities', 42 *New York University Journal of International Law & Politics* 741 (2010), pp. 753–758.
62 See for example, Common Article 3, Geneva Conventions and Protocol II.
63 Common Article 3, Geneva Conventions; Article 13, Protocol II and Rule 1, ICRC Study.
64 Common Article 3, Geneva Conventions; Article 7(1), Protocol II and Rule 47, ICRC Study.
65 Common Article 3, Geneva Conventions; Article 9(1), Protocol II and Rules 25 and 27, ICRC Study.
66 See for example: Watkin, *supra* FN 60; Michael Schmitt, 'Deconstructing Direct Participation in Hostilities: The Constitutive Elements', 42 *New York University Journal of International Law & Politics* 697 (2010); Boothby, *supra* FN 61; Hays Parks, *supra* FN 40; 'Keeping the Balance between Military Necessity and Humanity: A Response to Four Critiques of the ICRC's Interpretive Guidance on the Notion of Direct Participation in Hostilities', 42 *New York University Journal of International Law & Politics* 831 (2010); Geoffrey Corn and Chris Jenks, 'Two Sides of the Combatant Coin: Untangling Direct Participation in Hostilities from Belligerent Status in Non-international Armed Conflicts', 33 *University of Pennsylvania Journal of International Law* 313 (2011).
67 ICRC Guidance, pp. 30–31. Also see Dieter Fleck, 'The Law of Non-International Armed Conflict', in Dieter Fleck (ed.), *The Handbook of International Humanitarian Law* (Oxford University Press, 2013), para. 1203.

membership, in that membership is generally determined by domestic law and is expressed through formal integration into permanent units, distinguished by uniform, insignia and equipment. Members recover their civilian protection only once they disengage from active duty and re-integrate into civilian life, whether through a full discharge or as a deactivated reservist.

(ii) Members of an organised armed group

Organised armed groups constitute the armed forces of the non-state party to the conflict. In order to qualify as an organised armed group, its members must be armed, organised and under responsible command, although this need not be to the same level of sophistication as state armed forces.[68]

Members of organised armed groups are not civilians. However, membership of such groups can be difficult to define, as there are rarely formalised rules regarding membership, and there are frequently none regarding uniform, distinctive fixed signs or identification cards.[69] There can also be different degrees of affiliation.[70] The Guidance's approach is to determine membership of these groups in a 'functional sense', meaning that:

> membership must depend on whether the continuous function assumed by the individual corresponds to that collectively exercised by the group as a whole, namely the conduct of hostilities on behalf of a non-State party to the conflict.[71]

The Guidance terms this as having a 'continuous combat function'. For an individual to have a continuous combat function there must be evidence of their lasting integration into the organised armed group. The Guidance explains:

> individuals whose continuous combat function involves the preparation, execution, or command of acts or operations amounting to direct participation in hostilities are assuming a continuous combat function.[72]

Individuals who accompany or support an organised armed group, but who do not have a function to DPH, remain civilians.[73] Whether an individual has a continuous combat function can be openly expressed by the carrying of uniforms, distinctive signs or certain weapons. It can also be assessed on the basis of behaviour, for example if a person repeatedly DPH, rather than doing so on a spontaneous, sporadic or temporary basis.[74] Those individuals who are deemed to have a

68 Melzer, *supra* FN 45, p. 314.
69 ICRC Guidance, pp. 31–32.
70 Ibid., p. 33.
71 Ibid., p. 33.
72 Ibid., p. 34.
73 Ibid., pp. 34–35.
74 Ibid., p. 35.

continuous combat function are deprived of protection from direct attack for as long as they remain members of that group.[75] Reaction within the academic community to the continuous combat function test has been mixed,[76] and it is important to remember that there are other approaches that can be taken when distinguishing between civilians and fighters during a NIAC.[77]

The following chapter considers how some of these rules from IHL have been applied by ICTs within the context of ICL.

75 Ibid., p. 72.

76 Corn and Jenks are of the view that continuous combat function test 'provides a logical and workable method to status based targeting authority in NIAC'. Corn and Jenks, *supra* FN 66, p. 338. Watkin, on the other hand, argues that the approach 'creates a bias against State armed forces', in that it construes membership too narrowly, compared to the concept of membership of state armed forces. Watkin, *supra* FN 60, p. 694.

77 See for example Jann K. Kleffner, 'From "Belligerents" to "Fighters" and Civilians Directly Participating in Hostilities – on the Principle of Distinction in Non-International Armed Conflicts One Hundred Years after the Second Hague Peace Conference', 54(2) *Netherlands International Law Review* 315–336 (2007).

2 Untangling victims of war crimes from lawful casualties of war

IHL endeavours to take into account the realities of armed conflict. At its most dramatic, it must be understood and applied by military personnel in the middle of fast-developing, dangerous combat situations, when it should give them recourse to clear rules that are both easy to understand and flexible enough to apply in the particular situation they are facing. IHL was not primarily[1] drafted to be applied by lawyers acting with the benefit of hindsight in a courtroom setting.[2] This juxtaposition, between the application of IHL on the battlefield and its application after the event, perhaps becomes most evident when ICTs are being asked to rule on questions surrounding the lawfulness of targeting decisions.

The issue of who can be targeted and when in IHL is not as simple in practice as it may appear on paper. As Boothby notes, questions surrounding the targeting of individuals are 'easy to pose, but difficult to answer'.[3] Matters become more challenging when cases concerning violations of the laws on targeting enter the criminal arena. Such cases involve courts determining whether military decisions, often made under extreme circumstances, violated IHL. ICTs have to reconcile IHL and ICL, by interpreting the rules of IHL in a realistic way, so that it remains relevant for those who have to apply the rules on the ground,[4] and yet meets the

1 An exception being the grave breach provisions of the Geneva Conventions and Protocol I, see Chapter 3.

2 Rogier Bartels, 'Discrepancies Between International Humanitarian Law on the Battlefield and in the Courtroom: The Challenges of Applying International Humanitarian Law During International Criminal Trials', in M. Matthee *et al* (eds), *Armed Conflict and International Law: In Search of the Human Face, Liber Amicorum in Memory of Avril McDonald* (Asser Press, 2013).

3 William H. Boothby, *The Law of Targeting* (Oxford University Press, 2012), p. 141.

4 ICTs are not unaware of this problem. An example is the 'Rendulic Rule', which provides that when addressing the question of whether or not an act on the battlefield is unlawful, the question to be addressed by the court is 'whether the defendant at the time of its occurrence acted within the limits of honest judgment on the basis of the conditions prevailing at the time'. *United States v Wilhelm List et al*, XI Trials of War Criminals Before the Nuernberg Military Tribunals under Control Council Law No 10, US Govt Printing Office, Washington DC, 1947–1951, para. 1297; and see Brian J. Bill, 'The Rendulic "Rule": Military Necessity, Commander's Knowledge, and Methods of Warfare', 12 *Yearbook of International Law* 119 (2009).

requirements of ICL.[5] It is partly for this reason that although the principle of distinction is one of the most important principles in IHL, there have been relatively few cases brought before ICTs involving its violation.[6]

When determining whether a war crime has been committed during hostilities against persons, the focus should be upon two different, yet related, aspects, and the weight to be attached to each aspect differs according to which war crimes charge is under consideration. The first aspect is the status of the alleged victim at the time they were attacked. A correct determination as to the alleged victim's status as civilian or combatant (in the generic sense) is vital for some war crimes, marking the difference between an individual being an unlawful target, and therefore a potential victim of a war crime; or a legitimate target, and therefore a lawful casualty of war. Reaching a legal finding as to the status of an alleged victim after the event can be exceptionally difficult, as Hayashi explains: 'determining the status of persons in combat often involves dealing with factual uncertainties and legal presumptions. Judges must adjudicate these matters with caution.'[7]

However, while it is important that judges use caution when considering the status of an alleged victim, it is also necessary that they give the issue sufficient attention, and this has not always been the case. A prime example of the ICTY failing to do this can be found in one of the Trial Chamber's earlier judgments, the case of *Kordić and Čerkez*. In its Judgment, the Trial Chamber made no determination as to the status of individual victims, referring to them all as 'Bosnian Muslims' and implicitly treating them as civilians.[8] On appeal, the Appeals Chamber was required to re-examine the evidence to determine the status of the individual victims concerned, resulting in the findings of the Trial Chamber being overturned in some instances.[9] This example illustrates the need for a court to make a correct determination as to the status of alleged victims at the outset.

5 ICTs have not always achieved the right balance here. See for example the criticism following the *Gotovina* Judgment,*Prosecutor v Ante Gotovina et al*, ICTY, IT-06-90-T, Trial Chamber, 15 April 2011; and see Laurie R. Blank, 'Operational Law Experts Roundtable on the Gotovina Judgment: Military Operations, Battlefield Reality and the Judgment's Impact on the Effective Implementation and Enforcement of International Humanitarian Law', *Public Law & Legal Theory Research Paper Series*, Research Paper no 12-186 (2012); and Janine Natalya Clark, 'Courting Controversy: The ICTY's Acquittal of Croatian Generals Gotovina and Markač', 11(2) *Journal of International Criminal Justice* 399–423 (2013).

6 Regarding the difficulties of prosecuting such cases see William J. Fenrick, 'The Prosecution of Unlawful Attack Cases Before the ICTY', 7 *Yearbook of International Humanitarian Law* 153–189 (2004); and Carolin Wuerzner, 'Mission Impossible? Bringing Charges for the Crime of Attacking Civilians or Civilian Objects before International Criminal Tribunals', 90(872) *International Review of the Red Cross* 907–930 (2008).

7 Nobuo Hayashi, 'The Role of Judges in Identifying the Status of Combatants', 2 *Acta Societatis Martensis* 69–92 (2006), p. 70.

8 See *Prosecutor v Dario Kordić and Mario Čerkez*, ICTY, IT-95-14/2-T, Trial Judgment, 26 February 2001 (*Kordić and Čerkez* TC), paras 147, 149, 520, 646, and 800.

9 See *Prosecutor v Dario Kordić and Mario Čerkez*, ICTY, IT-95-14/2-A, Appeal Judgment, 17 December 2004 (*Kordić and Čerkez* AC), paras 450, 446, 524, 517, 603, 607 and 616–619.

The status of an alleged victim is only part of the puzzle that a court has to solve in these types of cases. A second aspect must also be addressed, namely the conduct of the victim and whether they were APH/DPH[10] at the time they were attacked. If the alleged victim was a civilian and their conduct amounted to APH/DPH, they were a legitimate military target rather than a victim of a war crime.[11] Alternatively, if the victim did not have civilian status, but was *hors de combat*, they could potentially be a victim of a war crime, depending on the crime charged.[12] As this chapter will illustrate, this distinction between the *status* of an alleged victim and their *conduct* has not always been fully appreciated by ICTs.

The chapter is divided into five sections. The first clarifies how the terms of a war crimes charge determine which persons qualify as victims of a particular war crime. Section two focuses upon war crimes where the civilian status of the victim is the decisive issue, and asks how civilian status has been defined in ICL and how ICTs have determined who had civilian status in practice. Section three considers war crimes where the conduct of the victim is the decisive issue, namely those that require that the alleged victim had been not APH/DPH at the time of the offence. Section four of the chapter explores how ICTs have determined who is a legitimate target, before conclusions are drawn in section five.

2.1 War crimes concerning persons

While the ICTY, the ICTR and the ICC have jurisdiction over war crimes involving persons, their precise jurisdiction differs. A line can be drawn in this respect between the ICTY and the ICTR, on the one hand, and the ICC on the other.

2.1.1 The ICTY and ICTR

Article 3 of the ICTY Statute and Article 4 of the ICTR Statute list a number of specific war crimes over which the tribunals have jurisdiction. They also contain a residual clause to the effect that the tribunals' jurisdiction 'shall include, but [shall] not be limited to' the specific war crimes listed, helping to ensure that no serious violation of the laws or customs of war escapes their jurisdiction.[13] War crimes charges brought under these articles are founded upon different IHL provisions, and the IHL roots upon which the crimes are based determine who can be victims of the crime.

10 Treaty law uses both the phrases 'active participation in hostilities' and 'direct participation in hostilities'. The predominant view has been that these phrases are interchangeable (*Prosecutor v Jean-Paul Akayesu*, ICTR-96-4-T, Trial Judgment, 2 September 1998 (*Akayesu* TC), para. 629; and *Prosecutor v Germain Katanga and Mathieu Ngudjolo Chui*, Decision on Confirmation of Charges, Case no ICC-01/04-01/07, Pre-Trial Chamber I, 30 September 2008 (*Katanga* Decision), para. 266), and the phrases are used interchangeably in this chapter.

11 Article 51(3), Protocol I.

12 See discussion below.

13 *Prosecutor v Duško Tadić*, ICTY, IT-94-1-AR72, Decision on the Defence Motion for Interlocutory Appeal on Jurisdiction, 2 October 1995 (*Tadić* Decision), para. 89.

In respect of the targeting of individuals during hostilities, there are two categories of war crimes.[14] The first encompasses crimes founded on Articles 48 and 51 of Protocol I and Article 13 of Protocol II, which protect 'civilians' and the 'civilian population'. Examples include the war crime of attacking civilians or the civilian population[15] and terrorising civilians.[16] These require that the victims concerned had civilian status. However, evidence of civilian status is insufficient in itself for the persons to constitute victims of the crime. As the Appeals Chamber in *Milošević* explains:

> to establish that the crimes of terror and unlawful attacks against civilians had been committed, the Trial Chamber was required to find beyond reasonable doubt that the victims of individual crimes were civilians *and* that they were not participating directly in the hostilities.[17]

When establishing whether an alleged victim qualifies as a victim of this category of war crimes, a two-stage test should therefore be applied: first, it must be established that the alleged victim had civilian status. If the answer to this is in the affirmative, the second stage of the test requires an examination of their conduct to ascertain whether they were not APH/DPH at the time they were attacked. It is only then that they can qualify as a victim of this class of crime.

The second category of war crimes encompasses charges founded on Common Article 3 of the Geneva Conventions and Article 4(1) of Protocol II. These provisions protect those who were not APH/DPH at the time of the alleged crime, including members of the armed forces who have laid down their weapons and persons *hors de combat*.[18] Examples of crimes founded on these provisions include murder, cruel treatment, torture and the taking of hostages. A broader range of victims are encompassed within this category than those included under the first. Here, the focus is upon the conduct of the alleged victim, namely whether they had been not APH/DPH at the time of the alleged crime. However, status continues to play a part in the determination, in that even if the alleged victim had not been engaging in an act of APH/DPH at the time they were attacked, if they had combatant status[19] they were a legitimate military target unless they were *hors de combat*.

14 Iain Bonomy, *Principles of Distinction and Protection at the ICTY* (Torkel Opsahl Academic EPublisher, Oslo, 2013), p. 10.

15 See *Prosecutor v Stanislav Galić*, ICTY, IT-98-29-T, Trial Judgment, 5 December 2003 (*Galić* TC), para. 27, and see *Tadić* Decision, para. 127, *Kordić and Čerkez* TC, para. 328, *Prosecutor v Zoran Kupreškić et al*, ICTY, IT-95-16-T, Trial Judgment, 14 January 2000 (*Kupreškić* TC), para. 521, and *Prosecutor v Pavle Strugar*, IT-01-42-AR72, Decision on Interlocutory Appeal, 22 November 2002 (*Strugar* Decision), para. 10.

16 *Galić* TC, paras 65, 133 and 138.

17 *Prosecutor v Dragomir Milošević*, ICTY, IT-98-29-A, Appeal Judgment, 12 November 2009 (*Milošević* AC), para. 57, emphasis added.

18 The relevant section of Common Article 3 reads 'persons taking no active part in the hostilities, including members of armed forces who have laid down their arms and those placed hors de combat by sickness, wounds, detention or any other cause'.

19 Or potentially if they had a continuous combat function, see Chapter 1.

2.1.2 The ICC

Article 8 of the ICC Statute contains a definitive list of war crimes over which the court has jurisdiction and specifies who constitutes a victim of each crime. Thus, the war crimes of 'intentionally directing attacks against the civilian population as such or against civilians not taking direct part in hostilities',[20] and 'intentionally launching an attack in the knowledge that such attack will cause incidental loss of life or injury to civilians ... which would be clearly excessive in relation to the concrete and direct overall military advantage anticipated',[21] need evidence that the alleged victims were civilian.

Two provisions of the ICC Statute require the victim to have been a combatant, '[k]illing or wounding a combatant who, having laid down his arms or having no longer means of defence, has surrendered at discretion'[22] and '[k]illing or wounding treacherously a combatant adversary'.[23] In addition, Article 8(2)(c), which applies in NIACs, gives the court jurisdiction over violations of Common Article 3, and requires that the victim had been not APH at the time they were attacked.

To summarise, war crimes concerning attacks against individuals can be divided into two categories: first, those that require it to be shown that the alleged victim had civilian status, but also that they were not APH/DPH at the time; and second, crimes where the focus is on the conduct of the victim, that they were not APH/DPH, with status playing a part in that determination. The following section discusses war crimes where the focus is on civilian status.

2.2 War crimes focusing on civilian status

The term 'civilian' is not defined in any ICT Statute; it has been left to the courts to clarify the concept. In doing this, ICTs have largely had recourse to Article 50(1) of Protocol I, which states that '[a] civilian is any person who does not belong to one of the categories of persons referred to in Article 4(A)(1),(2),(3) and (6) of the Third Convention and in Article 43 of this Protocol'. This excludes military personnel, including persons *hors de combat* from being included within the term.[24] In

20 Articles 8(2)(b)(i) and 8(2)(e)(i), ICC Statute.
21 Articles 8(2)(b)(iv), ICC Statute.
22 Article 8(2)(b)(vi), ICC Statute.
23 Article 8(2)(e)(ix), ICC Statute.
24 In *Galić* the Trial Chamber stated: 'For the purpose of the protection of victims of armed conflict, the term "civilian" is defined negatively as anyone who is not a member of the armed forces or of an organized military group belonging to a party to the conflict.' *Galić* TC, para. 47, and see *Kordić and Čerkez* AC, para. 97, *Prosecutor v Tihomir Blaškić*, ICTY, IT-95–14-T, Trial Judgment, 3 March 2000 (*Blaskić* TC), para. 180, and *Prosecutor v Clément Kuyishema and Obed Ruzindana*, ICTR-95-1-T, Trial Judgment, 21 May 1999 (*Kayeshima* TC), para. 179. However, see *Prosecutor v Pavle Strugar*, ICTY, IT-01-42-T, Trial Judgment, 31 January 2005 (*Strugar* TC), paras 277 and 282, which included those who are *hors de combat* within the definition of civilian. At the ICC, in the *Katanga*, Decision of the Confirmation of Charges, the Pre-Trial Chamber indicated that it would interpret 'civilian' in accordance with

order for an ICT to determine whether an individual can qualify as a victim of this category of war crime, it must address two things: did the alleged victim have civilian status, and, if so, were they not APH/DPH at the time?

2.2.1 Did the alleged victim have civilian status?

Determining who is entitled to civilian status is not always easy in practice. The ICTY has found that 'the clothing, activity, age, or sex of a person are among the factors which may be considered in deciding whether he or she is a civilian'.[25] In practice, the level of detail that the tribunal has gone into when determining the status of a victim or group of victims in a particular incident, has varied from case to case. Children,[26] the elderly[27] and women[28] have generally been presumed to be civilian.[29] The fact that an alleged victim was wearing civilian clothing at the time they were attacked has not tended to be determinative in itself. In addition, the opinion of one witness as to the status of victims has generally been deemed to be insufficient.[30]

Examining a combination of factors in order to determine status is a sensible and intuitive method. The implicit presumptions taken by the ICTY as regards children, women and the elderly being civilian, should not operate as a blueprint for other ICTs operating in a different context. The fact that an individual was wearing civilian clothes, was a child or was female may not necessarily be an indication that they were a civilian in the circumstances of a different armed conflict.

Article 50(1) of Protocol I, but the Chamber then stated that it defined the concept of 'civilians', in relation to Article 8(2)(b)(i) as 'being any persons not taking a direct part in hostilities', thereby including persons *hors de combat*. In the event, the Trial Judgment did not follow this approach, defining civilian to mean 'any persons who are not members of either State or non-State armed forces'. *Katanga* Decision, para. 266 at FN 366 and para. 276 at FN 375; and *Prosecutor v Germain Katanga*, Judgment pursuant to article 74 of the Statute, Case no ICC-01/04-01/07, 7 March 2014 (*Katanga* TC), paras 788 and 801.

25 *Galić* TC, para. 50.

26 For example, see *Galić* TC, para. 268. Also see *Prosecutor v Jadranko Prlić et al*, ICTY, IT-04-74-T, Trial Chamber, 29 May 2013 (Prlić, TC), Vol. III, paras 953 and 1003.

27 *Kordić and Čerkez* AC, para. 515:

28 Ibid., paras 486–488.

29 The SCSL held that armed law enforcement agencies of the state are generally presumed to be civilian, excepting military police or *gendarmerie* who operate under control of the military; however, 'the status of police officers in a time of armed conflict must be determined in light of an analysis of the particular facts of a case. A civilian police force, for example, may be incorporated into the armed forces, which will cause the police to be classified as combatants instead of civilians. This incorporation may occur *de lege*, by way of a formal Act, or *de facto*'. *Prosecutor v Moinina Fofana and Allieu Kondewa*, SCSL-04-14-T, Trial Judgment, 2 August 2007 (*CDF* case TC), para. 137, and see para. 136; and *Prosecutor v Issa Hassan Sesay, Morris Kallon and Augustine Gbao*, SCSL-2004-15-T, Trial Judgment, 2 March 2009 (*RUF* case TC), para. 102.

30 *Kordić and Čerkez* AC, para. 603.

When assessing whether an alleged victim had civilian status, an ICT must also take into account the presumption in IHL that in case of doubt as to whether a person is a civilian, they should be presumed to be so.[31] However, in the context of ICL, this requirement has to be weighed against the principle of *in dubio pro reo*, that in cases of doubt as to the appraisal of evidence, any uncertainties are to be interpreted in favour of the accused. This means that the IHL presumption in favour of civilian status, which in IHL works in favour of the victim and their need for protection, is interpreted in ICL in favour of the accused and their right to a fair trial.[32] In *Galić*, the Trial Chamber considered how the presumption of civilian status should be applied in ICL. Referring to the ICRC Commentary to Protocol I, it found that a person shall not be made the object of attack when it is not reasonable to believe, in the circumstances of the person contemplating the attack, including the information available to the latter, that the potential target is a combatant.[33] The Prosecution was required to show that the perpetrator was aware or should have been aware of the civilian status of the persons attacked. In case of doubt as to the status of a person, that person shall be considered to be a civilian. However, in such cases, the test is whether in the given circumstances a reasonable person could not have believed that the individual he or she attacked was a combatant.[34] The Trial Chamber therefore tried to reconcile the IHL rule that in cases of doubt, the presumption is in favour of the person being civilian, with the criminal law requirement that any uncertainties in interpretation be interpreted in favour of the accused.[35]

In order to determine whether the accused could reasonably ascertain the civilian status of the victim, the ICTY has taken into account factors[36] such as the distance between the victim and the alleged perpetrator;[37] whether there was combat activity going on at the time, or whether there were military targets nearby;[38] the visibility at the time of the incident[39] and whether the alleged perpetrator had an unobstructed line of sight; and the activity in which the victim was engaged.[40]

31 Article 50 (1), Protocol I. The ICRC Guidance states: 'All feasible precautions must be taken in determining whether a person is a civilian and, if so, whether that civilian is directly participating in hostilities. In cases of doubt, the person must be presumed to be protected against direct attack.' ICRC Guidance, p. 74. Once a person falls into the hands of the enemy, there is a legal presumption in favour of them being a POW, see Article 45(1), Protocol I. Also see Hayashi, *supra* FN 7, p. 76.

32 Hayashi, *supra* FN 7, pp. 76–84; and Bartels, *supra* FN 2, pp. 345–346.

33 *Galić* TC, para. 50.

34 *Galić* TC, para. 55; and see *Prosecutor v Pavle Strugar*, ICTY, IT-01-42-A, Appeals Judgment, 17 July 2008 (*Strugar* AC), para. 271.

35 See *Prosecutor v Tihomir Blaškić*, ICTY, IT-95-14-A, Appeals Judgment, 29 July 2004 (*Blaškić* AC), para. 111; and Hayashi, *supra* FN 7, pp. 78–79.

36 *Galić* TC, para. 188; Wuerzner, *supra* FN 6, pp. 913–915.

37 *Galić* TC, para. 520.

38 Ibid., paras 428 and 433.

39 Ibid., paras 311, 519 and 522.

40 Ibid., para. 520.

2.2.2 Was the alleged victim not actively/directly participating in hostilities at the time?

Determining whether an individual was a victim of this category of war crimes also requires an assessment as to whether their conduct at the time amounted to APH/DPH. This was acknowledged by the *Galić* Trial Chamber,[41] which considered the specific activities that the alleged victims were engaged in when making its determination as to whether the attacks against them constituted war crimes. For example, it found people engaged in the activities of riding a tram,[42] loading rubbish,[43] playing football,[44] fetching water,[45] picking lettuces[46] and riding a bicycle[47] were all engaged in civilian activities.

However, the Trial Chamber did not always make a sufficiently clear distinction between the status of the victim on the one hand, and their conduct on the other. This is illustrated in one incident, where the Trial Chamber found that there was reasonable doubt as to whether a witness's civilian status was clear at the time they were attacked. The incident concerned a witness, Witness L, who had been hit by sniper fire whilst pulling a trolley.[48] The Defence argued that his civilian status had not been established, in that he may have been transporting goods or necessities for the army at the time. The Chamber noted that pulling a cart was not in itself something to put one on notice that a 'combatant' was approaching.[49] Witness L had been dressed in civilian clothing and had not been carrying a weapon at the time he was attacked. Despite this, the Trial Chamber stated that it was left:

> with some doubt as to whether (Witness L's) status of civilian was reasonably clear to any armed force on that morning. Witness L testified that the incident occurred in the 'early morning hours', that although there was no fighting in the area, the area was full of troops. The evidence also shows that there was a check-point in the vicinity of the incident. Because it is reasonably possible that, in view of the location of the victim and other conditions such as the presence of troops and a check-point in the vicinity, SRK forces reasonably considered Witness L to be an enemy soldier advancing toward the frontline, the Trial Chamber is left with some doubt as to whether Witness L was deliberately targeted as a civilian.[50]

In its analysis of the situation, the Trial Chamber was looking to answer the wrong question, namely whether Witness L's civilian status was clear. Rather, the

41 *Galić* TC, para. 50.
42 Ibid., para. 258.
43 Ibid., para. 274.
44 Ibid., para. 386.
45 Ibid., para. 355.
46 Ibid., para. 548.
47 Ibid., para. 358.
48 Ibid., para. 556.
49 Ibid., para. 557.
50 Ibid., para. 557.

Chamber should have asked: first, was the victim a civilian, and, if so, second, were they not APH/DPH at the time of the attack?[51] The issue was not so much regarding the *civilian status* of Witness L; it had been established that he was wearing civilian clothing and was not carrying a weapon. Rather, the Trial Chamber should have posed a second question and asked whether the activity Witness L was engaged in, pulling a cart in that part of town at that time of the day, constituted APH/DPH. It was the conduct of Witness L which was really in doubt in this case, rather than his civilian status.

The incident serves to illustrate a situation where the Chamber's assessment could have benefited from a clearer, more structured application of the law to the facts.[52] While this more structured approach would no doubt have resulted in the Trial Chamber reaching the same conclusion here, it would have been a tidier way to resolve the matter, avoiding the need for awkward assessments as to whether the Witness could reasonably have been considered to be an 'enemy soldier advancing toward the frontline'.[53] Rather, the civilian status of the witness could have been confirmed, but his conduct as APH/DPH would bar him from being a victim of the crime.

To summarise, when determining whether an individual was a victim of war crimes which require that the victim have civilian status, ICTs would benefit from adopting a more structured approach. First, a determination as to whether the individual was a civilian is required. If civilian status is established, an assessment that their conduct at the time did not amount to APH/DPH is required. Adopting a structured approach when evaluating the evidence in these types of cases would ensure that the courts do not entangle themselves in questions of whether or not an alleged victim, whom the evidence suggests was a civilian, was a 'combatant'. They simply have to ask whether, despite their civilian status, the individual was APH/DPH, making them a legitimate target.

2.3 War crimes focusing on conduct

The second group of war crimes concerning attacks against individuals comprise war crimes where the emphasis is upon the conduct of the alleged victim at the time and whether they were not APH/DPH at the time they were attacked. These are crimes based on Common Article 3 and Protocol II. As the ICTR explains: 'The question to be answered simply is whether, at the time of the alleged offence, the alleged victim was directly participating in hostilities. If the answer is negative, the alleged victim was a person protected by Common Article 3 and Additional Protocol II.'[54]

51 *Milošević* AC, para. 57.
52 Hayashi, *supra* FN 7, pp. 80–82.
53 *Galić* TC, para. 557.
54 *Prosecutor v Semanza*, ICTR-97-20T, Trial Judgment, 15 May 2003 (*Semanza* TC), para. 366; *Prosecutor v Duško Tadić*, ICTY, IT-94-1-T, Trial Judgment, 7 May 1997 (*Tadić* TC), para. 615; *Blaskić* TC, para. 177; *Prosecutor v Goran Jelisić*, ICTY, IT-95-10-T, Trial Judgment, 14 December 1999 (*Jelisić* TC), para. 34; *Prosecutor v Zejnil*

This section explores, first, how APH/DPH has been defined by ICTs; second, how it has been determined whether a particular victim had been APH/DPH; third, how courts have determined whether members of organised armed groups were APH/DPH at the time they were attacked; fourth, what acts have been found to constitute APH/DPH in ICL; and finally, makes some comments concerning the *mens rea* requirement for these types of crimes.

2.3.1 Defining the concept of active/direct participation in hostilities

When defining what constitutes APH/DPH, ICTs have tended to refer to the definition provided within the ICRC Commentary, namely, that APH/DPH comprises 'acts of war which by their nature or purpose are likely to cause actual harm to the personnel and equipment of the enemy armed forces'.[55] In the event, few cases have considered the notion of APH/DPH in great depth, the exception being the case of *Strugar* from the ICTY,[56] where the Appeals Chamber held that:

> Conduct amounting to direct or active participation in hostilities is not … limited to combat activities as such … The notion of direct participation in hostilities must therefore refer to something different than involvement in violent or harmful acts against the adverse party. At the same time, direct participation in hostilities cannot be held to embrace all activities in support of one party's military operations or war effort … Moreover, to hold all activities in support of military operations as amounting to direct participation in hostilities would in practice render the principle of distinction meaningless.[57]

The Chamber fleshed out its definition by giving examples of what constituted direct and indirect participation. It examined military manuals, decisions of international bodies, and the Commentaries to the Geneva Conventions and their Protocols, to conclude that:

Delalić et al, ICTY, IT-96-21-A, Appeal Judgment, 20 February 2001 (*Čelebići* AC), para. 420; *Prosecutor v Miroslav Kvočka et al*, ICTY, IT-98-30/1, Trial Judgment, 2 November 2001 (*Kvočka* TC), para. 124; and *Prosecutor v Vidoje Blagojević and Dragan Jokić*, ICTY, IT-02-60-T, Trial Judgment, 17 January 2005 (*Blagojević* TC), para. 540.

55 ICRC Commentary to Protocol I, para. 1944; *Galić* TC, para. 48; and *Strugar* AC, para. 178.

56 The issue of what constitutes DPH was notably considered in *The Public Committee against Torture in Israel v Government of Israel*, HCJ 769/02 Supreme Court Sitting as High Court of Justice, 11 December 2005 (*Targeted Killings Judgment*); see William J. Fenrick, 'The Targeted Killings Judgment and the Scope of Direct Participation in Hostilities', 5(2) *Journal of International Criminal Justice* (2007) 332; Antonio Cassese, 'On Some Merits of the Israeli Judgment on Targeted Killings', 5(2) *Journal of International Criminal Justice* (2007) 339; and see the other articles in the same special issue of the *Journal of International Criminal Justice*.

57 *Strugar* AC, para. 176.

> Examples of active or direct participation in hostilities include: bearing, using or taking up arms, taking part in military or hostile acts, activities, conduct or operations, armed fighting or combat, participating in attacks against enemy personnel, property or equipment, transmitting military information for the immediate use of a belligerent, transporting weapons in proximity to combat operations, and serving as guards, intelligence agents, lookouts, or observers on behalf of military forces. Examples of indirect participation in hostilities include: participating in activities in support of the war or military effort of one of the parties to the conflict, selling goods to one of the parties to the conflict, expressing sympathy for the cause of one of the parties to the conflict, failing to act to prevent an incursion by one of the parties to the conflict, accompanying and supplying food to one of the parties to the conflict, gathering and transmitting military information, transporting arms and munitions, and providing supplies, and providing specialist advice regarding the selection of military personnel, their training or the correct maintenance of the weapons.[58]

According to the Appeals Chamber, APH/DPH includes activities that amount to more than just combat, but does not include activities that lend a supporting role to the war effort. However, it is one thing to provide general guidance as to the notion of APH/DPH, it is quite another to determine whether APH/DPH has actually occurred.

2.3.2 Determining whether an alleged victim was actively/directly participating in hostilities

The *Tadić* Trial Chamber provided some general guidance as to how to determine whether an individual was APH/DPH at the time they were attacked. It found that it is unnecessary to define precisely the line dividing those APH/DPH and those who are not; rather, it is sufficient to examine the relevant facts of each victim and to ascertain whether, in each individual's circumstances, that person was APH/DPH at the relevant time.[59]

The particular factors be taken into account when determining this have been found to include the activity the individual was engaged in; whether they were carrying weapons; and their clothing, age and gender.[60] This is similar to the list given by the Trial Chamber in *Galić* for determining whether a victim had civilian status. However, when determining whether an individual was APH/DPH or not, the primary focus should not be upon the status of the victim, which involves assessments as to their appearance, but rather upon whether their conduct amounted to APH/DPH at the time of the attack. Thus, if an alleged victim was

58 Ibid., para. 177.

59 *Tadić* TC, para. 616. Also see *Strugar* AC, para. 178; and *CDF* case TC, para. 134.

60 *Prosecutor v Sefer Halilović*, ICTY, IT-01-48-T, Trial Judgment, 16 November 2005 (*Halilović* TC), para. 34.

driving a truck full of ammunition to the front line at the time they were attacked, that would constitute APH/DPH, regardless of whether they were a woman, or elderly, or wearing civilian clothing: it is their conduct which is key.[61]

That is not to say that the status of an alleged victim has no part to play in a court's assessment as to whether an individual has been a victim of this category of war crime; rather, status plays a secondary role. If an individual was APH/DPH at the time they were attacked, they were a legitimate military target, not a victim of a war crime. On the other hand, if the alleged victim's conduct at the time did not amount to APH/DPH, their status must also be considered. If they were not APH/DPH and had civilian status, they are a potential victim of a war crime. However, if they did not have civilian status, matters become more complicated.

If the conflict in question was an IAC, and the alleged victim qualified for combatant status,[62] they constitute a legitimate military target at all times, unless *hors de combat*. Thus, even if a combatant is not engaging in a specific act of APH/DPH at the time they are attacked, their status means that they are a lawful target unless they are *hors de combat*. In NIACs, where combatant status does not exist,[63] the situation is more complex. In cases involving alleged victims who had been involved in the fighting, an ICT should consider at the outset how they will approach the matter of distinguishing between those who could be legitimately targeted and those who could not. This involves an assessment as to how to determine who constituted a member of an organised armed group and consideration as to what such membership entailed: did membership of the group entail loss of civilian protection, or was it only those members who, for example, had a continuous combat function which did so?[64] The following section discusses how ICTs have approached this issue.

2.3.3 Active/direct participation in hostilities and members of organised armed groups

In the event, ICTs have determined whether a member of an organised armed group had been APH/DPH for the purposes of this category of war crime in only a handful of cases. Different approaches have been taken concerning whether and when such individuals' conduct amounted to APH/DPH.

In the case of *Halilović*, the ICTY held that the fact of membership in the armed forces or an organised armed group is not sufficient in itself to constitute APH/DPH. The Trial Chamber stated:

> While membership of the armed forces can be a strong indication that the victim is directly participating in the hostilities, it is not an indicator which in

61 ICRC Guidance, p. 56; and *Targeted Killings* Judgment, para. 35.

62 Article 43(2), Protocol I.

63 See Chapter 1.

64 This is discussed further below. Also see Chapter 1 and see ICRC Guidance, pp. 30–36 and Boothby, *supra* FN 3, pp. 141–164.

> and of itself is sufficient to establish this. Whether a person did or did not enjoy protection of Common Article 3 has to be determined on a case-by-case basis.[65]

This approach is correct. If someone is a member of an armed force, then that is a good indication that they were APH/DPH at the time. In order for them to be a victim of this class of crime, it must be shown that they were *hors de combat*. Thus, in the *Tadić* case, the Trial Chamber considered whether detained fighters could be victims of violations of Common Article 3. It stated:

> Whatever their involvement in hostilities prior to that time, each of these classes of persons cannot be said to have been taking an active part in the hostilities. Even if they were members of the armed forces of the Government of the Republic of Bosnia and Herzegovina or otherwise engaging in hostile acts prior to capture, such persons would be considered 'members of armed forces' who are 'placed hors de combat by detention'.[66]

As soon as a member of an armed force is captured or detained, they are not APH/DPH, and are entitled to the minimum protections guaranteed by Common Article 3, violations of which amount to a war crime.[67] This fact has not always been sufficiently appreciated at the ICTY, however. An example of this can be found in the case of *Boškoski and Tarčulovski*, concerning charges of murder and cruel treatment founded on Common Article 3. In respect of one victim, Muharem Ramadani, who had been killed when in police custody, the Appeals Chamber confirmed the Trial Chamber's view that he had not been APH/DPH at the time. It stated that the Trial Chamber:

> based its finding on the fact that Ramadani was in the custody of the police members and on evidence indicating that he wore civilian clothes and the only weapon found in ... [the] house was a light shotgun for hunting birds, which had not been used or moved. The Appeals Chamber finds that on the basis of the evidence, the Trial Chamber was satisfied beyond reasonable doubt that the perpetrators were aware or should have been aware that Ramadani was taking no active part in the hostilities.[68]

In this instance, there was no need for the Tribunal to investigate whether the victim had been wearing civilian clothes or whether he had had a weapon. The fact

65 *Halilović* TC, para. 34, and see *Prosecutor v Milan Martić*, ICTY, IT-95-11-T, Trial Judgment, 12 June 2007 (*Martić* TC), para. 47.
66 *Tadić* TC, para. 616.
67 *Prosecutor v Radovan Karadžić*, IT-95-5/18-T Trial Judgment, 24 March 2016 (*Karadžić* TC), para. 5943.
68 *Prosecutor v Ljube Boškoski and Johan Tarčulovski*, ICTY, IT-04-82-A, Appeal Judgment, 19 May 2010 (*Boškoski and Tarčulovski* AC), para. 102, and see *Prosecutor v Ljube Boškoski and Johan Tarčulovski*, ICTY, IT-04-82-T, Trial Judgment, 10 July 2008 (*Boškoski and Tarčulovski* TC), para. 328.

that he was in the custody of the police when he was killed meant that he was not APH/DPH at the time.

The killing of another victim, Rami Jusufi, was considered in the same case. He was attacked while standing outside, near the open door of a house. He was unarmed and wearing civilian clothes.[69] The Defence argued that Rami Jusufi had been a member of an organised armed group called the NLA.[70] The Trial Chamber found that this was not the case,[71] stating:

> The evidence does not support a finding that Rami Jusufi was anything other than an unarmed civilian, and, *in any event*, not taking an active part in hostilities at the time he was shot with fatal consequences.[72]

This sentence is interesting, as the phrase 'in any event' suggests that as Rami Jusufi was not APH/DPH at the time he was killed, even if he had been a member of the NLA,[73] he would have been viewed by the Chamber as not APH/DPH for the purposes of the crime. However, the evidence suggests that he was shot whilst standing in the doorway of a house; there is no indication that he had been detained or was *hors de combat* for any other reason. If he was a member of an organised armed group, he arguably[74] did not have civilian status, meaning that his death in those circumstances would not have amounted to a war crime.[75]

A third alleged victim in the same case, Sulejman Bajrami, had been killed whilst in custody, although there was some evidence that he may have been killed while trying to escape. Again, the Defence argued that he had been a member of the NLA, or at least was 'involved' in the NLA.[76] The Appeals Chamber held that:

> Considering that Bajrami had been mistreated right before he was killed, as well as the circumstances in which he was shot, the Trial Chamber did not err in failing to find that his black t-shirt would have given rise to any reasonable doubt that Bajrami's conduct at the time of his death was connected to the activities of the NLA.[77]

69 *Boškoski and Tarčulovski* TC, para. 312.
70 The National Liberation Army of Macedonia.
71 *Boškoski and Tarčulovski* TC, paras 310 and 311.
72 Ibid., para. 311.
73 The Trial Chamber had found that the NLA sufficiently demonstrated the characteristics of an organised armed group or force. See *Boškoski and Tarčulovski* TC, para. 291, emphasis added.
74 This is a situation where the tribunal could have considered what the consequences of membership within the NLA were as regards loss of civilian status. See discussion below.
75 On Appeal, the Prosecution argued for a specific acts approach, stating: 'the issue to be decided by the Trial Chamber was not whether Rami Jusufi was a member of the NLA, but whether he was taking an active part in hostilities at the time he was shot.' However, this was not investigated by the Appeals Chamber. *Boškoski and Tarčulovski* AC, para. 80.
76 Ibid., para. 90.
77 Ibid., para. 92.

Once again in this incident, there was no need for the Tribunal to enquire into whether the alleged victim had been a member of the NLA, as the fact that he had been in the custody of the perpetrators meant that he was not APH/DPH. Had he been killed whilst escaping, that would have changed the situation somewhat.[78] However, the evidence showed that even if he did escape, this was only for a matter of moments,[79] and, at the very least, under IHL he was entitled to a warning before weapons were used against him.[80]

Another relevant case is that of *Halilović*, where the Trial Chamber of the ICTY considered a curious situation whereby certificates in the name of some of the victims had been issued by the Croatian Defence Council (HVO). These certificates provided that the victim in question had been mobilised in the army and had been killed, for example, 'while carrying out an order on the defence front line',[81] or that they were 'killed … by … [Army of the Republic of Bosnia and Herzegovina – ABiH] forces … while performing a task ordered by Commander Josip Prskalo'.[82] The purpose of these certificates was to entitle the victims' families to financial aid.[83] The Chamber found that the alleged victims in question had been engaged in civilian activities at the time they were attacked and had been wearing civilian clothes; however, the contents of the certificates cast doubt on whether they had been APH/DPH at the time they were killed.[84] Thus, in respect of one victim, the Trial Chamber stated:

> The Trial Chamber notes that Kata Ljubić was wearing civilian clothes at the time of her death, that the evidence does not establish that she had any weapons and that she was killed behind her house. However, the Trial Chamber cannot disregard the clear wording of the certificate that Kata Ljubić was carrying out an order as a member of the HVO at the time of her death. The Trial Chamber therefore finds that the Prosecution has not proven beyond reasonable doubt that Kata Ljubić was taking no active part in the hostilities at the time of her death.[85]

The Trial Chamber undoubtedly reached the correct decision in this case. As the certificates identified the alleged victims as being members of HVO and stated that they had been carrying out orders at the time they were killed, there was a reasonable doubt as to whether they had been APH/DPH at the time they were attacked. Accordingly, they could not be victims of a war crime founded on Common Article 3 unless the evidence showed that they had been *hors de combat* at the relevant time.

78 For example, see Article 42, Geneva Convention III.
79 *Boškoski and Tarčulovski* TC, paras 314 and 316.
80 Article 42, Geneva Convention III.
81 *Halilović* TC, para. 643.
82 Ibid., para. 637.
83 Ibid., para. 637.
84 Ibid., paras 642, 642 and 637.
85 Ibid., para. 643.

To summarise, as soon as a member of an organised armed group becomes *hors de combat*, they can be victims of war crimes that focus on the conduct of the victim as having been not APH/DPH. Once this is established, enquiries into, for example, the clothing of the victim or whether they had had a weapon up until that point are completely unnecessary. The fact of their being *hors de combat* is sufficient.

2.3.4 What has amounted to active/direct participation in hostilities in international criminal law?

The issue of what constitutes APH/DPH has risen infrequently before ICTs. The leading case is that of *Strugar* from the ICTY. It concerned an attack by the Yugoslav People's Army (JNA) on the Croatian town of Dubrovnik. One specific incident in the case concerned an individual, Valjalo, who was employed as a driver for the Dubrovnik Municipal Crisis Staff. His duties required him to drive local and foreign officials around the town. He was injured during the attack on the town while on his way to work. During the trial, Valjalo gave evidence that he was a civilian, and that at the time he was attacked he was wearing civilian clothes and was unarmed.[86] The Trial Chamber found, with no analysis,[87] that 'there is nothing in the evidence to suggest that, as a driver, in this capacity, he was taking an active part in the hostilities'.[88] On Appeal, Strugar challenged the Trial Chamber's finding. The Appeals Chamber considered evidence that Valjalo had been granted the status of a 'disabled veteran of the Croatian war of defence' by the Dubrovnik Secretariat for Health, Social Welfare, Labour Soldiers and Disability Affairs.[89] It found that:

> it was open to a reasonable trier of fact to find that Valjalo's status as a disabled veteran did not raise a reasonable doubt as to his non-participation in acts of war which by their nature or purpose were intended to cause actual harm to the personnel or equipment of the JNA forces in the Dubrovnik region at the time he was injured.[90]

The Appeals Chamber then considered whether Valjalo had APH/DPH by driving members of the Crisis Staff and other officials to their war tasks during the attack on the city.[91] It stated:

86 *Strugar* AC, para. 182.
87 William J. Fenrick, 'Riding the Rhino: Attempting to Develop Usable Legal Standards for Combat Activities', 30 *Boston College International & Comparative Law Review* 111 (2007), p. 120.
88 *Strugar* TC, para. 274.
89 *Strugar* AC, para. 183.
90 Ibid., para. 183.
91 Ibid., para. 184.

> there is no reasonable doubt that the required nexus is lacking between Valjalo's activities at the time of the offence (he was injured near his home while on his way to work) and any possible participation of the Dubrovnik Municipal Crisis Staff, municipal officials and officials of the Republic of Croatia in acts of war which by their nature or purpose were intended to cause actual harm to the personnel or equipment of the JNA forces in the Dubrovnik region.[92]

The Appeals Chamber confirmed the Trial Chamber's finding that a reasonable trier of fact could have concluded beyond a reasonable doubt that at the time of the alleged offence Valjalo was not APH/DPH.[93]

Although the Tribunal reached the correct decision in this case, it would have benefited from taking a more structured approach to the facts. The first consideration was that at the time of the attack, the conduct of the alleged victim, that of driving to work, did not amount to APH/DPH. The second consideration was whether he had civilian status or whether he was a person *hors de combat*. On the available evidence, he was a civilian, meaning that he was a victim of the war crime.

Other ICTs have also considered what amounts to APH/DPH. In the *CDF* case, the Trial Chamber of the SCSL considered whether collaborating with a government or armed forces amounts to APH/DPH under Common Article 3. It held that:

> Persons accused of 'collaborating' with the government or armed forces would only become legitimate military targets if they were taking direct part in the hostilities. Indirectly supporting or failing to resist an attacking force is insufficient to constitute such participation.[94]

The issue of whether the possession of weapons constitutes APH/DPH was considered by the ICTR in the case of *Bagosora*. It concerned the massacre of a group of refugees, some of whom had been in possession of weapons at the time they were killed. The Trial Chamber found:

> There is evidence that the refugees … used traditional weapons to defend themselves against repeated attacks by militiamen. The Chamber is not satisfied that the use of rudimentary defensive weapons changes the status of the victims. Even if those with weapons for self-defence could be characterized as combatants, their possible presence within groups of refugees does not deprive those who are non-combatants of their protected status.[95]

92 Ibid., para. 184.
93 Ibid., para. 185.
94 *CDF* case TC, para. 135.
95 *Prosecutor v Bagosora et al*, ICTR-98-41-T, Trial Judgment, 18 December 2008 (*Bagosora* TC), para. 2238.

This passage evidences some confusion between the notions of the victims' status and their conduct. The appropriate question here was not whether the use of weapons by the victims to defend themselves altered their status from civilian to 'combatant'; rather, the question was whether the act of their possessing weapons could be construed as APH/DPH. IHL allows for the use of force in self-defence in limited situations, when one's life or the life of others is seriously at risk, and this may have applied in the circumstances of this case.[96] The ICTR could have found the alleged victims to be civilians, and held that the victims' use of rudimentary weapons in that situation to defend themselves against the attackers did not constitute APH/DPH because they were acting in self-defence. Although the Chamber would have reached the same conclusion, it would have avoided any uncertainty concerning the status of the victims by listing as potential 'combatants'. Rather, all of those involved would unequivocally have been found to have been victims of the crime.

2.3.5 Mens rea

Finally, a brief word on the *mens rea* requirement for war crimes founded on Common Article 3, namely that the perpetrator knew, or should have been aware, that the victim was not APH/DPH at the time the crime was committed.[97] In the case of *Boškoski and Tarčulovski*, the Defence counsel for Tarčulovski called this formulation into question. They argued that the Trial Chamber had erred in both law and fact in deciding that in order to incur criminal liability for acts prohibited under Common Article 3, it must merely be established that the victims of the alleged violation were not APH/DPH at the time the crime was committed. Rather, the prosecutor must also show that the perpetrator 'was aware or should have been aware of the status of the victim'. Furthermore, in case of doubt, the Prosecution must show that a reasonable person could not have believed that the individual he or she attacked was a combatant.[98] Thus, for example, in the incident concerning the victim Rami Jusufi, discussed above, the Defence argued that the *mens rea* of the perpetrator should be shown to be whether he knew that Jusufi was a civilian or could not reasonably have believed otherwise.[99]

In response, the Prosecution argued that the Appeal Chamber's jurisprudence does not explicitly mention the victim's status as an element of the *mens rea* to be established for Common Article 3 offences. However, the *mens rea* must include that the victim was taking no active part in the hostilities at the time of the offence which requires the awareness of (or reckless indifference as to) the factual circumstances establishing that the victim was taking no active part in the hostilities at the time of the crime. It is not necessary to prove knowledge of this legal

96 See discussion below.

97 See *Čelebići* AC, paras 420 and 423–424; *Strugar* AC, para. 172; and *Prosecutor v Mladen Naletilić and Vinko Martinović*, ICTY, IT-98-34-A, Appeal Judgment, 3 May 2006 (*Naletilićand Martinović* AC), paras 118–12.

98 *Boškoski and Tarčulovski* AC, para. 61, referring to *Tarčulovski* Appeal Brief, paras 139–141 and 181.

99 Ibid., para. 84.

status.[100] The Appeals Chamber confirmed the Prosecution's view of the matter, stating:

> It is well established in the Tribunal's jurisprudence that the elements of a Common Article 3 crime encompass the requirement that the victim did not take an active part in the hostilities at the time when the crime was committed. Therefore, the Appeals Chamber is satisfied that the principle of individual guilt requires that the perpetrator of a Common Article 3 crime knew or should have been aware that the victim was taking no active part in hostilities when the crime was committed.[101]

It is submitted that the Appeals Chamber's finding is correct, and there is no requirement to show that the victim was a civilian for this category of war crimes. In cases where the alleged victim was not in the hands of the perpetrator at the time they were attacked, the status of the alleged victim is of some relevance, as if the alleged victim was a member of an armed group then they are legitimate military targets unless *hors de combat*. However, if the alleged victim has surrendered, or is wounded, sick or captured, all questions as to status are irrelevant, the alleged victim was not APH/DPH and is a potential victim of this class of war crimes.

2.4 Determining who was a legitimate target in international criminal law

IHL provides that in IACs, all members of the armed forces of a party to the conflict, except medical and religious personnel, are combatants.[102] Combatants have the right to DPH and a consequence of this right is that opposing forces may target them legitimately at all times, unless *hors de combat*. In NIACs, the predominantly accepted position is that members of state armed forces of a party to a conflict are legitimate military targets at all times, unless *hors de combat*.[103] The situation of members of non-state armed groups is less clear. The ICRC has advanced the view that only those members who have a continuous combat function lose their civilian protection, but this is not universally accepted.[104] In view of these uncertainties in IHL, it is interesting to explore how ICTs have identified who constitutes a lawful military target and when.

2.4.1 Identifying legitimate military targets

Only a handful of cases have made explicit findings concerning whether members of organised armed groups had been legitimately targeted. More frequently, the

100 Ibid., para. 63, referring to Prosecution Response Brief, para. 116.
101 Ibid., para. 66.
102 Article 43(2), Protocol I and Rule 3, ICRC Study.
103 ICRC Guidance, pp. 30–31 and see Chapter 1.
104 ICRC Guidance, pp. 31–36 and see Chapter 1.

matter has been dealt with implicitly in the judgment of the court. A good example of the ICTY doing this can be found in *Galić*.

In *Galić*, the Trial Chamber considered one particular incident, where SRK[105] forces had shelled a football tournament taking place in a car park. An estimated 200 spectators were attending the match, consisting of a mix of ABiH soldiers and civilians.[106] There was conflicting evidence as to how many soldiers were present, but the Chamber found that military personnel had been off-duty, unarmed and had not been engaged in any military activity.[107] It made no determination as to whether the conflict at the time of the events under consideration was classified as an IAC or a NIAC.[108] The Chamber held that the attack breached the principle of proportionality and constituted an indiscriminate attack, stating:

> there is no evidence on the Trial Record that suggests that the SRK was informed of the event taking place in the parking lot. However, had the SRK troops been informed of this gathering and of the presence of ABiH soldiers there, and had intended to target these soldiers, this attack would nevertheless be unlawful. Although the number of soldiers present at the game was significant, an attack on a crowd of approximately 200 people, including numerous children, would clearly be expected to cause incidental loss of life and injuries to civilians excessive in relation to the direct and concrete military advantage anticipated.[109]

Another incident considered in the case concerned a bus carrying several passengers, which was hit by sniper fire.[110] The bus driver was a military conscript who was employed by a public transport company to drive civilians on a regularly scheduled bus route during ceasefires.[111] At the time of the attack he was not wearing a uniform and was not carrying a weapon.[112] The Trial Chamber found that 'the civilian passengers of a civilian vehicle were deliberately targeted from SRK-controlled territory',[113] and that the passengers were the victim of an unlawful attack.[114]

In both these incidents, the Trial Chamber implicitly held that the members of ABiH, which was the military force of the Republic of Bosnia and Herzegovina, were legitimate targets, despite the fact that they were not engaging in a specific act of DPH at the time. This reflects the view that members of state armed

105 Sarajevo Romanija Corps, a branch of the Bosnian Serb Army.
106 *Galić* TC, para. 372.
107 Ibid., para. 386.
108 Ibid., para. 22.
109 Ibid., para. 387; and see Daniela Kravetz, 'The Protection of Civilians in War: The ICTY's *Galić* case', 17(3) *Leiden Journal of International Law* 521–536 (2004), pp. 532–533.
110 *Galić* TC, para. 362.
111 Ibid., para. 362.
112 Ibid., para. 364.
113 Ibid., para. 367.
114 Ibid., para. 366.

forces are always a legitimate military target in both IACs and NIACs, unless *hors de combat*.[115]

One case that explicitly considered whether members of irregular armed groups constituted legitimate military targets is *Kordić and Čerkez*, where the Appeals Chamber of the ICTY considered the status of members of the Territorial Defence (TO). The TO was a system of defence peculiar to the former Yugoslavia, whereby individual villages had their own TO unit consisting of part-time soldiers and conscripts.[116] During the hostilities, the TO of each village was aligned to one of the parties to the conflict. The military capabilities of these units often varied considerably, as Olásolo explains:

> The members of the defence systems were poorly equipped, as they typically only had hunting rifles and lacked uniforms. They usually carried out duty guards and gathered information from the surroundings of their village, which included, whenever necessary, shooting at enemy forces approaching the village.[117]

In *Kordić and Čerkez*, the Appeals Chamber paid specific consideration as to whether members of the TO constituted legitimate military targets at all times, or only when they were engaging in a specific act of APH/DPH. The Appeals Chamber agreed with the Trial Chamber's finding that the conflict in question was an IAC,[118] and noted the provisions of Article 43 of Protocol I, and Article 4 of Geneva Convention III. It found that read together, they establish that members of armed forces (other than medical personnel and chaplains) and members of militias or volunteer corps forming part of such armed forces are 'combatants' and cannot claim civilian status. Neither can members of organised resistance groups, provided that they are commanded by a person responsible for his or her subordinates, that they have a fixed distinctive sign recognisable at a distance, that they carry arms openly, and that they conduct their operations in accordance with the laws and customs of war.[119] The Chamber noted that:

> Particular attention has to be paid to the situation of members of a Territorial Defence (TO) and as to whether they are to be considered as combatants at all times during the conflict or only when they directly take part in hostilities, that is, when they participate in acts of war which by nature or purpose are likely to cause actual harm to the personnel and equipment of the enemy's armed forces.[120]

115 ICRC Guidance, pp. 30–31.
116 See *Prosecutor v Zejnil Delalić et al*, ICTY, IT-96-21-T, Trial Judgment, 16 November 1998 (*Čelebići* TC), paras 93–95; and see Héctor Olásolo, *Unlawful Attacks in Combat Situations: From the ICTY's Case Law to the Rome Statute* (Martinus Nijhoff Publishers, 2008), pp. 111–113.
117 Olásolo, ibid., p. 112.
118 *Kordić and Čerkez* TC, para. 145, confirmed in *Kordić and Čerkez* AC, para. 374.
119 *Kordić and Čerkez* AC, para. 50.
120 Ibid., para. 51, referring to ICRC Commentary to the Protocols, p. 515, para. 1677.

It concluded:

> the Appeals Chamber considers that members of the armed forces resting in their homes in the area of the conflict, as well as members of the TO residing in their homes, remain combatants whether or not they are in combat, or for the time being armed.[121]

The Chamber therefore regarded members of the TO as targetable at all times by virtue of their membership in the organisation. The consequences of this became clear when the Appeals Chamber applied its reasoning to a specific incident: a man and a women who were at home in their apartment were shot through their apartment door by HVO soldiers and killed. The male victim had been an assistant commander in the TO, whereas the female victim had worked as a member of the TO Municipal staff. The title of 'assistant commander' suggests that the male victim had a combat role within the organisation. The situation is less clear regarding the role of the female victim who worked on the TO Municipal staff; no information is provided in the Judgment as to what her duties had been or what her role involved. The Appeals Chamber, applying its earlier finding to the facts, held that:

> there is no doubt that the soldiers who shot both victims had the intent to kill them or to inflict them serious injury in the reasonable knowledge that it was likely to result in death. However, the Appeals Chamber considers that as TO members, the two victims are to be considered as 'combatants' and cannot claim the status of civilians.[122]

The couple's membership within the TO meant that they could be targeted at all times. Had the Appeals Chamber adopted a function-based approach, for example the ICRC's continuous combat function approach, a different conclusion could conceivably have been reached. The male victim would likely have been found to constitute a legitimate target as he had a combat role within the organisation, whereas the female victim may have been deemed to have had civilian status, as her role within the organisation was administrative. The incident serves to illustrate the consequences that can arise from applying a membership-based, as opposed to a function-based, approach when determining who can be targeted and when in an organised armed group.

A different approach was taken by the ICTY in the *Milošević* case, where the Trial Chamber considered the legality of the shooting of a witness by a sniper. The witness had been employed as a 'cook assistant' by the ABiH.[123] At the time she was shot, she was dressed in civilian clothing, was unarmed and was engaged

121 *Kordić and Čerkez* AC, para. 51.
122 Ibid., para. 458.
123 *Prosecutor v Dragomir Milošević*, IT-98-29/1-T, Trial Judgment, 12 December 2007 (*Milošević* TC), para. 362.

in the activity of gathering firewood in a private garden.[124] The Defence argued that the witness had been a member of the ABiH and was therefore a lawful target. This argument was rejected by the Chamber, which found her to be a civilian.[125] Although there was evidence that the witness was employed by ABiH as a cook and had some form of uniform, the Trial Chamber focused on the fact that at the time she was shot she was 'an unarmed cook'.[126] The Chamber concentrated on her role within the organisation, and that at the time she was shot she was in civilian clothing and engaged in a civilian activity. Unlike the *Kordić and Čerkez* case, where the tribunal treated all members of the armed group as being legitimate targets, irrespective of their function in the group, the *Milošević* case focused on the victim's function. As she had the appearance of a civilian and was engaged in a civilian activity when she was attacked, and as she had a non-combat role within the group, she continued to have civilian protection.

The contrasting outcomes in these two cases serve to illustrate that the ICTY has not applied a consistent approach when assessing when members of armed groups can be lawfully attacked. There are benefits to be had from adopting a more structured and considered approach when determining issues surrounding who constitutes a legitimate target and when. In cases involving members of organised armed groups as alleged victims of war crimes, the court should actively consider whether an individual's membership within the group results in a loss of civilian status, or whether their function within the group is key. IHL does not provide a definitive answer to this, and ICTs may have a part to play in resolving outstanding issues. At the very least, ICTs should be more conscious of the debates within IHL when considering these cases.

2.4.2 Civilians who actively/directly participate in hostilities

The final part of this chapter considers the phenomenon of civilians who APH/DPH on a more spontaneous basis, and when they constitute legitimate military targets. Once again, the ICTY's approach has been interesting in this regard.

The tribunal had to consider attacks against members of the TO in several cases, and has not always taken the approach of the Appeals Chamber in *Kordić and Čerkez* in finding members of the TO to be legitimate targets unless *hors de combat*. Rather, it has drawn a distinction between TO defences that were more military in nature, as was the case in *Kordić and Čerkez*, and those that were more *ad hoc* and 'civilian' in nature.

An example of the ICTY adopting the latter approach can be found in *Blaškić*, where the Trial Chamber was concerned with the question of whether there had been a military objective within the geographical area in question which justified the military attack that had occurred. Witness evidence was presented that:

124 Ibid., paras 362 and 365.
125 Ibid., para. 366.
126 Ibid., para. 366.

> the territorial defence was starting to organise in the area and consisted of about 120 men whose main task was to carry out night watches … their participation was purely voluntary and there was no disciplinary sanction for those who failed to take their turn on guard. It was therefore a sort of civil defence rather than an army strictly speaking. The members of the territorial defence were very badly equipped and most of them were dressed as civilians and did not think of themselves as soldiers.[127]

The Trial Chamber also made reference to another witness's evidence that:

> he joined the TO voluntarily and nonetheless thought of himself as a civilian when he was not in uniform. In fact, he only wore his uniform during the day and in the evening went back home and did not exercise any official function. In other words, he thought of himself as a soldier when he was in uniform and as a civilian when he was not.[128]

The Chamber found that there was no military objective in the village in question justifying the subsequent attacks.[129] Although it did not make any concrete findings as to the status of the members of the TO, it cites with approval the evidence given by the witnesses, implying that the members of the TO in this case were not, to quote the Appeals Chamber in *Kordić and Čerkez*, '"combatants" in the legal sense', but were civilians.

The conclusion that there was no military objective in the village justifying an attack, despite the fact that there was a defence of some description in the area, albeit a weak one, is an example of the Tribunal equating a weak defence as no defence. However, as Olásolo explains, this approach is contrary to IHL, which makes no such distinction:

> It is one thing for the inhabitants of a village, hamlet or apartment building not to have combatant status and not to actively participate in hostilities, it is a completely different thing for them to be so poorly equipped and instructed as to prevent them from mounting an effective defence against an enemy. In the first scenario, they are not military objectives and cannot be attacked. Concerning the second scenario, any organised defence against the attack of the armed forces of a party to the conflict, no matter how weak and ineffective it might be, amounts to an active participation in hostilities unless it constitutes an isolated act of self-defence. As a result, those participants in such an organized defence become military objectives and can be attacked.[130]

127 *Blaškić* TC, para. 407.

128 Ibid., p. 135, FN 816.

129 Ibid., para. 410.

130 Olásolo, *supra* FN 116, pp. 116–117. On Appeal, the Chamber in *Blaškić* found that the evidence before the Trial Chamber had not supported their finding that ABiH forces were not preparing for combat within the area; however, they did not disagree

Although a right of self-defence exists under IHL, it is limited and occurs when persons who are not military objectives take up arms against enemy armed forces which are unlawfully attacking them, or are about to do so, in order to save their own lives or those of third persons.[131]

An example of the ICTY implicitly finding that civilians were exercising their right to self-defence rather than APH/DPH can in fact be found in the Appeals Chamber's judgment in *Kordić and Čerkez*. The Chamber, when examining evidence regarding an attack in the town of Busovača, noted that:

> The witness agreed that although there was no armed unit of the Patriotic league or the TO in Busovača, but in Kaćuni, young men of the Muslim part of Busovača … had weapons and gathered during the night of the attack in various houses of Kadića Strana. Asked whether he would agree that these were combat positions, the witness answered 'Do you think we should have just waited for somebody to attack us?' At trial even the Prosecution conceded that there was some resistance to the … attack.[132]

This seems to be a genuine case of self-defence. There was an imminent attack and civilians had tried to mobilise to defend themselves. Accordingly, their resistance would not qualify as APH/DPH, a fact which seems to have been taken on board by the Appeals Chamber which found that numerous civilians were targeted and killed during the attack.[133]

In contrast, in the *Blaškić* case the indications are that the defence mounted was out with the narrow limits of self-defence provided for in IHL. Regular watches had been organised and the indications are that some of the civilians were armed. Arguably, the participants were civilians APH/DPH, meaning they would constitute legitimate targets while so participating.

2.5 Conclusion

The issue of who is a legitimate military target and when has not always received the attention from ICTs that it warrants. This chapter has argued that cases involving these types of war crimes would benefit from a more structured approach being taken.

First, courts need to be clear and consistent in their findings as to who is included within the definition of a 'civilian'. Persons *hors de combat* are not

with their finding as regards the status of the TO members within the town. *Blaškić* AC, paras 332–333.

131 Olásolo, *supra* FN 116, p. 107, and see p. 108. Also see Fenrick, *supra* FN 6, p. 173: 'Civilians who take up arms to defend themselves and others may retain their protected status and not be regarded as taking a direct part in hostilities in certain limited circumstances, although, as a purely practical matter, they may increase the risk they will be attacked by mistake by combatants on the opposing side.'

132 *Kordić and Čerkez* AC, para. 412.

133 Ibid., para. 413.

civilians, and cannot be victims of war crimes which require that the victim had civilian status.

Second, notions of status and conduct have become entangled in some cases, and ICTs have, at times, tied themselves in knots when trying to describe why an alleged victim was or was not a victim of a war crime. A better strategy would be to separate these two aspects. Thus, for war crimes which require that the victim have civilian status, ICTs should systematically answer two questions. Did the alleged victim have civilian status? If so, were they not APH/DPH at the time of the attack? It is only if the answer to both these questions is in the affirmative, that those concerned can be victims of this class of war crime. When considering war crimes that require the victim to have been not APH/DPH at the time of the offence, the emphasis of the court should be on the victim's conduct, with status playing a secondary role, in that if the alleged victim had been a combatant (in the generic sense), they may only be a victim if *hors de combat* at the time of the attack.

Finally, in cases involving alleged victims who were members of organised armed groups in NIACs, ICTs should be cognisant of the debates that take place in IHL as to when such persons constitute legitimate targets. They should consider whether to apply a membership approach, meaning that all members of the group lose their civilian status, or whether to apply a functional approach, meaning that only those with a combat function lose civilian protection, when determining whether they were victims of a war crime. ICTs should be more mindful of the debates in IHL concerning these issues and should explicitly address the matter in their judgments.

3 Fighting and war crimes involving prohibited means and methods of warfare

IHL places restrictions on the means and methods that can be used by parties during hostilities. Some of these restrictions apply regardless of whether those who are attacked are fighters or civilians, whereas others apply only as regards civilians. This chapter explores the ways in which war crimes involving prohibited means and methods of warfare are affected if the victims had been involved in fighting at the time. First, the chapter discusses weapons, the use of which has been prohibited or restricted under IHL. While it is the use of the weapon that constitutes the war crime, the status of those who are attacked with the weapon can be important when determining whether the war crime occurred. Second, two methods of warfare are discussed: perfidy, and ordering that no quarter be given.

3.1 Means of warfare

IHL prohibits the use of certain types of weapon and restricts the use of others. Two ICTs currently have jurisdiction over war crimes concerning the use of weapons: the ICTY and the ICC. Article 3(a) of the ICTY Statute gives the Tribunal jurisdiction over the 'employment of poisonous weapons or other weapons calculated to cause unnecessary suffering'. The Tribunal has never been required to rule on this provision.[1] At the ICC, one of the more controversial issues concerning the jurisdiction of the court has concerned the weapons prohibitions of Article 8 of its Statute.[2] Originally, the court was given jurisdiction over a limited number of war crimes involving the use of certain prohibited weapons in IACs only;[3] however, following the Kampala Review Conference in 2010, state parties

1 The Tribunal did consider the issue of prohibited weapons in *Tadić*, see *Prosecutor v Duško Tadić*, ICTY, IT-94-1-AR72, Decision on the Defence Motion for Interlocutory Appeal on Jurisdiction, 2 October 1995, paras 119–124.

2 See Michael Cottier, 'War Crimes', in Otto Triffterer, *Commentary on the Rome Statute of the International Criminal Court* (C.H. Beck, Hart, Nomos, 2nd edition, 2008), para. 177.

3 Articles 8(2)(b)(xvii), (xviii), (xix) and (xx), ICC Statute. Until a late stage in the negotiations for the ICC Statute, provision had been made for the ICC to have jurisdiction over war crimes involving certain weapons in NIACs. However, they were deleted from the final version, see UN.Doc.A/CONF.183/C.1/L.53 (6 July 1998).

amended the Statute to give the court jurisdiction over (most) of the same war crimes if committed in the context of a NIAC.[4]

Two fundamental rules of IHL underpin the prohibition or restriction of the use of certain weapons. The principle of distinction prohibits weapons that cause indiscriminate harm to civilians and the civilian population,[5] while the principle prohibiting the use of weapons that cause superfluous injury and unnecessary suffering prohibits injury that lacks military utility. It is this second principle which determines whether a particular weapon may be used against fighters. This section begins by discussing the prohibition concerning weapons that cause superfluous injury and unnecessary suffering; it then considers existing war crimes provisions concerning the use of prohibited weapons; finally, weapons prohibitions and restrictions under customary law, the use of which may constitute a war crime, are explored.

3.1.1 Superfluous injury and unnecessary suffering

The notion that weapons which cause superfluous injury and unnecessary suffering are prohibited has existed for centuries.[6] The reasoning behind the principle was eloquently expressed in the Preamble to the St Petersburg Declaration of 1868 to be as follows:[7]

> Considering that the progress of civilization should have the effect of alleviating as much as possible the calamities of war; That the only legitimate object that States should endeavour to accomplish during war is to weaken the military forces of the enemy; That for this purpose it is sufficient to disable the greatest possible number of men; That this object would be exceeded by the employment of arms which uselessly aggravate the sufferings of

4 *Amendments to Article 8 of the Rome Statute*, Resolution RC/res.5, 10 June 2010, and see Amal Alamuddin and Philippa Webb, 'Expanding Jurisdiction over War Crimes under Article 8 of the ICC Statute', 8 *Journal of International Criminal Justice* 1219–1243 (2010); Robin Geiß, 'Poison, Gas and Expanding Bullets: The Extension of the List of Prohibited Weapons at the Review Conference of the International Criminal Court in Kampala', 13 *Yearbook of International Humanitarian Law* 337–352 (2011); and Roger S. Clark, 'Building on Article 8(2)(b)(xx) of the Rome Statute of the International Criminal Court: Weapons and Methods of Warfare', 12(3) *New Criminal Law Review* 366–389 (2009).

5 *Legality of the Threat or Use of Nuclear Weapons*, ICJ Advisory Opinion, 8 July 1996 (*Nuclear Weapons*), para. 257; and see Yoram Dinstein, *The Conduct of Hostilities under the Law of International Armed Conflict* (Cambridge University Press, 2010), p. 62.

6 M. Cherif Bassiouni, 'The Regulation, Control and Prohibition of the Use of Certain Weapons in the Context of War', in M. Cherif Bassiouni, *International Criminal Law, Volume I: Sources, Subjects and Contents* (Martinus Nijhoff, 2008), p. 378.

7 Also see Article 16, Instructions for the Government of Armies of the United States in the Field, 1863 (Lieber Code) and Article 23(e), Convention (IV) Respecting the Laws and Customs of War on Land with its Annex, Regulations concerning the Laws and Customs of War on Land (Hague Regulations, 1907).

> disabled men, or render their death inevitable; That the employment of such arms would therefore be contrary to the laws of humanity.

The most recent formulation of the principle can be found in Article 35(2) of Protocol I, which states: 'It is prohibited to employ weapons, projectiles and material and methods of warfare of a nature to cause superfluous injury or unnecessary suffering.' The principle is customary international law.[8] However, while the concept of superfluous injury or unnecessary suffering is universally accepted, it is difficult to define in practice.[9] The UK Ministry of Defence *Manual of the Law of Armed Conflict* explains:

> The law does not specify the permissible level of disablement. In contemporary military operations, while the killing of enemy combatants is still contemplated, so is wounding them to put them out of action. This may cause them permanent injury. In either case suffering is implicit. But the law does not define unnecessary suffering, and views can differ markedly. Some are horrified by the prospect of blindness, others by the blast injuries caused by mines, and many regard burn injuries as particularly serious, but it is difficult to compare one type of injury with another and say that it signifies unnecessary suffering.[10]

Due to the nebulousness of the notion, the rule tends to be viewed as a guiding principle upon which prohibitions regarding specific weapons can be founded.[11]

In the context of ICL, Article 3(a) of the ICTY Statute refers to the principle by listing the 'employment of poisonous weapons or other weapons calculated to cause unnecessary suffering' as a violation of the laws or customs of war. The ICC Statute too refers to the principle in Article 8(b)(xx),[12] which gives the court jurisdiction over the acts of:

8 *Nuclear Weapons*, para. 78 and Rule 70, ICRC Study.

9 In 1997, a report was published by the ICRC, known as the 'SIrUS project', which sought to clarify what constitutes superfluous injury and unnecessary suffering based on data collected on the health effects of weapons used during conflicts during the past 50 years. See International Committee of the Red Cross, *The SIrUS Project: Towards a Determination of which Weapons Cause 'Superfluous Injury or Unnecessary Suffering'* (1997), available at: www.loc.gov/rr/frd/Military_Law/pdf/SIrUS-project.pdf. Also see Robin Coupland and Peter Herby, 'Review of the Legality of Weapons: A New Approach – The SIrUS Project', 835(1) *International Review of the Red Cross* 583 (1999); and Major Donna Marie Verchio, 'Just Say No! The SIrUS Project: Well-Intentioned, but Unnecessary and Superfluous', 51 *The Air Force Law Review* 183 (2001).

10 UK Ministry of Defence, *The Manual of the Law of Armed Conflict* (Oxford University Press, 2004), para. 6.1.2.

11 Ibid., para. 6.1.5.

12 During the negotiations for the weapons provisions of the ICC Statute, it was debated whether the Statute should have an exhaustive list of weapons, or should contain a generic category of weapons which could evolve over time: see *Decisions taken by the Preparatory Committee at its Session Held from 1 to 12 December 1997*, A/AC.249/

> Employing weapons, projectiles and material and methods of warfare which are of a nature to cause superfluous injury or unnecessary suffering or which are inherently indiscriminate in violation of the international law of armed conflict, provided that such weapons, projectiles and material and methods of warfare are the subject of a comprehensive prohibition and are included in an annex to the Statute.

Rather than being an embodiment of the general IHL prohibition against weapons that cause superfluous injury or unnecessary suffering,[13] the article merely addresses specific weapons that are deemed to fall foul of the general principle, and which, most importantly, are listed in an annex to the Statute.[14] At present, the provision is an 'empty shell',[15] in that no such annex exists.[16]

ICTs have yet to make a ruling as to whether the use of a particular means of warfare was a war crime because it was of a nature to cause superfluous injury or unnecessary suffering.[17] In view of the difficulties in defining the concept precisely, it is doubtful whether individual criminal responsibility could arise on the basis of this principle alone, without there being a corresponding treaty or customary obligation concerning the specific means of warfare that was used.

3.1.2 The ICTY and ICC Statutes

War crimes involving the use of weapons can be divided into those that currently fall within the jurisdiction of an ICT, and those that do not explicitly fall under

1997/L.9/Rev.1, which proposed four different options. Cottier writes that '[a] general clause was supported by many delegations but rejected by others, arguing, *inter alia*, that its vagueness did not allow combatants to know what weapons would fall under ICC jurisdiction', Cottier, *supra* FN 2, para. 177.

13 Cryer explains that 'States were simply unwilling to pass jurisdiction to the ICC to use such a broad principle, as it could be used by the ICC to deliver opinions on the legality of a number of controversial weapons, such as landmines, cluster weapons, incendiary weapons or depleted uranium weapons. Some states and scholars seem to view this prospect with horror'. Robert Cryer, 'Hague Law Comes Home: Prosecuting Weapons Offences at the International Criminal Court', *Acta Juridica* 238 (2003), pp. 250–251.

14 Schabas refers to this provision as 'the only really important provision dealing with prohibited weapons', William Schabas, *Prohibited Weapons and the Belgian Amendment: Symbolic, but of what?* 22 May 2010, available at: http://iccreviewconference.blogspot.no/search?q=weapons.

15 Geiß, *supra* FN 4, p. 351.

16 Cottier explains that the provision was inserted due to the disagreements among delegates at the Rome Conference regarding which weapons should be prohibited under the Statute, and was inserted as a 'reminder' that further weapons and methods of warfare could be brought within the jurisdiction of the court at a later date. Cottier, *supra* FN 2, para. 177. The provision applies only in IACs, there is no equivalent provision that applies in NIACs. The possibility of inserting an equivalent provision in Article 8(2)(e) was not considered at the Kampala Review Conference. However, see *Belgium Proposal of Amendments*, Reference C.N.733.2009.TREATIES-8 (Depositary Notification).

17 However see *Nuclear Weapons Advisory Opinion*, para. 238.

the jurisdiction of an existing ICT, but which may nevertheless constitute a war crime under customary international law.

There are three specific weapons prohibitions under the ICC Statute: employing poison or poisoned weapons; the use of asphyxiating, poisonous or other gases; and the use of bullets that expand or flatten easily in the human body. These apply in both IACs and NIACs.[18] Each of the prohibitions is absolute, and applies regardless of whether it is used against civilians or fighters.

(i) *Employing poison or poisoned weapons*

The prohibition against the use of poison and poisoned weapons in armed conflict is one of the oldest weapons prohibition in IHL.[19] The ICRC Study found it to be prohibited under customary international law in both IACs and NIACs,[20] and this finding is widely accepted.[21] Article 3(a) of the ICTY Statute and in Articles 8 (b)(xvii) and 8(e)(xiii) of the ICC Statute[22] list employing poison or poisoned weapons as being a war crime.[23]

(ii) *The use of asphyxiating, poisonous or other gases*

Although the use of asphyxiating, poisonous or other gases, and all analogous liquid materials or devices, was prohibited in Declaration IV of the Hague Declarations of

18 For IACs see Articles 8(2)(b)(xvii), (xviii) and (xix), and for NIACs, see 8(2)(e)(xiii), (xiv) and (xv), ICC Statute.

19 Geiß, *supra* FN 4, p. 341. 'The prohibition against poison is … probably the most ancient prohibition of a means of combat in international law. Since the late Middle Ages, the use of poison has always been strictly prohibited … Beyond any doubt, the ancient prohibition of poison is still valid today.' Stefan Oeter, 'Methods and Means of Combat', in Dieter Fleck, *The Handbook of International Humanitarian Law* (Oxford University Press, 2008), para. 429. For early treaty provisions see Articles 16 and 70, Lieber Code; Article 12, Project of an International Declaration concerning the Laws and Customs of War, 1874; Article 8(a), Oxford Manual 1880 and Article 23(a), Hague Regulations 1907.

20 Rule 72, ICRC Study.

21 For example, Geiß, *supra* FN 4, pp. 218–220; William H. Boothby, *Weapons and The Law of Armed Conflict* (Oxford University Press, 2009), pp. 119–121; Steven Haines, 'Weapons, Means and Methods of Warfare', in Wilmshurst and Breau, *Perspectives on the ICRC Study on Customary International Law* (Cambridge University Press, 2007), pp. 267–268.

22 The definition of what constitutes a poison is considered in Cottier, *supra* FN 2, para. 178, and Knut Dörmann, *Elements of War Crimes under the Rome Statute of the International Criminal Court* (Cambridge University Press, 2003), pp. 282–284.

23 Boothby, *supra* FN 21, p. 121. Garraway observes '[a]lthough the weaponry provisions were the subject of heated debate at the Rome Conference, this particular prohibition received general agreement from the start and was never challenged'. Charles Garraway, 'Elements of War Crimes', in Roy S. Lee *et al*, *The International Criminal Court: Elements of Crimes and Rules of Procedure and Evidence* (Transnational Publishers Inc., 2001), p. 178.

1899,[24] it failed to prevent the use of poisonous gases during the First World War. Following the war, a further attempt was made to prohibit such weapons in the 1925 Geneva Gas Protocol, which extended the prohibition to 'the use of bacteriological methods of warfare'. The prohibition is customary international law in both IACs and NIACs.[25] Articles 8(b)(xviii) and 8(e)(xiv) of the ICC Statute adopt the wording of the Hague Declaration IV of 1899, in prohibiting the employment of 'asphyxiating, poisonous or other gases and all analogous liquids, materials or devices'.[26]

(iii) The use of bullets that expand or flatten easily in the human body

This type of ammunition is prohibited due to its increased ability to harm in comparison with ordinary bullets. The use of such ammunition has been prohibited under IHL since the 1899 Hague Conference,[27] and the prohibition was found to be a rule of customary law by the ICRC Study.[28] This finding is, again, relatively uncontroversial. Articles 8(b)(xix) and 8(2)(e)(xv) of the ICC Statute list 'employing bullets which expand or flatten easily in the human body, such as bullets with a hard envelope which does not entirely cover the core or is pierced with incisions' as being a serious violation of the laws and customs of war.[29]

3.1.3 Customary international law

The use of this group of weapons does not currently fall under the jurisdiction of an ICT as a war crime.[30] A discussion as to whether these weapons prohibitions constitute war crimes under ICL[31] is therefore largely academic at present, as no forum exists at an international level in which to hold individuals who violate the prohibitions criminally responsible. The following discussion therefore explores whether in theory the use of these weapons constitutes a war crime when those against whom they are used have been fighting. In the event that these weapons are used, it does not necessarily mean that there is no recourse under ICL. It may be possible to prosecute the perpetrator for the harm the weapons caused, rather than for the actual use of the weapon, for example as the war crime of directly

24 Declaration IV on Asphyxiating Gases, 1899.
25 Rule 73, ICRC Study.
26 Garraway, *supra* FN 23, pp. 179–180.
27 Final Act of the International Peace Conference, The Hague 29 July 1899, Declaration IV 3.
28 Rule 77, ICRC Study. See Haines, *supra* FN 21, p. 271; and Boothby, *supra* FN 21, pp. 146–150.
29 The Elements of Crimes require that the perpetrator was aware that the nature of the bullets was such that their employment would uselessly aggravate suffering or the wounding effect. There is therefore a particular mental element to this offence. Garraway, *supra* FN 23, p. 182, and Cottier, *supra* FN 2, pp. 422–423.
30 An exception potentially being Article 3, ICTY Statute.
31 The use of prohibited weapons can be prosecuted under national laws. See for example the Dutch case of *Van Araat v The Netherlands*, ECtHR Application no 65389/09, 6 July 2010.

attacking civilians, or indiscriminate attacks against civilians.[32] Clearly, this applies only if the weapons were used against civilians. As has been discussed, no ICT has jurisdiction over crimes that cause superfluous injury and unnecessary suffering which would allow for prosecution for the harm caused by prohibited weapons if those harmed were fighters.[33]

In the following discussion, reliance is placed upon the ICRC's Study on customary international law. The Study's conclusions concerning the customary status of the rules concerning means of warfare have been subject to some criticism.[34] It is important to bear in mind that the Study conveys the ICRC's views as to what the customary law position is, and it does not necessarily follow that an ICT would reach the same conclusion.

Furthermore, although the use of a certain weapon may be prohibited or restricted under customary international law, for the present purposes its use must also constitute a war crime under ICL. In order to determine whether an act constitutes a war crime, recourse can be had to the four conditions laid down by the Appeals Chamber in the *Tadić* Decision, namely: that the violation constitutes an infringement of a rule of IHL; that the rule is customary in nature or part of treaty law; that the violation is serious in that it protects important values and involves grave consequences for the victim; and that breach of the rule entails individual criminal responsibility.[35] If one assumes that the use of prohibited or restricted weapons infringes IHL and is sufficiently serious, it must be asked whether the specific prohibition or restriction constitutes a violation of customary or treaty law under IHL and whether those who violate the rule incur individual criminal responsibility as a result. In addition, for present purposes, it is necessary to establish whether the war crime of using a specific weapon applies also if the victims involved had been involved in the fighting.

(i) Chemical and biological weapons

The development, production and use of chemical and bacteriological or biological weapons[36] is prohibited under treaty law,[37] and this was found by the ICRC

32 Articles 8(2)(b)(i), 8(2)(b)(iv) and Article 8(2)(e)(i), ICC Statute.

33 Robert Cryer, 'Of Custom, Treaties, Scholars and the Gavel: The Influence of the International Criminal Tribunals on the ICRC Customary Law Study', 11(2) *Journal of Conflict and Security Law* 239–263 (2006), p. 252. Cryer argues that prosecuting a perpetrator on the basis of the harm caused by such weapons rather than the use of the weapon themselves falls foul of the principle of fair labelling, in that the conviction entered for a person accurately reflects the precise wrongdoing that was involved in the offence.

34 Cryer, ibid.; David Turns, 'Weapons in the ICRC Study on Customary International Humanitarian Law', 11(2) *Journal of Conflict and Security Law* 201–237 (2006).

35 See *Tadić* Decision, para. 94.

36 Although the use of such weapons is not explicitly prohibited under the Biological Weapons Convention, it is prohibited to possess them. See the preamble to Convention on the Prohibition of the Development, Production and Stockpiling of Bacteriological (Biological) and Toxin Weapons and on their Destruction ('Biological Weapons Convention').

37 For chemical weapons: 1925 Gas Protocol and Article 1, Chemical Weapons Convention. For biological weapons: Geneva Protocol for the Prohibition of the Use of

Study to be a rule of customary international law in both IACs and NIACs.[38] It is highly likely that the use of these types of weapon constitutes a war crime under ICL.[39] Indeed, some commentators opine that it may be the case that the use of some of these types of weapons fall under the jurisdiction of the ICC as poison or poisonous weapons under Articles 8(2)(b)(xvii) or 8(e)(xiii),[40] or as an asphyxiating, poisonous or other gas under Articles 8(2)(b)(viii) or 8(e)(xiv).[41] However, this has to be balanced against the drafting history of the Statute, which suggests that states parties to the ICC have a contrary view. The issue of whether the use of chemical or biological weapons should constitute a war crime under the jurisdiction of the ICC was discussed during the Rome Conference. The penultimate draft of the Statute contained specific prohibitions on both types of weapons, but these were deleted from the final draft.[42] At the Kampala Review Conference, Belgium proposed that the Statute be amended to prohibit the use of biological and chemical weapons in IACs or NIACs,[43] but again the proposal was rejected. Clearly, the view of the states parties is that these types of weapons are presently out with the jurisdiction of the court.[44] In order to avoid the court addressing whether the use of these types of weapons falls within its jurisdiction, cases could be brought

Asphyxiating, Poisonous or Other Gases, and of Bacteriological Methods of Warfare ('1925 Gas Protocol') and Article 1, Biological Weapons Convention. The Convention does not explicitly prohibit the use of such weapons, but this has been found to be implicit in Article 1, UK Manual, *supra* FN 10, para. 6.5, note 8.

38 For chemical weapons see Rule 74, Rule 75 (the use of riot-control agents as a method of warfare) and Rule 76 (regarding the use of herbicides as a method of warfare), ICRC Study. Also see *Tadić* Decision, para. 124. For biological weapons see Rules 73 and 74, ICRC Study.

39 See Annita Larissa Sciacovelli, 'The Criminalization of the Use of Biological and Chemical Weapons', in Fausto Pocar *et al*, *War Crimes and the Conduct of Hostilities: Challenges to Adjudication and Investigation* (Edward Elgar, 2013), pp. 212–227.

40 For chemical weapons see Gerhard Werle, *Principles of International Criminal Law* (TMC Asser Press, 2005), p. 376. However, see William Schabas, 'Attacking Syria? This is the Crime of Aggression', http://humanrightsdoctorate.blogspot.com.au/2013/08/attacking-syria-this-is-crime-of.html. For biological weapons see Boothby, *supra* FN 21, p. 129. However, Cryer is of the view that biological weapons do not fall under the ICC Statute, see Cryer, *supra* FN 33, p. 251.

41 Cottier, *supra* FN 2 pp. 415–419; and Cryer, *supra* FN 33, p. 251.

42 *Report of the Drafting Committee, Draft Statute for an International Criminal Court*, reprinted in Official Records from the UN Diplomatic Conference of Plenipotentiaries on the Establishment of an International Court at 149–180, UN Doc. A/CONF.183/13 (Vol. III) (1998).

43 Rome Statute of the International Criminal Court, Belgium: Proposal of Amendments, 29 October 2009, Ref. C.N.733.2009.TREATIES-8 (Depositary Notification), p. 12. Available at http://iccreviewconference.blogspot.no/2010/05/prohibited-weapons-and-belgian.html.

44 A number of blog posts have discussed the matter in the context of the use of chemical weapons in Syria, see Schabas, *supra* FN 40; Dapo Akande, *Can the ICC Prosecute for Use of Chemical Weapons in Syria?*, available at www.ejiltalk.org/can-the-icc-prosecute-for-use-of-chemical-weapons-in-syria/; Kevin Jon Heller, *Syria, Chemical Weapons and the Incoherence of the VCLT*, available at http://opiniojuris.org/2013/08/23/syria-chemical-weapons-incoherence-vclt/; Beth Van Schaak,

under other provisions of the Statute based on the harm the weapons caused rather than upon their use, for example as an indiscriminate attack against civilians.[45]

(ii) The anti-personnel use of bullets that explode within the human body

This prohibition stems from the St Petersburg Declaration, and was found by the ICRC Study to be a rule of customary international law.[46] In 1999, an expert meeting found the 400-gramme limit provided for within the St Petersburg Declaration to be obsolete. Instead, it was agreed that targeting combatants with bullets, the foreseeable effect of which was to explode upon impact with the human body, is contrary to the object and purpose of the St Petersburg Declaration.[47] It is likely that this constitutes a war crime under customary law in international criminal law.

(iii) The use of weapons the primary effect of which is to injure by fragments that are not detectable in the human body by X-rays

The use of these types of weapons is prohibited under Protocol I of the Convention on Certain Conventional Weapons (CCW),[48] and was found to be a rule of customary international law.[49] It is likely that violation of the rule would amount to a war crime under customary international law.

(iv) Blinding laser weapons

The use of these weapons is prohibited by Protocol IV of the CCW[50] and was found to be customary international law by Rule 86 of the ICRC Study.[51] This

Chemical Weapons Use Returns to Syria, available at www.justsecurity.org/32309/chemical-weapons-returns-syria/.

45 Articles 8(2)(b)(i) and 8(2)(e)(i), ICC Statute; and see Cottier, *supra* FN 2, para. 181 and Dörmann, *supra* FN 22, p. 288. Also see the *Anfal* case, from the Iraqi High Tribunal where the accused was convicted of intentionally directing attacks against a civilian population for using chemical weapons, which failed to distinguish between civilians and military individuals, *Al Anfal, Iraqi High Tribunal*, Case No 1/CSecond/2006, 24 June 2007, p. 582.

46 Rule 78, ICRC Study. The prohibition against these types of bullets is not absolute – they are sanctioned for use by aircraft (Article XVIII, Hague Rules of Warfare, 1923); and see Dinstein, who writes that 'State practice shows the widespread use of explosive bullets by aircraft strafing enemy personnel'. Dinstein, *supra* FN 5, p. 69.

47 ICRC Study, discussion to Rule 78.

48 Protocol on Non-Detectable Fragments (Protocol I), Convention on Prohibitions or Restrictions on the Use of Certain Conventional Weapons which may be deemed to be Excessively Injurious or to have Indiscriminate Effects, 1980.

49 Rule 79, ICRC Study. The ICRC's finding in this regard is disputed by some; for example, Turns argues that the rule is expounded on the basis of a very recent treaty and in the absence of any meaningful State practice. Turns, *supra* FN 34, p. 226–227.

50 CCW Protocol on Blinding Laser Weapons (Protocol IV), 1995.

51 The customary nature of the rule has been questioned. Haines, *supra* FN 21, p. 277, Boothby, *supra* FN 21, p. 213.

type of weapon is prohibited only if it causes permanent blindness, as this is regarded as breaching the principle of causing superfluous injury or unnecessary suffering.[52] It is likely that use of these weapons constitutes a war crime under customary law.

(v) Booby traps

The use of booby traps is restricted rather than prohibited under IHL. Article 6 of CCW Protocol II and Article 7 of CCW Amended Protocol II[53] provide lists of objects that are prohibited for use as booby traps.[54] The ICRC Study found a rule of customary law to the effect that:

> The use of booby-traps which are in any way attached to or associated with objects or persons entitled to special protection under international humanitarian law or with objects that are likely to attract civilians is prohibited.[55]

However, while the restrictions on the use of booby traps primarily exist to protect civilians, they also operate to protect those who fight. Kalshoven, for example, writes of the list of prohibited items that:

> While the children's toys and other similar objects included in the list clearly envisage the protection of the civilian population, some other (dead or living) objects mentioned here belong to the category of objects the soldier might be expected to regard as safe. To booby trap such objects may therefore be regarded as perfidy.[56]

52 Dinstein, *supra* FN 5, p. 79.

53 CCW Protocol on Prohibitions or Restrictions on the Use of Mines, Booby-traps and other Devices, 1980 (Protocol II); and Protocol on Prohibitions or Restrictions on the Use of Mines, Booby-traps and other Devices, as amended, 1996.

54 For example, Article 6 (1) provides: 'Without prejudice to the rules of international law applicable in armed conflict relating to treachery and perfidy, it is prohibited in all circumstances to use: (a) any booby-trap in the form of an apparently harmless portable object which is specifically designed and constructed to contain explosive material and to detonate when it is disturbed or approached, or (b) booby-traps which are in any way attached to or associated with: (i) internationally recognized protective emblems, signs or signals; (ii) sick, wounded or dead persons; (iii) burial or cremation sites or graves; (iv) medical facilities, medical equipment, medical supplies or medical transportation; (v) children's toys or other portable objects or products specially designed for the feeding, health, hygiene, clothing or education of children; (vi) food or drink; (vii) kitchen utensils or appliances except in military establishments, military locations or military supply depots; (viii) objects clearly of a religious nature; (ix) historic monuments, works of art or places or worship which constitute the cultural or spiritual heritage of peoples; (x) animals or their carcasses.'

55 Rule 80, ICRC Study.

56 Frits Kalshoven, 'Conventional Weapons in the "Reaffirmation and Development of the 1970s"', in *Arms, Armaments and International Law*, Collected Courses of the Hague Academy of International Law 191 (Martinus Nijhoff Publishers, 1985), p. 255; and see Boothby, *supra* FN 21, p. 176.

Dinstein also is of the view that while most of the protection from booby traps is established with civilians in mind, some protection is also conferred on combatants.[57] He explains that:

> The degree of combatants' protection from booby-traps varies with circumstances. Thus, it is permitted in Article 6 of Protocol II to booby-trap a kitchen appliance (such as a refrigerator) in a military location, but not food or drink. The fact that combatants are not entirely protected from booby-traps indicates that booby-traps *per se* are not deemed to contravene the principle of unnecessary suffering.[58]

Several items on the lists of prohibited objects could apply to military personnel: internationally recognised protective emblems, signs or signals; or sick, wounded or dead persons, for example. However, it is unlikely that a war crimes charge could be brought for the use of a booby trap against military personnel, unless the object used invited the victim to believe they were entitled to protection under IHL, for example by using protective emblems, signs or signals, which would constitute the war crime of perfidy.[59]

(vi) Incendiary weapons

The use of incendiary weapons[60] is restricted under Protocol III of the CCW.[61] During the Preparatory Conference for the CCW, there was a push by some states to prohibit the use of such weapons completely. When it became clear that consensus on this point would be impossible, a number of states tried to agree a prohibition of their use against military personnel, with some exceptions.[62] This proposal was also ultimately unsuccessful.[63] The ICRC Study notes that:

> The fact that this prohibition was not included in the Protocol does not mean, however, that the use of incendiary weapons against combatants is lawful in all circumstances.
>
> Several States have specified the few restricted situations in which incendiary weapons may be used, namely when combatants are under armoured

57 Dinstein, *supra* FN 5, p. 71.
58 Ibid.
59 Article 8(2)(b)(vi), ICC Statute, discussed in more detail below.
60 CCW Protocol on Prohibitions or Restrictions on the Use of Incendiary Weapons, 1980 (Protocol III). Incendiary weapons include napalm and flame throwers, for a more comprehensive list, see Boothby, *supra* FN 21, pp. 200–201.
61 Article 2, Protocol III to CCW, and see Rules 84 and 85, ICRC Study.
62 ICRC Study, pp. 289–290.
63 For example, the UK position on the use of incendiary weapons is that '[a]lthough these weapons can cause severe injury to personnel, their use is lawful provided the military necessity for their use outweighs the injury and suffering which their use may cause'. UK Manual *supra* FN 10, para. 6.12.1.

> protection or in field fortifications. Others have stated that incendiary weapons may not be used in a way that would cause unnecessary suffering. Several military manuals and a number of official statements make the point that the use of incendiary weapons against combatants is prohibited because it causes unnecessary suffering.

As there have been very few reports of the use of such weapons against combatants, the Study concluded that the anti-personnel use of incendiary weapons is prohibited, unless it is not feasible to use a less harmful weapon to render a person *hors de combat.*[64] The Study's findings have been criticised. Aldrich, for example, argues:

> it seems that the authors believe that incendiary weapons, particularly air-delivered napalm and ground-delivered flame throwers, cause unnecessary suffering to the affected combatants since they could have been killed or wounded by other weapons. That may well sometimes be true, but it cannot always be true. In any event, this proposed rule has no treaty precedent and can only be seen as an effort to propose a new rule of law.[65]

In view of the uncertainties surrounding the existence of a customary rule in IHL regarding the use of incendiary weapons against military personnel, it would be challenging to prosecute such a case in an ICL context.[66] It would have to be shown that the way in which the weapon had been used breached the general principle of unnecessary suffering and superfluous injury.

64 ICRC Study, pp. 290–291. Rule 85 of the Study states: 'The anti-personnel use of incendiary weapons is prohibited, unless it is not feasible to use a less harmful weapon to render a person hors de combat.' Also see ICRC Commentary to Protocol I, para. 1424, which states: 'It is worth noting that none of the rules explicitly protects combatants from incendiary weapons such as flame-throwers or napalm. However, it is generally admitted that these weapons should not be used in such a way that they will cause unnecessary suffering, which means that in particular they should not be used against individuals without cover.'

65 G.H. Aldrich, 'Customary International Humanitarian Law: An Interpretation on Behalf of the International Committee of the Red Cross', 76 *British Yearbook of International Law* 521. For a response by one of the authors of the ICRC Study, see J.-M. Henckaerts, 'Customary International Law – A Rejoinder to Judge Aldridge', 76 *British Yearbook of International Law* 525 (2005).

66 An example of a state using an incendiary weapon against fighters is the US Military's use of white phosphorus in the Iraqi city of Falluja in 2004. The US argued that white phosphorus is classified as an incendiary weapon, rather than a chemical weapon, and it could therefore be used against fighters. They also argued that the primary reason that that particular weapon had been used in Falluja was for illumination and as a smoke screen, rather than as a weapon to be used directly against people. See BBC News, 'US used White Phosphorus in Iraq', 16 November 2005, available at: http://news.bbc.co.uk/2/hi/4440664.stm.

(vii) Landmines

The use of landmines is restricted under Protocol II to the CCW, while under the Ottawa Convention, the use of anti-personnel mines is banned.[67] These weapons restrictions primarily exist because their effects are indiscriminate.[68] The ICRC Study found customary rules restricting the way these weapons are used;[69] however, their use is not a war crime under customary international law at present.[70]

3.2 Methods of warfare

Two methods of warfare constitute war crimes if committed against those involved in fighting: perfidious killing or wounding, and ordering that no quarter be given.

3.2.1 Perfidious killing or wounding

The prohibition against perfidy is a well-established principle of IHL and is widely accepted to be customary international law.[71] It was incorporated into treaty law by Article 23(b) of the Hague Regulations, which states that it is forbidden 'to kill or wound treacherously individuals belonging to the hostile nation or army'. The current formulation is contained in Article 37(1) of Protocol I.[72] Three requirements need to be fulfilled for a claim of perfidy to be made. First, the adversary must be entitled to, or is obliged to be accorded, protection under a rule of IHL; second, an act must be committed which causes, or induces, the adversary to believe that he or she will be protected according to that rule; and third, there must be an intent to betray the confidence of the adversary. As Dinstein explains, '[p]erfidy is thus all about the creation of a false impression of legal entitlement (on either side) to exemption from attack'.[73]

67 Article 1, Convention on the Prohibition of the Use, Stockpiling, Production and Transfer of Anti-Personnel Mines and of their Destruction, 1997 (Ottawa Convention).

68 Rule 85 of the ICRC Study states: 'When landmines are used, particular care must be taken to minimize their indiscriminate effects.' Also see Article 3(8), CCW, Amended Protocol II.

69 Rules 81, 82 and 83, ICRC Study.

70 Werle, *supra* FN 40, para. 1126.

71 Rule 65, ICRC Study states that '[k]illing, injuring or capturing an adversary by resort to perfidy is prohibited'.

72 Article 37(1) provides: 'It is prohibited to kill, injure or capture an adversary by resort to perfidy. Acts inviting the confidence of an adversary to lead him to believe that he is entitled to, or is obliged to accord, protection under the rules of international law applicable in armed conflict, with intent to betray that confidence, shall constitute perfidy. The following acts are examples of perfidy: (a) the feigning of an intent to negotiate under a flag of truce or of a surrender; (b) the feigning of an incapacitation by wounds or sickness; (c) the feigning of civilian, non-combatant status; and (d) the feigning of protected status by the use of signs, emblems or uniforms of the United Nations or of neutral or other States not Parties to the conflict.'

73 Dinstein, *supra* FN 5, p. 231. Also see Rule 65, ICRC Study: 'The essence of perfidy is thus the invitation to obtain and then the breach of the adversary's confidence, i.e., an abuse of good faith.'

Perfidy is to be distinguished from ruses of war, which are a lawful means of warfare.[74] For perfidy to occur, there must be an indication that the adversary will receive protection under IHL, whereas ruses of war, while involving deception, do not involve the abuse of protected status.[75] Thus, while a combatant may pretend to be wounded, sick or dead to avoid being captured, it is perfidy if they do so with the intention of wounding, killing or capturing enemy combatants who come to their aid, and the intent is carried out.[76]

Articles 8(2)(b)(xi) and 8(2)(e)(ix) of the ICC Statute contain different expressions of the crime. Article 8(2)(b)(xi) echoes the language of Article 23(b) of the Hague Regulations in listing the war crime of '[k]illing or wounding treacherously individuals belonging to the hostile nation or army'. The Elements of Crimes clarify the provision by using the substance and language of Article 37(1).[77] Article 8(2)(e)(ix), on the other hand, lists '[k]illing or wounding treacherously a combatant adversary' as being a violation of the laws and customs applicable in NIACs. Despite the difference in language, the elements of the crime are almost identical to those of its IAC equivalent. Cottier explains that a 'careful distinction' was made by using the phrase 'combatant adversary' in order to avoid the impression that there might exist the notion of 'combatants' in NIACs.[78]

The ICC Statute specifies that it is only the acts of killing or wounding by perfidy which constitute a war crime. This aligns with the ICRC Study, which found that while killing, injuring or capturing by resort to perfidy is illegal under customary international law, only acts that result in serious bodily injury, namely killing or injuring, constitute war crimes.[79]

3.2.2 Denying quarter

The denial of quarter to enemies is prohibited under IHL.[80] Moir explains:

74 Article 37(2), Protocol I and Rule 57, ICRC Study. See Oeter, *supra* FN 19, para. 471; and Cottier, *supra* FN 2, paras 120–121.

75 A.P.V. Rogers, *Law on the Battlefield* (Juris Publishing, 2004), p. 37.

76 Dinstein, *supra* FN 5, p. 233.

77 The ICC Elements of Crimes lists the elements for Article 8(2)(b)(xi) as follows: '1 The perpetrator invited the confidence or belief of one or more persons that they were entitled to, or were obliged to accord, protection under rules of international law applicable in armed conflict. 2 The perpetrator intended to betray that confidence or belief. 3 The perpetrator killed or injured such person or persons. 4 The perpetrator made use of that confidence or belief in killing or injuring such person or persons. 5 Such person or persons belonged to an adverse party. 6 The conduct took place in the context of and was associated with an international armed conflict. 7 The perpetrator was aware of factual circumstances that established the existence of an armed conflict.' The Elements of Crimes for Article 8(2)(ix) contain similar wording. Also see Dörmann, *supra* FN 22, p. 240.

78 Cottier, *supra* FN 2, para. 332.

79 See discussion regarding Rule 65, ICRC Study; and see John C. Dehn, 'Permissible Perfidy? Analysing the Colombian Hostage Rescue, the Capture of Rebel Leaders and the World's Reaction', 6(4) *Journal of International Criminal Justice* 627 (2008).

80 Article 23(d), Hague Regulations; Article 40(1), Protocol I; Article 4(1), Additional Protocol II. Also see ICRC Commentary to Protocol I, paras 1589–1590; and Cottier *supra* FN 2, para. 130.

> It is a logical corollary of the principle of proportionality, and of the rule that the lawful use of force is strictly controlled by the requirements of military necessity. Enemy *hors de combat* take no active part in hostilities, and so killing them cannot be necessary or proportionate as it offers no military advantage.[81]

While the offence featured in trials following the First[82] and Second World Wars,[83] there have been no instances of it being charged in contemporary ICL. The crime is listed in Articles 8(2)(b)(xii) and 8(2)(e)(x) of the ICC Statute,[84] both of which provide that '[d]eclaring that no quarter will be given' constitutes a violation of the laws and customs of war. There is no need to show a result for the crime to have occurred; it need only be shown that the alleged perpetrator declared or ordered that there shall be no survivors.[85]

3.3 Conclusion

IHL prohibits the use of some weapons and restricts the use of others. For prohibited weapons, who they are used against, whether civilian or fighter, is irrelevant. However, restricted weapons, such as landmines and incendiary weapons, can be used against fighters, and it is then that the status of those against whom the weapon was used becomes important. Those who fight can also be victims of war crimes concerning prohibited methods of warfare, namely the crimes of perfidy and ordering that there be no quarter. The jurisprudence in this area is underdeveloped, both due to general difficulties in prosecuting cases concerning war crimes committed during hostilities,[86] and perhaps also due to the tendency to focus on crimes involving civilian victims of atrocity.

81 Lindsay Moir, 'Conduct of Hostilities – War Crimes', in José Doria *et al*, *The Legal Regime of the International Criminal Court: Essays in Honour of Professor Igor Blishchenko: In Memoriam Professor Igor Pavlovich Blishchenko (1930–2000)* (Martinus Nijhoff, 2009), p. 518.

82 See *Llandovery Castle* case, German Supreme Court of Leipzig, 26 *American Journal of International Law* (1922) Supp. 708–723. Also see Claud Mullins, *The Leipzig Trials* (H.F. & G. Witherby, London, 1921), p. 168; and John Horne and Alan Kramer, *German Atrocities 1914: A History of Denial* (Yale University Press, 2001), pp. 349–350.

83 See *Von Ruchteschell*, British Military Court at Hamburg 21 May 1947; *Wickman*, British Military Court at Hamburg, 26 November 1947; *Eck* case (The Peleus Trial), British Military Court at Hamburg, 20 October 1945.

84 Both provisions use identical language and list the crime of '[d]eclaring that no quarter will be given'; see Cottier, *supra* FN 2, paras 130–135 and 334–335.

85 Elements of Crimes for Article 8(2)(b)(xii).

86 Paola Gaeta, 'Serious Violations of the Law on the Conduct of Hostilities: A Neglected Class of War Crimes?' in Fausto Pocar *et al*, *supra* FN 39.

4 War crimes and persons *hors de combat*

The treatment of persons *hors de combat*[1] has always been one of IHL's chief concerns.[2] Originally, this emphasis was reflected in the cases that appeared before criminal courts: the maltreatment of POWs featured heavily in the trials held following the First[3] and Second[4] World Wars, for example. In contrast, cases focusing on persons *hors de combat* are less prevalent in contemporary case law. This chapter explores how issues surrounding persons *hors de combat* have been addressed in ICL and considers some of the more interesting issues that have arisen in the jurisprudence to date.

1 Article 41(2) of Additional Protocol I states: 'A person is hors de combat if: (a) he is in the power of an adverse Party; (b) he clearly expresses an intention to surrender; or (c) he has been rendered unconscious or is otherwise incapacitated by wounds or sickness, and therefore is incapable of defending himself provided that in any of these cases he abstains from any hostile act and does not attempt to escape.'

2 See Convention for the Amelioration of the Condition of Wounded in Armies in the Field, 1864 and Convention for the Amelioration of the Condition of the Wounded and Sick in Armies in the Field, 1906.

3 See Claud Mullins and E.M. Pollock, *The Leipzig Trials an Account of the War Criminals' Trials and a Study of German Mentality* (London, H.F. & G. Witherby, 1921), pp. 173–177; and H. Jones, *Violence against Prisoners of War in the First World War: Britain, France and Germany, 1914–1920* (Cambridge University Press, 2011).

4 The International Military Tribunal for the Far East summarised some of the atrocities committed against POWs within its jurisdiction as follows: 'Ruthless killing of prisoners by shooting, decapitation, drowning, and other methods; death marches in which prisoners including the sick were forced to march long distances under conditions which not even well-conditioned troops could stand, many of those dropping out being shot or bayonetted by the guards; forced labor in tropical heat without protection from the sun; complete lack of housing and medical supplies in many cases resulting in thousands of deaths from disease; beatings and torture of all kinds to extract information or confessions or for minor offences; killing without trial of recaptured prisoners after escape or for attempt to escape; killing without trial of captured aviators; and even cannibalism.' Judgment of the International Military Tribunal of the Far East in judgment of 12 November 1948, in John Pritchard and Sona M. Zaide (eds), *The Tokyo War Crimes Trial*, at 49, 593, cited in Howard S. Levie, 'Penal Sanctions for Maltreatment of Prisoners of War', 56 *American Journal of International Law* 433 (1962), p. 439.

War crimes involving persons *hors de combat* can be prosecuted as grave breaches of the Geneva Conventions and Protocol I, or as other serious violations of the laws and customs of war. Grave breaches of the Geneva Conventions comprise those violations of the Conventions and their Protocol I deemed to be the most serious.[5] Three ICTs have jurisdiction over this class of crime: the ICTY,[6] the ICC[7] and the Extraordinary Chambers in the Courts of Cambodia (ECCC).[8] In order for a crime to constitute a grave breach, two evidential requirements must be satisfied.[9] First, the conflict must be an IAC.[10] Second, victims must qualify as protected persons under the respective Convention at the time of the alleged offence. To constitute a protected person under Geneva Convention III, the person must qualify for POW status under Article 4A;[11] whereas in order to

5 Articles 49–50, Geneva Convention I; Articles 50–51, Geneva Convention II; Articles 129–130, Geneva Convention III; Articles 146–147, Geneva Convention IV, and Articles 11 and 85, Protocol I.

6 Article 2, ICTY Statute.

7 Article 8(2)(a), ICC Statute.

8 Article 6, ECCC Law.

9 *Prosecutor v Tihomir Blaškić*, ICTY, IT-95-14-T, Trial Judgment, 3 March 2000 (*Blaškić* TC), para. 74.

10 *Prosecutor v Duško Tadić*, ICTY, IT-94-1-AR72, Decision on the Defence Motion for Interlocutory Appeal on Jurisdiction, 2 October 1995 (*Tadić Decision*), para. 84, and see paras 46–83. Also see *Prosecutor v Duško Tadić*, ICTY, IT-94-1-A, Appeals Judgment, 15 July 1999 (*Tadić* AC), para. 80, and Article 8(2)(a), ICC Statute. The *Tadić* Appeals Chamber suggested that the day may come when the grave breach regime will apply in NIACs, but given that the ICC Statute also requires that grave breaches be committed in IACs, it would seem that we are not yet at that stage. For articles considering whether grave breaches can be committed in NIACs, see Sonja Boelaert-Suominen, 'Grave Breaches, Universal Jurisdiction and International Armed Conflict: Is Customary Law Moving Towards a Uniform Enforcement Mechanism for All Armed Conflicts?', 5 *Journal of Conflict and Security Law*, 63–103 (2000); and Lindsay Moir, 'Grave Breaches and Internal Armed Conflicts', 7 *Journal of International Criminal Justice* 763–787 (2009).

11 Article 4A states: 'Prisoners of war, in the sense of the present Convention, are persons belonging to one of the following categories, who have fallen into the power of the enemy: (1) Members of the armed forces of a Party to the conflict as well as members of militias or volunteer corps forming part of such armed forces. (2) Members of other militias and members of other volunteer corps, including those of organized resistance movements, belonging to a Party to the conflict and operating in or outside their own territory, even if this territory is occupied, provided that such militias or volunteer corps, including such organized resistance movements, fulfill the following conditions: (a) that of being commanded by a person responsible for his subordinates; (b) that of having a fixed distinctive sign recognizable at a distance; (c) that of carrying arms openly; (d) that of conducting their operations in accordance with the laws and customs of war. (3) Members of regular armed forces who profess allegiance to a government or an authority not recognized by the Detaining Power. (4) Persons who accompany the armed forces without actually being members thereof, such as civilian members of military aircraft crews, war correspondents, supply contractors, members of labour units or of services responsible for the welfare of the armed forces, provided that they have received authorization from the armed forces which they accompany, who shall provide them for that purpose with an identity card similar to the annexed

benefit from the protection of Geneva Convention IV, it must be shown that an individual was 'in the hands of a Party to the conflict or Occupying Power of which they are not nationals'.[12] These two requirements can present substantial evidential hurdles for prosecutors to clear when trying to prove that a grave breach has occurred.[13]

At the ICTY, this has led to the prosecutor bringing charges under Article 3 of the ICTY Statute, as violations of the laws or customs of war, in order to avoid the additional evidential burdens that Article 2 entails.[14] Founding a war crimes charge, for example, on Common Article 3, avoids the need for the Tribunal to waste valuable court time in classifying the conflict, given that Common Article 3 applies in both IACs and NIACs.[15] It also only requires the prosecutor to prove that the victims had been not APH/DPH at the time, rather than the somewhat heavier burden of showing that they were protected persons. Consequently, relatively few cases have been brought under Article 2 of the ICTY Statute.

At the ICC, the terms of Article 8 mean that the ICC must always classify the armed conflict it is dealing with. Articles 8(a) (grave breaches of the Conventions) and Article 8(b) (other serious violations of law and customs of war) of the Statute apply only in conflicts classified as IACs; whereas Articles 8(c) (violations of Common Article 3) and (e) (other serious violations of law and customs of war) apply only in conflicts classified as NIACs. This makes it likely that there will be a steady stream of grave breach cases emanating from the ICC in the years to come.

For other violations of the laws and customs of war, as Chapter 2 explained, persons *hors de combat* are not civilians,[16] meaning they cannot be victims of war

model. (5) Members of crews, including masters, pilots and apprentices, of the merchant marine and the crews of civil aircraft of the Parties to the conflict, who do not benefit by more favourable treatment under any other provisions of international law. (6) Inhabitants of a non-occupied territory, who on the approach of the enemy spontaneously take up arms to resist the invading forces, without having had time to form themselves into regular armed units, provided they carry arms openly and respect the laws and customs of war.' Also see Article 44(1), Protocol I.

12 Article 4, Geneva Convention IV. The ICTY has interpreted this provision flexibly, see *Tadić* AC, paras 164–169; *Prosecutor v Zejnil Delalić et al*, ICTY, IT-96-21-T, Trial Judgment, 16 November 1998 (*Čelebići* TC), paras 245–266 and 274–275; *Prosecutor v Zejnil Delalić et al*, ICTY, IT-96-21-A, Appeal Judgment, 20 February 2001 (*Čelebići* AC), paras 54 and 99; *Blaškić* TC, paras 126 and 127; and *Prosecutor v Zlatko Aleksovski*, ICTY, IT-95-14/1-A, Appeal Judgment, 24 March 2000 (*Aleksovski* AC), para. 153.

13 James G. Stewart, 'The Future of the Grave Breaches Regime: Segregate, Assimilate or Abandon?' 7(4) *Journal of International Criminal Justice* 855–877 (2009), pp. 860–862.

14 See for example, *Prosecutor v Milorad Krnojelac*, ICTY, Motion to Withdraw Article 2 Counts, 27 October 2000, Article 2 Counts, 27 October 2000.

15 Certain Military and Paramilitary Activities in and against Nicaragua (*Nicaragua v United States of America*) Judgment (Merits), International Court of Justice, 27 June 1986 (*Nicaragua*), para. 218 and *Tadić* Decision, paras 128–134.

16 Article 50(1) and (2), Protocol I.

crimes which require that victims had civilian status. However, by being *hors de combat*, they are no longer DPH/APH, and can be victims of crimes founded on, for example, Common Article 3, which offers protection based on the conduct of those involved. This was confirmed by the ICTY in *Karadžić*,[17] which considered whether peacekeepers could be victims of the crime of hostage-taking under Common Article 3. Karadžić argued that, in the particular circumstances of the case,[18] the peacekeeping personnel had been APH/DPH and consequently were not protected by Common Article 3 upon detention.[19] The argument was rejected by the Trial Chamber, which stated:

> even if the UN personnel had been combatants prior to their detention, as the Accused argues, they were in any event rendered *hors de combat* by virtue of their detention and thus were also entitled to the minimum protections guaranteed by Common Article 3.[20]

Thus, once a person is rendered *hors de combat*, they can be victims of violations of the laws and customs of war which focus on the conduct of the victim as not APH/DPH.

This chapter will argue that although once a person becomes *hors de combat*, they can be victims of many of the same crimes as civilians, some important differences remain. It begins by examining how ICTs have determined who qualifies for POW status and the importance POW status has in ICL. It then examines the differences that can arise in war crimes cases when the alleged victim is a person *hors de combat* rather than a civilian.

4.1 International criminal law and POW status

The right to POW status is jealously controlled by states, being restricted to those who fulfil the requirements of Article 4A of Geneva Convention III or Article 44 (1) of Protocol I.[21] Traditionally, the right to become a POW when captured has been regarded as being a vital element of combatant status, and 'conventional wisdom maintains that denial of POW status to combatants has drastic protective and policy consequences'.[22] In recent years, however, its importance has been called into question by some. Jinks, for example, argues that while POW status

17 *Prosecutor v Radovan Karadžić*, IT-95-5/18-T Trial Judgment, 24 March 2016 (*Karadžić* TC).
18 The case is discussed further in Chapter 7.
19 Ibid., para. 5942; and see *Prosecutor v Radovan Karadžić*, Case no IT-95-5/18-AR73.9, Appeal from Denial of Judgment for Acquittal for Hostage-Taking, 25 July 2012.
20 *Karadžić* TC, para. 5934.
21 For a brief outline of the requirements for POW status, see Chapter 1.
22 Derek Jinks, 'The Declining Significance of POW Status', 44 *Harvard International Law Journal* 367 (2004), p. 368.

grants several important rights and privileges, it carries no significant, unique protective consequences.[23]

In the context of ICL, entitlement to POW status becomes important if grave breaches of the Geneva Conventions are alleged, and, as will be discussed below, it can also be of relevance in relation to certain war crimes. This section explores how ICTs have determined whether an alleged victim had POW status. It begins by analysing jurisprudence from the post-Second World War era, before moving to case law from the ICTY, which is the ICT that has devoted most time to considering this issue in recent years.

4.1.1 Post-World War II cases

Throughout the Second World War, many different groups resisted the Nazis and their allies. Upon becoming *hors de combat*, those belligerents who did not meet the requirements of the Hague Regulations[24] were not entitled to POW status, and it was accepted practice that they could be executed for their participation in hostilities.[25] These belligerents were viewed by the parties to the conflict as criminals, no matter how honourable their cause.[26] Consequently, during the

23 Jinks writes: 'Without question, the Geneva Conventions guarantee POWs several important rights and privileges. It is a mistake, however, to infer from this proposition that the denial of POW status carries significant detrimental consequences for the scope and content of detainee rights. In fact, careful analysis of the text, structure, and history of the Geneva Conventions demonstrates that the Conventions provide a robust rights regime for all war detainees.' Ibid., p. 374, and see p. 442. Also see Emily Crawford, *The Treatment of Combatants and Insurgents under the Law of Armed Conflict* (Oxford University Press, 2010), pp. 78–116.

24 'The laws, rights, and duties of war apply not only to armies, but also to militia and volunteer corps fulfilling the following conditions: 1. To be commanded by a person responsible for his subordinates; 2. To have a fixed distinctive emblem recognizable at a distance; 3. To carry arms openly; and 4. To conduct their operations in accordance with the laws and customs of war. In countries where militia or volunteer corps constitute the army, or form part of it, they are included under the denomination "army."' Article 1, Annex to Convention (IV) respecting the Laws and Customs of War on Land, 1907 (Hague Regulations, 1907).

25 '[C]aptured members of these unlawful groups were not entitled to be treated as prisoners of war. No crime can properly be charged against the defendants for the killing of such captured members of the resistance forces, they being francs-tireurs.' *United States v Wilhelm List et al*, XI Trials of War Criminals Before the Nuernberg Military Tribunals under Control Council Law No 10, US Govt Printing Office, Washington DC, 1947–1951 (*Hostages* case), p. 1244 and see p. 1269. Although the Tribunals deemed that it was legal to sentence resistance fighters to death, they did not accept that summary execution was lawful. However, Heller explains that, 'the tribunals were maddeningly vague concerning what the "accepted trial requirements" actually were'. Kevin John Heller, *The Nuremberg Military Tribunals and the Origins of International Criminal Law* (Oxford University Press, 2011), p. 210.

26 The prevailing view at that time as regards the resistance fighter was summarised by the Tribunal in the *Hostages* case: 'guerrillas may render great service to their country and, in the event of success, become heroes even, still they remain war criminals in the eyes of the enemy and may be treated as such. In no other way can an army guard and

trials following the war, accused persons sought to label these victims as guerrillas, partisans or *francs-tireurs*, arguing that they had not been lawful combatants and that it had not been unlawful to execute them. Having lawful belligerent status was therefore hugely important, as it meant entitlement to POW status upon capture.

Heller, writing of the 12 US trials held before the Nuremberg Military Tribunals, is of the view that they, 'embraced a very conservative reading of the Hague Regulations'[27] when determining entitlement to POW status. Certainly, it is true that some post-Second World War cases applied the Hague Regulations conservatively. An example of this is the *Hostages* case, where the US Military Tribunal considered whether bands of Yugoslavian and Greek resistance fighters, thousands of whom had been executed by the Nazis, had been partisans, as the defendants argued, or whether they had been lawful belligerents. In that case, the Tribunal took the view that if the requirements of the 1907 Hague Regulations were met, a lawful belligerency exists; if they were not met, it is an unlawful one.[28] It systematically applied the four conditions for belligerent status listed in the Hague Regulations,[29] to the evidence before it. The Tribunal found that the bands of resistance fighters were sometimes designated as units common to a military organisation, and that there was evidence of a centralised command in some instances. However, they had no common uniform and generally wore civilian clothes, although German, Italian and Serbian uniforms were worn when they could be found. They wore an insignia – the Soviet star – but there was no evidence that it could be seen from a distance. They did not carry arms openly unless it was to their advantage to do so.[30] The Tribunal held that although it was evident that some partisan bands met the requirements of lawful belligerency, those they were dealing with in the case before it did not meet the requirements and were not entitled to POW status.[31] Accordingly, the partisan bands had not been entitled to POW status.[32]

The strict application of the Hague Regulations in the *Hostages* case can be contrasted with the approach of the Tribunal in the *Einsatzgruppen* case, which pursued a more liberal approach when determining who had been a lawful

protect itself from the gadfly tactics of such armed resistance. And, on the other hand, members of such resistance forces must accept the increased risks involved in this mode of fighting. Such forces are technically not lawful belligerents and are not entitled to protection as prisoners of war when captured.' *Hostages* case, p. 1255.

27 Heller, *supra* FN 25, p. 209.

28 *Hostages* case, p. 1246.

29 Namely: (1) to be commanded by a person responsible for his subordinates; (2) to have a fixed distinctive emblem recognisable at a distance; (3) to carry arms openly; and (4) to conduct their operations in accordance with the laws and customs of war.

30 *Hostages* case, p. 1244.

31 Ibid., p. 1244.

32 The decision in the *Hostages* case regarding Greek and Yugoslavian fighters, represents the only instance in the cases before the US Nuremberg Military Tribunals, where a claim by a defendant that the victims were partisans succeeded. See *Hostages* case, pp. 1292–1293; and Heller, *supra* FN 25, p. 209.

belligerent. The *Einsatzgruppen* case was partly concerned with the deaths of thousands of people in the Soviet Union. The accused argued that their deaths had been lawful as they had been partisans. The Tribunal considered Article 1 of the Hague Regulations and held that:

> It is unnecessary to point out that, under these provisions, an armed civilian found in a treetop sniping at uniformed soldiers is not such a lawful combatant and can be punished even with the death penalty if he is proved guilty of the offense.
>
> But this is far different from saying that resistance fighters in the war against an invading army, if they fully comply with the conditions (of Article 1), can be put outside the law by the adversary. As the Hague Regulations state expressly, if they fulfill the four conditions, 'the laws, rights and duties of war' apply to them in the same manner as they apply to regular armies.
>
> Many of the defendants seem to assume that by merely characterizing a person a partisan, he may be shot out of hand. But it is not so simple as that. If the partisans are organized and are engaged in what international law regards as legitimate warfare for the defense of their country, they are entitled to be protected as combatants.[33]

The Tribunal found that the 'so-called partisans' had been carrying out a regular act of war in trying to regain control of territory from the Germans and had been punished simply for having fought against the enemy, in contravention of the laws of war. Rather than strictly applying Article 1 of the Hague Regulations to the facts of the case to establish whether the resistance fighters complied with each individual requirement, the Tribunal took a broader, more flexible approach.

These two cases serve to illustrate the importance of POW status in war crimes cases following the Second World War and the different levels of analysis that courts applied when establishing entitlement to POW status. The *Hostages* case applied the terms of the Hague Regulations strictly to the facts of the case, whereas the *Einsatzgruppen* case took a more liberal approach.

4.1.2 POW status at the ICTY

The ICTY has considered entitlement to POW status in a handful of cases. This is partly due to the paucity of grave breach charges brought before the ICTY, and partly due to the approach taken by the Tribunal towards who is protected under the Conventions. The general approach taken by the Tribunal will be discussed first, before a specific case is explored, that of *Mrkšić*, where the Tribunal found that a special agreement had existed concerning POW status.

33 *United States of America v Otto Ohlendorf et al*, IV Trials of War Criminals before Nuernberg Military Tribunals under Control Council Law No 10, US Govt Printing Office, Washington DC, 1951 (*Einsatzgruppen* case), p. 491.

(i) The ICTY's general approach to POW status

The leading case at the tribunal concerning the determination of POW status is *Čelebići*. It centred around events that took place in Čelebići village in central Bosnia and Herzegovina. Bosniak and Bosnian Croat forces had taken control over the predominantly Serbian villages in the area. Bosnian Serb residents had been expelled from their homes and detained in detention camps, including the one at Čelebići, where they were alleged by the Prosecution to have been 'killed, tortured, sexually assaulted, beaten, and otherwise subjected to cruel and inhuman treatment'.[34] The accused were charged with having committed violations of the laws of customs of war and grave breaches of the Geneva Conventions in relation to those detained.

The armed conflict was found to have been an IAC at the time of the events in question.[35] The evidence showed that some of the detainees had been fighting against the detaining forces when captured, and the Chamber had to determine whether they qualified for POW status under Geneva Convention III. It began by considering the terms of Article 4A, noting that:

> Article 4(A) of the Third Geneva Convention sets rather stringent requirements for the achievement of prisoner of war status … this provision was drafted in the light of the experience of the Second World War and reflects the conception of an international armed conflict current at that time. Thus, the various categories of persons who may be considered prisoners of war are narrowly framed.[36]

The Chamber systematically applied the provisions of Article 4A to the facts to ascertain whether the detainees qualified for POW status under one of the six sub-paragraphs. It observed that the alleged victims were not contended to be members of the regular armed forces, as defined in Article 4A(1),[37] and that sub-paragraphs 3, 4 and 5 also did not apply.[38] Two alternatives remained: first, that the detainees qualified as POWs under Article 4A(2), as members of militias or volunteer corps belonging to a party which: (a) was commanded by a person responsible for his subordinates; (b) had a fixed sign recognisable at a distance; (c) carried arms openly; and (d) conducted their operations in accordance with the laws and customs of war;[39] or second, that the detainees qualified as participants in a *levée en masse* under Article 4A(6).[40]

34 *Prosecutor v Zejnil Delalić et al*, ICTY, IT-96-21-I, Indictment, 19 March 1996, para. 2.
35 *Čelebići* TC, para. 234.
36 Ibid., para. 267.
37 'Members of the armed forces of a Party to the conflict as well as members of militias or volunteer corps forming part of such armed forces.' Article 4A(1), Geneva Convention III.
38 Ibid., para. 268.
39 Ibid., para. 268.
40 Ibid., para. 268.

In relation to the claim that the detainees were POWs under Article 4A(2), the Prosecution argued that Protocol I, which adopts a more liberal approach to entitlement to POW status than Geneva Convention III, could be used to interpret the provision. Whilst the Trial Chamber did not reject this proposal, it stated:

> Even should this be accepted, and despite the discussion above of the need to take a broad and flexible approach to the interpretation of the Geneva Conventions, the Trial Chamber finds it difficult, on the evidence presented to it, to conclude that any of the victims of the acts alleged in the Indictment satisfied these requirements. While it is apparent that some of the persons detained in the Čelebići prison-camp had been in possession of weapons and may be considered to have participated to some degree in 'hostilities', this is not sufficient to render them entitled to prisoner of war status.[41]

Thus, even based on a liberal construction of the facts of the case, the Chamber was unable to find that the detainees were able to qualify for POW status.

It then considered whether the detainees had been participants in a *levée en masse*. Article 4A(6) of Geneva Convention III confers POW status upon '[i]nhabitants of a non-occupied territory, who on the approach of the enemy spontaneously take up arms to resist the invading forces, without having had time to form themselves into regular armed units, provided they carry arms openly and respect the laws and customs of war'. The Chamber found that the facts of the case were difficult to fit into this scenario, as the 'aggressors', who were the local authorities, were not invading. There was also no evidence to show that the Bosnian Serbs as a group were at all times carrying their weapons openly and observing the laws or customs of war. The Chamber commented that 'Article 4(A)(6) undoubtedly places a somewhat high burden on local populations to behave as if they were professional soldiers'.[42] It concluded that the Bosnian Serb detainees were not entitled to POW status, either under Article 4(A)(2), as members of militias or volunteer corps, or under Article 4(A)(6), as members of a *levée en masse*.

The case illustrates the difficulties faced by prosecutors when trying to argue that fighters who were not members of state armed forces were entitled to protection as POWs under Geneva Convention III: the provisions of Article 4A set a high threshold. In reaching their decision, the Trial Chamber in *Čelebići* carried out a reasoned analysis, systematically applying the provisions of Article 4A to the facts of the case to reach their conclusion that the detainees did not qualify for protection as POWs. Crucially, however, the Chamber then made a further finding that:

> there is no gap between the Third and the Fourth Geneva Conventions. If an individual is not entitled to the protections of the Third Convention as a prisoner of war (or of the First or Second Conventions) he or she necessarily

41 Ibid., para. 269.
42 Ibid., para. 270.

> falls within the ambit of Convention IV, provided that its article 4 requirements are satisfied.[43]

This approach that if an individual does not fall within the ambit of the Third Convention, they are protected by the Fourth, feeds into the debate concerning whether there is a gap in the Conventions.[44] At the ICTY this has simply not been an issue;[45] the approach taken in *Čelebići* has been consistently followed in other cases.[46] The consequences of this will be considered shortly. First, another case will be discussed: that of *Mrkšić* from the ICTY, which considered when POW status can be conferred through a special agreement between the parties to the conflict.

(ii) Special agreements as to POW status and the Mrkšić *case*

Detainees can qualify for POW status if the parties to the conflict enter a special agreement to that effect. This possibility was considered in *Mrkšić*. First, a brief résumé of the facts of the case: the events occurred in Vukovar, a city lying in Croatian territory, close to the border with Serbia. Towards the end of August 1991, the JNA[47] laid siege to the city, which capitulated on 18 November 1991.

43 Ibid., para. 271.

44 See for example, Richard R. Baxter, 'The Duties of Combatants and the Conduct of Hostilities (Law of the Hague)', in *International Dimensions of Humanitarian Law* (Henry Dunant Institute, UNESCO ed., 1988), p. 106; G.I.A.D Draper, 'The Status of Combatants and the Question of Guerrilla Warfare', in Meyer and McCoubrey (eds), *Reflections on Law and Armed Conflicts: The Selected Works on the Laws of War by the late Professor Colonel G.I.A.D. Draper* (Kluwer Law International, 1998), p. 208; Knut Dörmann, 'The Legal Situation of "Unlawful/Unprivileged Combatants"', 85(849) *International Review of the Red Cross* 45–74 (2003); M. Sassòli, 'The Status of Persons held in Guantánamo under International Humanitarian Law', 2 *Journal of International Criminal Justice* 96–106 (2004); Ryan Goodman, 'The Detention of Civilians in Armed Conflict', 103(1)*American Journal of International Law* 48–74 (2009).

45 Stewart explains that 'in sharp contrast to the now extensive and deeply polarized political and academic debate surrounding the existence and scope of unlawful combatant status, the position adopted in international criminal precedents is markedly more uniform'. James G. Stewart, 'Rethinking Guantánamo: Unlawful Confinement as Applied in International Criminal Law', 4 *Journal of International Criminal Justice* 12–30 (2006), p. 18.

46 For example in *Blaškić*, the Prosecution contended that Bosnian Muslim combatants held by the HVO were entitled to POW status under Geneva Convention III. Rather than carrying out a detailed analysis applying the provisions of Article 4A in order to ascertain whether some of those who had been detained complied with the provision, the Trial Chamber simply stated that: 'The Trial Chamber is of the view that all the persons identified as prisoners of war did enjoy the protection accorded by the Third Geneva Convention and points out that those who did not enjoy this protection were civilians and thereby enjoyed the protection accorded by the Fourth Geneva Convention.' *Blaškić* TC, paras 146–147.

47 The military forces of the Socialist Federal Republic of Yugoslavia (SFRY).

The case centred upon what happened to a group of prisoners who were taken by the JNA from the hospital in Vukovar after the capitulation. Towards the end of the siege, many people had sought refuge at the hospital in the hope that it would be safely evacuated in the presence of international observers. The group comprised patients, family members of hospital staff, other civilians, and also members of Croat military groups, including some who were not wounded.[48] On 18 November 1991, an agreement was reached between the JNA and the Croatian government[49] regarding the evacuation of the wounded and sick from the hospital (the Zagreb Agreement).[50] The JNA took control of the hospital the next day and the evacuation commenced.

There were three accused in the case. Radić, a captain in the JNA, was found not guilty by the Trial Chamber. The other two were Mrkšić, the commander of OG South, and Šljivančanin, a major in the JNA. When the evacuation of the hospital began, Mrkšić ordered Šljivančanin to transport all 'war crimes suspects' from the hospital to a prison.[51] The phrase 'war crimes suspects' was interpreted to mean all members of the Croatian armed forces.[52] Initially, it was intended that these prisoners would be exchanged for Serb prisoners. Plans were changed, and it was decided that the prisoners should be tried locally.[53] They were taken to a JNA barracks where they were humiliated and threatened, and some were beaten. An order was given that the prisoners were to be transported to a hanger in a place called Ovčara, about four kilometres from Vukovar. Mrkšić then ordered Šljivančanin to withdraw the JNA soldiers guarding the prisoners, leaving them in the custody of other paramilitary forces.[54] That night the prisoners were transported in groups of ten to 20 to a nearby ravine, where they were executed and their bodies buried in a mass grave.[55]

The Trial Chamber established that it had jurisdiction over the alleged acts,[56] but chose to make no determination as to whether the conflict was an IAC or a NIAC at the relevant time.[57] Despite this, the Chamber reasoned that:

48 *Mrkšić* TC, para. 181.
49 Croatia had proclaimed its independence from SFRY on 8 October 1991.
50 The Zagreb Agreement was an agreement between representatives of the Republic of Croatia and the JNA on the evacuation of the sick and wounded from Vukovar Hospital under supervision of international observers from the ICRC and Médecins Sans Frontières. The Agreement concerned the evacuation of the wounded and sick undergoing medical treatment at the hospital who were judged by the authorities of the hospital to be fit to make the journey. It did not include evacuation of hospital staff, their families or other persons at the hospital. *Prosecutor v Mile Mrškić et al*, ICTY, IT-95-13/1-T, Trial Judgment, 27 September 2007 (*Mrkšić* TC), paras 130–131. A copy of the Zagreb Agreement can be found on the ICTY's Court Records database, available at http://icr.icty.org.
51 *Mrkšić* TC, para. 191.
52 Ibid., para. 191.
53 Ibid., paras 304–306.
54 Ibid., paras 275, 285, 293 and 321.
55 Ibid., para. 252.
56 Ibid., paras 406–428.
57 Ibid., paras 422 and 457.

> the evidence reveals that at least the vast majority of (the detainees), if not all, had been involved in Croat military formations active in the fighting at Vukovar. At the time all of them were thought by the JNA to have been so involved. The Chamber finds that at least by the time they were searched to ensure they were not armed and were under the guard of JNA soldiers, these men became prisoners of war.[58]

POW status applies only in IACs[59] or in situations where the parties to the conflict agree that it should apply.[60] However, as the Trial Chamber had made no determination that the armed conflict was an IAC, on what evidence did it rely to establish that the detainees in question were entitled to POW status?

In its Judgment, the Trial Chamber devoted minimal attention to this question. It referred to the surrender negotiations between the JNA and the Croatian government on 18 November 1991, culminating in the Zagreb Agreement. The Judgment states that as part of those negotiations, it was agreed that 'the Croatian forces were to be treated as prisoners of war in accordance with the Geneva Convention'.[61] It also referred to a fax received by monitors for the European Community Monitoring Mission (ECMM) from their tasking cell in Zagreb regarding the evacuation, informing them that the rules of the Geneva Conventions would be applied to all wounded POWs, and that the prisoners would be interviewed to ascertain where they wanted to go.[62] The Trial Chamber noted that the surrender took place in an organised manner, that witnesses observed that the prisoners were treated in accordance with IHL, and that the ICRC took a register of the prisoners.[63] The Chamber did not analyse whether this evidence was sufficient to conclude that the detainees had POW status. It simply proceeded on the basis that Geneva Convention III applied and the prisoners were POWs.

On Appeal, the Appeals Chamber gave more detailed consideration as to whether the detainees had been entitled to POW status. It noted that the Trial Chamber opted not to make a finding as to the character of the conflict; however, it recalled that 'even in the context of an internal armed conflict, Geneva Convention III applies where the parties to the conflict have agreed that the Convention shall apply'.[64] In making this statement, the Appeals Chamber referred in a footnote to Common Articles 2 and 3 of the Geneva Conventions. Common Article 2 provides (in part):

58 Ibid., para. 207. The Chamber found that 181 of the 194 identified persons held were known to be active in the Croat forces in Vukovar, while the remaining 13 had no known military involvement, ibid., para. 479.
59 Article 4A Geneva Convention III and Article 44(1), Protocol I.
60 *See* Common Articles 2 and 3, Geneva Conventions.
61 *Mrkšić* TC, para. 147.
62 Ibid., para. 144.
63 Ibid., para. 150.
64 Ibid., para. 69.

> Although one of the Powers in conflict may not be a party to the present Convention, the Powers who are parties thereto shall remain bound by it in their mutual relations. They shall furthermore be bound by the Convention in relation to the said Power, if the latter accepts and applies the provisions thereof.

However, in order for this part of Common Article 2 to apply, it is necessary that the rest of the Article applies, namely that the conflict in question be an IAC.[65] As neither the Trial Chamber nor the Appeals Chamber had made such a finding in this case, it is difficult to understand how this provision can be relied upon.[66]

The relevant part of Common Article 3(2) states: 'the Parties to the conflict should further endeavour to bring into force, by means of special agreements, all or part of the other provisions of the present Convention.' Was there evidence of a special agreement in this case? The Appeals Chamber believed so. It examined several different sources to conclude that a special agreement had been reached between the parties to the effect that the detainees were POWs. The Chamber noted that the Zagreb Agreement was concerned purely with the evacuation of the wounded and sick from Vukovar hospital, and contained nothing regarding whether those taken prisoner were to be regarded as POWs.[67] The Chamber then turned to three other different sources of evidence: first, instructions given by the ECMM to its monitors regarding the implementation of the Zagreb Agreement, which indicated that the Geneva Conventions were to be applied to the prisoners; second, an order from a Lieutenant-Colonel Panić, chief of staff of the Gmtbr and OG South, directing JNA units in the Vukovar area to observe all aspects of Geneva Convention III; finally, a statement by a Colonel Pavković to ECMM monitors that a General Rešeta had issued instructions that Croat forces were not to be evacuated with the rest of the humanitarian convoy, but were to remain as POWs, and that the Geneva Conventions would apply to them.[68] On the basis of these sources of evidence, the Appeals Chamber concluded that the JNA had agreed that the Croat forces were to be considered as POWs and that Geneva Convention III was to apply.[69]

The evidence relied on by the Appeals Chamber to conclude that a special agreement existed between the parties to the effect that the prisoners were to be treated as POWs is flimsy at best. First, as regards the instructions given by the

65 Common Article 2 also states: '… the present Convention shall apply to all cases of declared war or of any other armed conflict which may arise between two or more of the High Contracting Parties, even if the state of war is not recognized by one of them. The Convention shall also apply to all cases of partial or total occupation of the territory of a High Contracting Party, even if the said occupation meets with no armed resistance.'

66 See Giulia Pinzauti, 'Protecting Prisoners of War, The *Mrkšić et al* Appeal Judgment', 8 *Journal of International Criminal Justice* 199–219 (2010), p. 205.

67 *Prosecutor v Mile Mrškić et al*, ICTY, IT-95-13/1-A, Appeal Judgment, 5 May 2009 (*Mrkšić* AC), para. 69.

68 Ibid., para. 69.

69 Ibid., para. 69 and FN 239.

ECMM to its monitors, the ECMM was a third party, and while its views on the situation may have some evidentiary value, they cannot be taken as definitive proof as to what had been agreed between the parties. Also, the ECMM's instructions that the Zagreb Agreement indicated that the Geneva Conventions should apply to POWs is incorrect. The Zagreb Agreement merely concerned the evacuation of the hospital, and did not address whether or not the Geneva Conventions were applicable.

Second, as regards the order from Lieutenant-Colonel Panić, although this is indicative of an intention on the side of one party to the conflict, it can hardly be said to constitute a special agreement between the parties. The same can be said as regards General Rešeta's instructions relayed to the ECMM via Colonel Pavković. Pinzauti notes that two days before the events in question, the JNA and the Croat government had concluded an agreement in respect of a different area, Mitnica, where it was specifically stipulated that members of Croatian military formations were to be treated as POWs. As she explains, on the one hand, this could suggest that the JNA's practice was to treat captured enemy fighters as POWs. On the other hand, it could suggest the opposite: that if the parties had agreed to treat the prisoners at Vukovar as POWs, there would have been a specific clause to that effect within the Zagreb Agreement.[70]

Another factor suggesting that the detaining party did not regard the prisoners as POWs, is that they were referred to by Mrkšić and others as 'war crimes suspects',[71] and that the initial indications were that they were to be put on trial.[72] This language could indicate that the prisoners were viewed primarily as suspected criminals and not as POWs;[73] although the two categories are not mutually exclusive, POWs can be tried for violating IHL.[74] The evidence that there was a special agreement between the parties that the prisoners were to be treated as POWs does not, therefore, stand up to closer scrutiny.

In her article, Pinzauti examines whether it is possible for a party to make a unilateral declaration, whereby one party to a conflict undertakes to apply the Conventions in their entirety or only in part.[75] She explains that in order for this to occur, a consistent course of conduct is required. In this case, there is the evidence of the order from General Panić and the statement from Colonel Pavković. There is also evidence that another exchange of prisoners agreement was concluded for a different situation, under which the JNA and the Croatian authorities undertook to place all prisoners under the protection of the ICRC and to abide by

70 Pinzauti, *supra* FN 66, pp. 205–206.

71 'It is clear … in the Chamber's finding, that by his reference to war crime suspects, Mile Mrkšić was referring to all members of the Croat Forces at the hospital', *Mrkšić* TC, para. 191.

72 *Mrkšić* TC, paras 191, 295, 304 and 391. Pinzauti, *supra* FN 66, pp. 208–209.

73 The Trial Chamber considered the use of the phrase by Mrkšić, finding that 'by his reference to war crimes suspects, Mile Mrkšić is referring to all members of the Croat forces at the hospital'. *Mrkšić* TC, para. 191. Also see Pinzauti, *supra* FN 66, pp. 208–209.

74 Articles 82–88, Geneva Convention III.

75 Pinzauti, *supra* FN 66, pp. 207–210.

the ICRC's standards regarding the protection and accommodation of prisoners. Pinzauti writes: 'It is plausible to conclude from the totality of evidence … that the JNA's declarations were more than a mere political pledge; rather, they evidenced an intention to be bound.'[76] Thus, Pinzauti argues, it is possible to argue that there was sufficient evidence to conclude that the JNA agreed unilaterally that the Geneva Conventions were to apply to the prisoners at Vukovar. However, even if it is possible to view the actions of the JNA as constituting a unilateral declaration to treat the detainees as POWs, this was not the reasoning followed by the Appeals Chamber.[77] The Appeals Chamber's finding that the prisoners in this case were entitled to POW status is therefore questionable.[78]

To summarise, establishing whether detainees were entitled to POW status is not always an easy matter. The ICTY's approach that if an individual is not protected by Geneva Convention III they fall under the protection of Geneva Convention IV is to be commended. However, as the following section will demonstrate, this does not mean that the status of a detainee as a POW is of no relevance in ICL.

4.2 Special considerations concerning persons *hors de combat* and war crimes

Once a person becomes *hors de combat*, they can fall victim to many of the same crimes as civilians; however, their status is relevant as regards a number of war crimes. One area of variance concerns grave breaches of the Geneva Conventions. While some grave breaches are common to each of the Conventions – wilful killing, torture and inhuman treatment, for example – others are peculiar to a certain Convention, thus the grave breaches of unlawful deportation or transfer, or unlawful confinement of a protected person, are grave breaches of Geneva Convention IV only.[79] The standard of treatment due to a person protected by the Conventions can also vary depending on which Convention applies. Thus, if an alleged victim qualified for POW status, they cannot be a victim of certain crimes, or are subject to different standards. Also, that an alleged victim was a person *hors de combat* rather than a civilian can be relevant in other ways. This section discusses war crimes where the status of the alleged victim is important, namely, the crimes of unlawful confinement; unlawful deportation or transfer; hostage-taking; forced labour; and war crimes involving violation of the principle of proportionality. Finally, some aspects specific to the ICC Statute are addressed.

76 Ibid., p. 208.
77 Ibid., pp. 209–210.
78 This was to have important consequences for one of the accused, as it was found that he had a duty of protection to the POWs under Geneva Convention III which included the obligation to ensure that he did not allow the transfer of their custody to anyone without first assuring himself that they would not be harmed. *Mrkšić* AC, paras 72–74, and see Pinzauti, *supra* FN 66, pp. 209–210.
79 Article 147, Geneva Convention IV.

4.2.1 Unlawful confinement

Unlawful confinement is a grave breach of Geneva Convention IV,[80] whereas under Geneva Convention III, POWs can be detained until the cessation of hostilities.[81] This means that if detainees had POW status, the crime of unlawful confinement cannot have occurred. Persons *hors de combat* who are not POWs, but are protected persons under Geneva Convention IV, can in theory be victims of this crime. When assessing whether unlawful confinement has occurred, the ICTY has taken a two-step approach, first, assessing whether the initial confinement was legal and, second, examining whether sufficient procedural safeguards had been put in place following the initial confinement.

The leading case here is *Čelebići*, where some of those detained had been fighting the detaining forces prior to their detention, and, as we have seen, the Trial Chamber ruled that although these prisoners were not protected under Geneva Convention III, they qualified as protected persons under Geneva Convention IV. The accused were charged with unlawful confinement of these individuals as a grave breach under Article 2(g) of the ICTY Statute.[82]

The Trial Chamber considered under what circumstances it is permissible for a detaining power to detain protected persons under Geneva Convention IV. It noted that the Convention permits the confinement of civilians in certain limited situations.[83] Article 5 provides:

> Where, in the territory of a Party to the conflict, the latter is satisfied that an individual protected person is definitely suspected of or engaged in activities hostile to the security of the State, such individual person shall not be entitled to claim such rights and privileges under the present Convention as would, if exercised in the favour of such individual person, be prejudicial to the security of such State.

The Chamber analysed the notion of activities prejudicial or hostile to the security of the state. It acknowledged that the concept is difficult to define, and appears to include espionage, sabotage and intelligence activities for the enemy forces or enemy nationals. It does not simply refer to an individual's political attitude towards the state.[84] The Chamber noted that:

> Clearly, a civilian cannot shoot a passing enemy soldier, secrete a bomb in the enemy encampment, or otherwise directly and intentionally harm his enemy and hope to retain all the protections of the Fourth Geneva Convention. However, all of these acts involve material, direct harm to the adversary,

80 Article 147, Geneva Convention IV, and see Article 8(2)(a)(vii), ICC Statute.
81 Article 118, Geneva Convention III.
82 Count 48, *Čelebići* Initial Indictment, 19 March 1996.
83 *Čelebići* TC, para. 566; and see Articles 42 and 78, Geneva Convention IV.
84 Ibid., para. 567, referring to ICRC Commentary to Geneva Convention IV, p. 56.

> rather than merely granting support to the forces of the party with which the civilian is aligned.[85]

Article 27 of Geneva Convention IV permits parties to the conflict to 'take such measures of control and security in regard to protected persons as may be necessary as a result of the war'.[86] The Chamber noted that the Convention leaves a great deal of discretion to the parties to the conflict as regards the choice of means, and '[w]hat is essential is that the measures of constraint adopted should not affect the fundamental right of the persons concerned to be treated with humanity'.[87] The drafters of Geneva Convention IV, who were working against the background of the atrocities committed during the Second World War, intended that internment and assigned residence should take place as a last resort and subject to strict rules.[88] The Chamber concluded that:

> Clearly, internment is only permitted when absolutely necessary. Subversive activity carried on inside the territory of a party to the conflict, or actions which are of direct assistance to an opposing party, may threaten the security of the former, which may, therefore, intern people or place them in assigned residence if it has *serious and legitimate reasons* to think that they may seriously prejudice its security by means such as sabotage or espionage.[89]

This approach, which has been followed in subsequent cases at the ICTY,[90] gives states considerable leeway when determining what constitutes a threat to their security.[91] When assessing allegations of unlawful confinement, ICTs have not required a reappraisal of the grounds on which each and every individual is purportedly held; nor have they doubted that particular detention facilities where

85 Ibid., para. 568.
86 Ibid., para. 569.
87 Ibid., para. 570.
88 Ibid., para. 572 and Article 41–43 and 78, Geneva Convention IV.
89 Ibid., para. 576 and see para. 577. Also see *Čelebići* AC, para. 320.
90 For example, see *Čelebići* AC, paras 320–322; *Prosecutor v Dario Kordić and Mario Čerkez*, ICTY, IT-95-14/2-T, Trial Judgment, 26 February 2001 (*Kordić and Čerkez* TC), paras 280–285; and *Prosecutor v Dario Kordić and Mario Čerkez*, ICTY, IT-95-14/2-A, Appeal Judgment, 17 December 2004 (*Kordić and Čerkez* AC), para. 69–73, *Prlić*, TC (Vol. I), paras 133–139.
91 The Appeals Chamber made it clear that although the margin for discretion may be wide when detaining, it is limited, and there must be an assessment that each civilian taken into detention poses a particular risk to the security of the State. *Čelebići* AC, para. 327. Also see *Kordić and Čerkez*, where the Trial Chamber stated: 'if activities threatening the security of the State, such as subversive activities or direct assistance to the enemy, may permit a Party to intern people or place them in assigned residence – but only if it has a serious and legitimate reason to think that they are members of a subversive organization – the mere fact that a person is a national of the enemy cannot be considered as threatening the security of the country where he lives. Furthermore, the fact that a man is of military age should not necessarily be considered as justifying the application of these measures.' *Kordić and Čerkez* TC, para. 284.

unlawful detention has occurred contained large numbers of civilians who were detained legitimately.[92]

Where a large number of civilians were in possession of weapons at the time they were captured and were alleged to have committed acts of armed resistance through DPH/APH, the ICTY has refrained from determining whether the detaining power could have legitimately formed the view that their detention was necessary for the security of the state.[93] In *Čelebići*, for example, the Trial Chamber accepted that some of those detained had possessed a weapon at the time they were taken into detention, which could have, or had, been used against enemy forces. However, it avoided determining whether the possession of a weapon was sufficient in itself to constitute a security risk.[94]

Although Geneva Convention IV permits a detaining power to arrest, detain and confine individuals when it has reasonable grounds to believe that the security of the detaining power makes it absolutely necessary, initially lawful detention can become unlawful if the procedural safeguards detailed in Geneva Convention IV are not adhered to.[95] While the Convention leaves a great deal of discretion to the detaining party in the matter of the original internment, the party's decision that such measures of detention are required must be reconsidered as soon as possible by an appropriate court or administrative board.[96] The procedures established in Geneva Convention IV are a minimum, and the fundamental consideration must be that no civilian should be kept in detention any longer than the security of the detaining party absolutely demands.[97]

Thus, in *Simić*, the Trial Chamber of the ICTY found that while the initial arrest and detention of the members of a paramilitary group (the SDA), was lawful, the lack of procedural safeguards following detention was not. It stated:

> Although a small number of the arrests may not have been unlawful for persons belonging to the SDA paramilitary group, in so far as there may have been a well-founded suspicion that they committed crimes during their participation in these groups, the detention of these persons became unlawful when they were subjected to continued detention without respect for their rights to liberty and security of the person, and to a fair trial. The detainees in these facilities were not given any lawful reasons for their detention, and they were confined

92 Stewart, *supra* FN 45, p. 22.
93 Ibid.
94 *Čelebići* TC, para. 1131 and Article 42, Geneva Convention IV.
95 *Čelebići* AC, para. 322.
96 *Čelebići* TC, para. 580 and see *Čelebići* AC, para. 322 and 328–329.
97 Ibid., para. 581. In the case, it was held that although a Military Investigations Commission had been formed to review the detainees, and although the Commission had taken its duties seriously, it did not have the necessary power to decide upon the final release of prisoners. Other basic procedural rights of detainees had also not been respected and, as a result, the Commission failed to meet the requirements of Article 43. See *Čelebići* TC, paras 1135–1140; *Čelebići* AC, para. 327; *Kordić and Čerkez* AC, para. 609; and *Prosecutor v Blagoje Simić et al*, ICTY, IT-95-9-T, Trial Judgment, 17 October 2003 (*Simić* TC), para. 678.

> for considerable amounts of time without being charged ... Those few who were subject to criminal proceedings, did not receive trials or procedures in accordance with international human rights standards, and the guarantees as set out in the Geneva Conventions. The legality of their detention was never reviewed by the Serb authorities.[98]

Thus, although a party to a conflict has the right to arrest and detain on security grounds, the detention becomes unlawful if appropriate procedural safeguards are not in place to review the detention and to ensure that they receive a fair trial at a later stage.

To summarise, that a detainee had been involved in fighting before their detention is relevant in relation to war crimes concerning unlawful detention and confinement. Persons *hors de combat* who have POW status cannot be victims of the grave breach of unlawful confinement. For those who fall under the protection of Geneva Convention IV, it is permitted for a state to arrest and detain them for reasons of security; however, detainees can be unlawfully confined in the event that there are insufficient appropriate procedural safeguards in place to review their detention and to ensure that they receive a fair trial.

4.2.2 Unlawful deportation or transfer

Another instance where POW status becomes relevant is in relation to crimes of unlawful deportation or transfer.[99] Geneva Convention IV prohibits individual or mass forcible transfers, as well as deportations of protected persons from occupied territory across borders, regardless of motive.[100] Geneva Convention III, on the other hand, specifically allows for the transfer of POWs. For example, Article 19 of Geneva Convention III requires POWs to be evacuated from the combat zone and into internment facilities as soon as possible after capture, whereas Article 46 imposes conditions upon the detaining power when transferring POWs.[101] In *Stakić* the Appeals Chamber of the ICTY noted that international law recognises certain grounds permitting forced removals, and that 'if an act of forced removal is carried out on such a basis, the act cannot constitute the *actus reus* of the crime of deportation'.[102] As IHL permits the forcible transfer of POWs, they cannot be victims of these crimes.[103]

98 *Simić* TC, para. 681. This involved unlawful detention or confinement in the context of the crime of persecution as a crime against humanity under Article 5 of the ICTY Statute.

99 Articles 8(2)(a)(vii) and 8(2)(e)(viii), ICC Statute.

100 Article 49, Geneva Convention IV. Also see Article 17, Protocol II.

101 Also see Article 111, Geneva Convention III. The ICTY has held that deportation is the forced displacement of persons by expulsion or other coercive acts from the area in which they are lawfully present 'without grounds permitted under international law', see *Prosecutor v Milorad Krnojelac*, ICTY, IT-97-24-T, Trial Judgment, 15 March 2002, para. 474; *Blaškić* TC, para. 234; and *Prosecutor v Milomir Stakić*, IT-97-24-A, Appeal Chamber, 22 March 2006 (*Stakić* AC), para. 679.

102 *Stakić* AC, para. 284.

103 *Mrškić* TC, para. 458.

4.2.3 Hostage-taking

The crime of taking hostages is both a grave breach of Geneva Convention IV[104] and a violation of Common Article 3. Although POWs cannot be victims of the crime of hostage-taking as a grave breach, it has been found that they can be victims of the crime when charged as a violation of Common Article 3, in that they were not APH/DPH at the time. Some uncertainty had surrounded whether an element of the crime of hostage-taking was that the original detention be unlawful.[105] If so, as POWs were initially lawfully confined, they could not be victims of this crime. However, in the *Karadžić* case, concerning detained peacekeepers, the Trial Chamber found that they had been not APH/DPH at the time and that 'Common Article 3 applies to the detained UN personnel irrespective of their status prior to detention'.[106]

4.2.4 Unlawful labour

The use of detainees for forced labour can constitute a grave breach of the Conventions (inhuman treatment) or a violation of the laws and customs of war (cruel treatment, unlawful labour).[107] While those detained under both Geneva Conventions III and IV can be victims of these crimes, IHL imposes different standards concerning whether they can be compelled to work and what they can be compelled to do.[108] The use of POWs for forced labour is permitted under

104 Article 147, Geneva Convention IV and see Article 8(2)(a)(viii) and 8(2)(c)(iii), ICC Statute.

105 For example, Article 1 of the International Convention Against the Taking of Hostages does not specify that the detention of the individual be unlawful. Neither do the Elements of Crimes for the Statute of the International Criminal Court regarding Article 8(2)(c)(iii) However, see ICRC Position on Hostage-Taking, 846, *International Review of the Red Cross* 467 (2002); and see *Kordić and Čerkez*, TC, paras 312–314, *Blaškić* TC, para. 708, and *RUF* AC, paras 597–598.

106 *Karadžić* TC, para. 5943.

107 *Prosecutor v Mladen Naletilić and Vinko Martinović*, ICTY, IT-98-34-T, Trial Judgment, 31 March 2003 (*Naletilić* TC), para. 250. It can also be charged as a crime against humanity (inhumane act). The use of POWs for forced labour was an issue of contention in both the First and Second World Wars. For the First World War, see Alan R. Kramer, 'Prisoners in the First World War', in Sibylle Scheipers (ed.), *Prisoners in War* (Oxford University Press, 2010), pp. 81–82; and see *Karl Heynen*, Supreme Court at Leipzig, 26 May 1921, *Verhandlungen*, 2543–7, English translation available in 16 *American Journal of International Law* 674–84 (1922). For the Second World War see Howard S. Levie, 'The Employment of Prisoners of War', 57(2) *American Journal of International Law* 318 (1963). For examples of post-World War II cases considering the use of POWs for forced labour, see *USA v Carl Krauch et al*, VIII Trials of War Criminals Before the Nuernberg Military Tribunals under Control Council Law No 10, US Govt Printing Office, Washington DC, 1947–1951 (*I.G. Farben*), p. 1182; and *United States of America v Erhard Milch*, II Trials of War Criminals Before the Nuremberg Military Tribunals under Control Council Law No 10, US Govt Printing Office, Washington DC, 1947–1951 (*Milch* case), p. 866.

108 The ICTY has found that the crime of unlawful labour consists of any intentional act or omission whereby a POW or a civilian not DPH/APH at the time of the act or

Geneva Convention III,[109] whereas while compelling protected persons to work is permitted under Geneva Convention IV, the situations when it can occur are more limited.[110]

Although Geneva Convention III permits detaining powers to compel POWs (excepting officers) to work,[111] two sets of factors limit what they can do.[112] The first set relates to the prisoner. POWs (excepting officers) may be compelled to work, provided that it is in their own interest to do so, and considerations relating to their age, sex, physical aptitude and rank are taken into account.[113] The conditions in which the work is undertaken must also meet certain standards.[114]

The second group of factors relates to the nature of the work required. Geneva Convention III broadly prohibits using POWs in labour related to combat operations. Article 50 of Geneva Convention III provides a list of work that POWs can undertake, and this contains three exceptions: work in metallurgical, machinery and chemical industries; public works; and work in building operations that have no military character and purpose.[115] Furthermore, POWs cannot be compelled to engage in unhealthy or dangerous labour unless they volunteer to do so, nor can they be assigned labour that would be looked upon as humiliating for a member of the detaining power's own forces.[116]

The *Naletilić* Trial Chamber found that determination as to whether detainees had volunteered for labour or had been compelled to undertake it must be made on a case-by-case basis. In determining this, the criteria to be considered are: (a) the substantially uncompensated aspect of the labour performed; (b) the vulnerable position in which the detainees found themselves; (c) the allegations that detainees who were unable or unwilling to work were either forced to do so or put in solitary confinement; (d) claims of longer-term consequences of the labour; (e) the fact and the conditions of detention; and (f) the physical consequences of the work on the health of the internees.[117]

The ICTY has considered the lawfulness of different kinds of labour for POWs. In *Naletilić* the Trial Chamber had little hesitation in declaring the use of

omission is compelled to perform labour prohibited under the provisions of Articles 49, 50 and 52 of Geneva Convention III and Articles 40, 51 and 95 of Geneva Convention IV, respectively. *Naletilić* TC, para. 261, and *Prlić* TC (Vol. I), para. 163.

109 Articles 49–57, Geneva Convention III.

110 'Protected persons may be compelled to work only to the same extent as nationals of the Party to the conflict in whose territory they are.' Article 40 Geneva Convention IV and for internees see Article 95, Geneva Convention IV.

111 Article 49, Geneva Convention III, and *Naletilić* TC, para. 254.

112 *Naletilić* TC, para. 253.

113 Article 49, Geneva Convention III, and *Prlić* TC (Vol. I), para. 158.

114 Article 51 of Geneva Convention III requires that POWs must work under 'suitable working conditions, especially as regards to accommodation, food' and 'climatic conditions'. Also see *Naletilić* TC, para. 254.

115 *Naletilić* TC, para. 257, referring to pp. 268, 274, 275 and 277, of the ICRC Commentary relative to Geneva Convention III.

116 Article 52, Geneva Convention III.

117 *Naletilić* TC, para. 259.

internees on the frontline to be unlawful. The detainees had been exposed to shelling and gunfire while carrying out tasks such as transporting food and ammunition and collecting bodies, and there was no evidence that they had done so voluntarily.[118] In *Prlić*, the use of POWs to work on defensive structures for the detaining power was found to amount to prohibited labour.[119] In addition, acts which are themselves unlawful constitute forced labour, regardless of consent: thus, forcing POWs to assist in looting Bosnian Muslim properties constituted unlawful labour as '[t]he commission of looting being a crime in itself, the consent of prisoners may not render the labour lawful and is therefore irrelevant'.[120]

Article 51 of Geneva Convention IV, which governs the use of protected persons for forced labour, is restricted to protected persons in occupied territory. The ICTY has adopted a broad definition of occupation in this context, finding that 'occupation does not require an occupying power to wield actual authority over a territory but that a state of organisation exists when civilians have fallen "into the hands of an occupying power"'.[121] There is no need to establish the existence of a state of occupation within the meaning of Article 42 of the Hague Regulations; rather, unlawful labour is prohibited as soon as the persons 'fall into the hands of an occupying power, regardless of the phase of hostilities'.[122] The ICTY has held that application of the law of occupation established in Article 51 includes persons not DPH.[123] In *Prlić* the Trial Chamber held that 'when an enemy power interns persons not taking part in hostilities who fall into its power, such persons automatically enjoy the status of internees, irrespective of whether a state of occupation has been proved'.[124]

Article 95 of Geneva Convention IV provides that the detaining authority shall not employ detainees as labourers unless they so desire, and prohibits '[e]mployment which if undertaken under compulsion by a protected person not in internment, would involve a breach of Articles 40 or 51'. Employment on work that is of a degrading or humiliating character is also prohibited. Detaining authorities can compel internees to carry out tasks that contribute to the well-being of the interned population, such as using doctors or dentists in their professional capacity to assist fellow detainees, or the use of detainees for administrative or domestic tasks.[125]

118 Ibid., para. 302. For example, in one incident POWs had been handed imitation wooden rifles and military uniforms, before being made to walk alongside a tank towards enemy positions. Ibid., paras 274–289. The turning of an abandoned house into a military headquarters was found to be unlawful labour, as such work falls into the category of work which requires consent from the POWs involved (ibid., para. 311). The offences of inhuman treatment, cruel treatment and inhumane acts was also found to have occurred in this case, as the circumstances the POWs were used in and the nature of the work caused the prisoners serious mental suffering, see ibid., para. 303.
119 *Prlić* TC (Vol. I), para. 164, and see (Vol. III), para. 1503–1506.
120 Ibid., para. 308
121 Ibid., para. 153, referring to *Naletilić* TC, para. 221.
122 Ibid., TC, para. 153, referring to *Naletilić* TC, para. 221.
123 Ibid., para. 153.
124 Ibid., para. 155.
125 Article 95, Geneva Convention IV and *Prlić* TC, para. 156.

To summarise, in cases involving forced labour, those who qualify for POW status under Geneva Convention III are subject to different standards than those protected under Geneva Convention IV. Although POWs can be compelled to work, this is subject to restrictions concerning the POWs themselves and the nature of the work involved. Protected persons under Geneva Convention IV are subject to stricter rules concerning forced labour. Accordingly, at the ICTY when it has been unclear as to whether the detainees concerned were protected under Geneva Convention III or IV, Geneva Convention III has been applied to all alleged victims as being the standard more favourable to the accused.[126]

4.2.5 Proportionality and persons hors de combat

That victims of an attack were persons *hors de combat* rather than civilians is relevant in cases alleging that the principle of proportionality has been violated. The principle of proportionality is one of the fundamental principles of IHL. It requires that military measures taken by parties to the conflict be proportionate to the military aim which they seek to accomplish. The expected military advantage to be obtained must outweigh the harm to civilians and/or the damage to civilian objects that is likely to result from the military action. Thus, Protocol I lists an indiscriminate attack as being 'an attack which may be expected to cause incidental loss of civilian life, injury to civilians, damage to civilian objects, or a combination thereof, which would be excessive in relation to the concrete and direct military advantage anticipated'.[127] Bartels argues that the principle of proportionality is broader than this, and includes prohibited attacks on military objects which would cause excessive damage to any person who cannot be targeted directly under IHL, including persons *hors de combat*.[128] He writes that in practice military actors might well take into account the potential injury and death that could be caused to those who are *hors de combat* when making their proportionality assessments.[129] However, the ICC Statute lists the war crime concerning the violation of the principle of proportionality as consisting of:

> Intentionally launching an attack in the knowledge that such attack will cause incidental loss of life or injury to civilians or damage to civilian objects or widespread, long-term and severe damage to the natural environment, which would be clearly excessive in relation to the concrete and direct overall military advantage anticipated.[130]

126 See *Naletilić*, Prosecution Final Brief, pp. 200–201; and *Naletilić* TC, para. 252.
127 Article 51(5)(b), Protocol I, and see Article 57.
128 Rogier Bartels, 'Dealing with the Principle of Proportionality in Armed Conflict in Retrospect: The Application of the Principle in International Criminal Trials', 46(2) *Israel Law Review* 217–315 (2013), p. 304. However, see Rule 12, ICRC Study.
129 Bartels, *supra* FN 128, p. 305.
130 Article 8(2)(b)(iv), ICC Statute.

The provision accords with the principle of proportionality as codified in Protocol I, and applies solely to attacks against civilians.[131] This means that attacks which cause a disproportionate number of collateral casualties among persons *hors de combat*, such as an attack against a military target in the direct vicinity of a POW camp, would not fall under the ICC's jurisdiction.[132]

4.2.6 The ICC Statute and persons hors de combat

Finally, mention must be made of some issues concerning the ICC's jurisdiction over war crimes involving persons *hors de combat.* Article 8(2)(a) of its Statute includes the grave breaches of 'unlawful deportation or transfer or unlawful confinement'[133] and that of 'taking of hostages'.[134] That these crimes only constitute breaches of Geneva Convention IV is not made clear in the language of Article 8 (2)(a) itself, nor in the relevant entries in the Elements of Crimes. It is to be assumed that the ICC will interpret the grave breach provisions of its Statute in accordance with IHL, meaning that only those who constitute protected persons under Geneva Convention IV can be victims of these crimes.[135] This also means that in IACs the court has no jurisdiction in cases involving POWs who have been taken hostage, as in IACs it only has jurisdiction over this crime as a grave breach and not as a violation of Common Article 3.

Article 8(2)(b)(vi) of the Statute gives the court jurisdiction over the act of 'killing or wounding a combatant who, having laid down his arms or having no longer means of defence, has surrendered at discretion'. The provision is based on Article 23(d) of the Hague Regulations and uses the language of that provision.[136] Although the term '*hors de combat*' is not used in the Article itself, the Elements of Crimes head the offence as '[k]illing or wounding a person *hors de combat*', and

131 Bartels, *supra* FN 128, p. 304.

132 It may be possible that fighters who are *hors de combat* could fall under a different provision of the Statute, for example, Article 8(2)(b)(ix), 'Intentionally directing attacks against ... hospitals and places where the sick and wounded are collected, providing they are not military objectives'. See Michael Cottier, 'War Crimes', in Otto Triffterer, *Commentary on the Rome Statute of the International Criminal Court* (C. H. Beck, Hart, Nomos, 2nd edition, 2008), para. 64.

133 Article 8(2)(a)(vii), ICC Statute.

134 Article 8(2)(a)(viii), ICC Statute. The war crime of taking of hostages under Common Article 3 can be committed against those who are *hors de combat.*

135 Article 21, ICC Statute. Bothe writes: 'Although the list in paragraph 2(a) is a cumulation of the lists contained in the four Conventions, it must be read differently in relation to the different types of persons protected by each of them: a grave breach requires that the particular act must be included in the list contained in the particular Convention which protects the particular type of victim.' Michael Bothe, 'War Crimes' in Cassese *et al* (ed.), *The Rome Statute of the International Criminal Court: A Commentary*, Vol. I (Oxford University Press, 2002), p. 391.

136 Charles Garraway, 'Article 8(2)(b)(vi) – Killing or Wounding a Person Hors de Combat', in Lee *et al*, *The International Criminal Court: Elements of Crimes and Rules of Procedure and Evidence* (Ardsey NY, Transnational Publishers Inc., 2001), para. 1907.

lists as an element of the crime that the 'person or persons were *hors de combat*'. It is to be hoped that the ICC will have recourse to the terms of Article 41 of Protocol I when interpreting the provision, rather than relying solely on the rather antiquated language used in the provision itself.[137] Also, while the terms of the provision itself refer to 'combatant', the Elements of Crimes make reference to 'person or persons'. One would hope that the ICC will interpret widely the class of victims protected by the provision, to include others who had been involved in fighting who did not qualify for combatant status.[138]

4.3 Conclusion

Those who fight are legitimate military targets, but this changes once they become *hors de combat*. The ICTY's decision that those who are not protected by Geneva Convention III as POWs fall under the protection of Geneva Convention IV, has ensured that in IACs there is no gap between the Conventions, meaning that persons *hors de combat* are not left unprotected. This clarification has reduced the need to make investigations into whether a particular group of detainees was entitled to POW status, as several grave breaches provisions are the same in both Conventions. It remains to be seen whether other ICTs will adopt the ICTY's approach, but it is to be hoped that they will do so. The ICTY has also confirmed that as soon as fighters become *hors de combat* they are not APH/DPH and can qualify as victims of war crimes which focus on the victim's conduct, such as violations of Common Article 3 and Protocol II.

While persons *hors de combat* can be victims of many of the same crimes as civilians, differences do remain. Persons *hors de combat* are not civilians, and cannot be victims of crimes that apply to those who have civilian status, such as crimes violating the principle of proportionality. Furthermore, although POW status is of diminished importance, that detainees were POWs remains very relevant in relation to several crimes. That an alleged victim had POW status is a defence to charges of unlawful confinement and unlawful deportation or transfer. It also involves different standards being applied in relation to allegations of forced labour. POWs also cannot be victims of hostage-taking as a grave breach, although they can be if it is charged as a violation of Common Article 3. Thus, when dealing with cases where some of the victims may have been persons *hors de combat*, these differences in entitlement to protection under IHL must be borne in mind.

137 Cottier, *supra* FN 132, paras 64–69; and Bothe, *supra* FN 135, pp. 405–406.
138 Cottier, *supra* FN 132, para. 65.

5 Members of non-opposing forces as victims of war crimes

Atrocities can be committed not only by one side of a conflict against enemy fighters, but also by members of one side of a conflict against members of non-opposing forces. The issue of whether these can constitute war crimes is somewhat contentious. The traditional view is that war crimes cannot be committed against members of non-opposing armed forces. Cassese, for example, writes 'Crimes committed by servicemen against their own military (whatever their nationality) do not constitute war crimes.'[1] He bases his opinion primarily upon two cases from the post-Second World War period decided before national courts,[2] begging the question as to whether these cases represent the final word on the matter. In recent years, the issue has arisen before both the SCSL in the *RUF* case and the ICC in *Ntaganda*. This chapter begins by discussing the RUF case, before analysing whether IHL grants protection to members of non-opposing forces. Finally, it examines the *Ntaganda* case from the ICC.

5.1 The SCSL and the *RUF* case

The relevant part of the *RUF* case concerned the killings of three individuals, each of whom had been fighting on the same side as the Revolutionary United Front

1 Antonio Cassese, *International Criminal Law* (Oxford University Press, 2008), p. 82.

2 The first case is that of *Pilz* from the Dutch Special Court of Cassation. Pilz was a Dutch doctor working in the German army. He was accused of failing to provide medical help to a member of the German army who was also Dutch. The court held that once an individual joins an armed force, the protection of the laws of war is lost, regardless of the nationality one has. The legal position of members of a state's armed forces is a matter for the domestic law of that state and not international law. *Pilz*, Dutch Special Court of Cassation, 5 July 1950, NederJ (1950), No 681; 17 ILR (1950) 391–392; Cassese, ibid., p. 82 at FN 1; and Göran Sluiter, *Pilz* in Cassese (ed.), *The Oxford Companion to International Criminal Justice* (Oxford University Press, 2009), p. 872. The second case is that of *Motosuke*, which came before the Temporary Court Martial of the Netherlands East Indies. It involved a Japanese officer who was accused of shooting a Dutch national who had joined the Gunkes, a corps of volunteers who served with the Japanese army. The court held that by joining the Japanese forces he had lost his nationality, and his killing by the accused was not a war crime, see Cassese, ibid., p. 82 at FN 1.

(RUF) during the armed conflict in Sierra Leone.[3] The first incident concerned an Armed Forces Revolutionary Council (AFRC) fighter called Charles Kayioko.[4] He was arrested, together with 109 others, on suspicion of being a Kamajor.[5] He was initially released on parole as part of a larger group of civilian prisoners. The group was later re-arrested on the orders of Sam Bockarie, one of the senior RUF leaders, and all were subsequently killed.[6] The second incident concerned a senior AFRC fighter, Fonti Kanu. Bockarie ordered Kanu to be killed on the basis that he was deemed to be a security threat to the RUF. During the case, the accused, Issa Hassan Sesay, explained that execution was the standard punishment for members of the RUF who connived with the enemy.[7] The third incident, involved the killing of an AFRC leader, Foday Kallon. He was summarily executed after a dispute between himself, Sesay and Sam Bockarie, over money and the sharing of RUF information in Liberia. Following his execution, a radio message was sent to front lines informing them of his death and warning fighters against committing acts of betrayal or sabotage.[8]

All three of these victims were members of non-opposing forces. The question arose as to whether this meant that their killings could constitute a war crime. In its analysis, the Trial Chamber stated: 'The Chamber is of the opinion that the law of armed conflict does not protect members of armed groups from acts of violence directed against them by their own forces.'[9] It justified its conclusion by reference to the law applicable in IACs, despite having determined earlier in the Judgment that the conflict in Sierra Leone was a NIAC.[10] It (wrongly)[11] noted that the law

3 The issue was also briefly considered by the SCSL Trial Chamber in the *CDF* case. Two fighters, who, like the accused, had been members of the CDF, were killed as part of a Kamajor ritual killing. The Trial Chamber found that it did not constitute a war crime as they had been fighting on the same side as the accused. In their closing argument, the Prosecutor agreed that the killings were not war crimes, but argued that they constituted evidence of the accused's standing in the hierarchy of the CDF, in that it showed that they were in absolute control and could perform acts without sanction from anyone else. See *Prosecutor v Moinina Fofana and Allieu Kondewa*, SCSL-04-14-T, Trial Judgment, 2 August 2007 (*CDF* case TC), paras 632–633 and 925.

4 The AFRC were allies of the RUF from the late 1990s onwards.

5 The Kamajors were a group of traditional hunters from a particular ethnic group in Sierra Leone who were incorporated into the security forces during the conflict.

6 *Prosecutor v Issa Hassan Sesay, Morris Kallon and Augustine Gbao*, SCSL-2004-15-T, Trial Judgment, 2 March 2009 (*RUF* case TC), paras 1389, 1396.

7 Ibid., para. 1399.

8 Ibid., paras 1400–1402.

9 Ibid., para. 1451.

10 Ibid., para. 977.

11 Ibid., para. 1452. This statement by the Trial Chamber that, 'persons who are *hors de combat* who do not belong to any of the armed groups participating in the hostilities' is inaccurate; in fact, it is persons who are *hors de combat* who *belong* to the armed groups who are participating in hostilities who are protected by IHL. See Article 41 (2), Protocol I. Also see Jann K. Kleffner, 'Friend or Foe? On the Protective Reach of the Law of Armed Conflict: A Note on the SCSL Trial Chamber's Judgment in the Case of *Prosecutor v Sesay, Kalon and Gbao*', in M. Matthee *et al* (eds), *Armed*

in IACs 'regulates the conduct of combatants *vis-à-vis* their adversaries and persons *hors de combat* who do not belong to any of the armed groups participating in the hostilities'. The Trial Chamber continued:

> It is trite law that an armed group cannot hold its own members as prisoners of war. The law of international armed conflict was never intended to criminalise acts of violence committed by one member of an armed group against another, such conduct remaining first and foremost the province of the criminal law of the State of the armed group concerned and human rights law. In our view, a different approach would constitute an inappropriate re-conceptualisation of a fundamental principle of international humanitarian law. We are not prepared to embark on such an exercise.[12]

The Trial Chamber held that as Charles Kayioko, Fonti Kanu and Foday Kallon had been fighting on the same side as those who had killed them, their deaths could not constitute a war crime.[13] The matter was not appealed, meaning that the finding stands.

5.2 IHL and the protection of members of non-opposing forces

The protection accorded to individuals by IHL varies to some degree depending upon whether the conflict in question is an IAC or a NIAC. In IACs, some IHL provisions clearly apply between members of opposing forces only, as with Article 4A of Geneva Convention III, to which the Trial Chamber refers: only enemy combatants may qualify for POW status.[14] This was confirmed in the *Prlić* case, which concerned the status of Muslim members of the HVO who had been detained by the HVO. The defence argued that these persons could not constitute protected persons under the Geneva Conventions and that Article 2 of the ICTY Statute pertaining to grave breaches could not apply to them.[15] The Trial Chamber confirmed that a teleological interpretation to establish the objective of the Third Convention 'unambiguously leads to the conclusion that only those persons belonging to the armed forces of a Party *other than* the detaining party are concerned. The fact that the HVO ... detained its own soldiers weighs against the notion that these detainees could be characterised as prisoners of war'.[16] The Chamber recalled that the purpose of the protection afforded to POWs is to allow belligerents to place members of enemy forces *hors de combat* while conflict is

Conflict and International Law: In Search of the Human Face, Liber Amicorum In Memory of Avril McDonald (Asser Press, 2013), pp. 292–294.

12 Ibid., para. 1453.

13 *RUF* case TC, paras 1454, 1455 and 1457, respectively.

14 Ibid., para. 1452.

15 *Prosecutor v Jadranko Prlić et al*, ICTY, IT-04-74-T, Trial Chamber, 29 May 2013 (*Prlić*, TC), para. 592.

16 Ibid., para. 603.

ongoing. It concluded that members of non-opposing forces cannot be POWs when detained by their own forces.[17]

However, the Trial Chamber then found that members of non-opposing forces can qualify as protected persons under Geneva Convention IV, as having fallen into the hands of a party to the conflict of which they were not nationals. The Chamber confirmed that the proper criterion to establish protection under the Convention is not nationality but allegiance.[18] The Chamber noted that from 1993, the HVO Muslims were perceived as constituting a threat to the security of the HVO[19] and from at least 30 June 1993, they were perceived by the HVO as being loyal to the ABiH.[20] The Chamber concluded that from this time, the detained HVO Muslims had fallen into the hands of an enemy power and were thus protected persons under Geneva Convention IV.[21] Thus, members of non-opposing forces can in the right circumstances qualify for protected person status under Geneva Convention IV.

There are also other provisions that apply in IACs which do not restrict the protection they give to members of adverse forces.[22] For example, protections for the wounded, sick and shipwrecked granted in Geneva I and II and Protocol I apply to all such persons. Geneva Conventions I and II state that they apply to 'members of the armed forces of *a* Party to the conflict',[23] and 'Members of other militias and members of other volunteer corps … belonging to *a* Party to the conflict'.[24] In contrast, Article 14 of Geneva Convention I provides that: 'the wounded and sick of a belligerent who fall into *enemy hands* shall be prisoners of war',[25] thereby implying that references within the Convention to 'a Party to the conflict' includes the party to which the individual belongs.[26] Article 12 of Geneva Convention I provides that members of the armed forces shall be 'respected and protected in all circumstances'; of this the ICRC explains that '[t]he wounded are to be respected just as much when they are with their own army or in no man's land as when they have fallen into the hands of the enemy'.[27]

17 Ibid., para. 604.
18 Ibid., para. 608.
19 Ibid., para. 609.
20 Ibid., para. 610.
21 Ibid., para. 611.
22 Kleffner, *supra* FN 11, pp. 294–300.
23 Article 13(1), Geneva Convention I and Article 13(1), Geneva Convention II, emphasis added. Also see Article 5 Geneva Convention I, which states: 'For the protected persons who have fallen into the hands of the enemy, the present Convention shall apply under their final repatriation.'
24 Article 13(2), Geneva Convention I and Article 13(2), Geneva Convention II, emphasis added.
25 Also see Article 16, Geneva Convention II.
26 Kleffner, *supra* FN 11, pp. 294–296.
27 ICRC Commentary to Geneva Convention I, p. 135; and see Sandesh Sivakumaran, *The Law of Non-International Armed Conflict* (Oxford University Press, 2014), pp. 247–248.

Turning to Protocol I, its provisions regarding the wounded, sick and shipwrecked apply: 'without any adverse distinction founded on race, colour, sex, language, religion or belief, political or other opinion, national or social origin, wealth, birth or other status, or on any other similar criteria';[28] while Article 10 states that '[a]ll the wounded, sick and shipwrecked, *to whichever Party they belong*, shall be respected and protected' (emphasis added). Thus, the duties owed under the Geneva Conventions and Protocol I to respect and protect the wounded, sick and shipwrecked arguably apply both to opposing and non-opposing military personnel.[29]

What about members of non-opposing forces who are detained, rather than being wounded, sick or shipwrecked? As the Trial Chamber noted in the *RUF* case, treaty law is clear that POW status applies only to those 'who have fallen into the power of the enemy'.[30] However, IHL allows for certain fundamental guarantees that apply to persons who are in the power of a party to the conflict and who do not benefit from more favourable treatment under the Conventions.[31] In IACs, these fundamental guarantees are to be found in Article 75 of Protocol I,[32] which provides that violence to life and outrages upon personal dignity are prohibited at any time and in any place whatsoever. Article 75 is contained within Part IV of Protocol I, which is headed 'Civilian Population'; however, the text of the Article itself states that the Article applies to '*persons* who are in the power of a Party to the conflict and who do not benefit from more favourable treatment under the Conventions or under this Protocol', suggesting that it is not just civilians who are protected by the provision.[33] This is the view taken in the ICRC Study, which finds these fundamental guarantees to be customary law, applying both to civilians and persons *hors de combat*.[34] However, this begs the question of whether a member of a military force can be described as being '*hors de combat*' when detained by members of their own side.

The term '*hors de combat*' is defined in Article 41(2) of Protocol I, and one of the requirements of being *hors de combat* is that the person is 'in the power of an adverse party'. Thus, one could argue that, according to the ICRC Study, under customary law, the fundamental guarantees apply to members of opposing forces only, as only they can be *hors de combat* according to a strict interpretation of the wording of Article 41(2). An alternative argument is that the ICRC Study uses the phrase '*hors de combat*' in a more generic sense, to describe a person who is no longer able to wage war due to being wounded, sick or detained, whether they be members of enemy forces or not. Indeed, it is in this sense that the phrase is used in the *RUF* Trial Judgment, which refers to the three victims (all of whom

28 Article 9(1), Protocol I.
29 Article 12, Geneva Convention I and II.
30 Article 4A, Geneva Convention III, and see Articles 44(1), 44(4) and 45(1), Protocol I, and *Prlić* TC, paras 603–604.
31 See Kleffner, *supra* FN 11, pp. 296–297.
32 They have also been found to be part of customary law. See ICRC Study, chapter 32.
33 Article 75(1), Protocol I.
34 ICRC Study, Introduction to the Fundamental Guarantees.

belonged to non-opposing forces) as having been *hors de combat* at the time they were killed.[35]

Furthermore, if the statement in the ICRC Study that the fundamental guarantees apply to those who are *hors de combat* were interpreted in a way that excludes members of non-opposing forces, this would contradict the position taken by the ICRC in its Commentary to Article 75. The ICRC Commentary to Protocol I explains that in order to benefit from the protection of Article 75, three conditions must be fulfilled: first, the individual must be in the power of a party to the conflict; second, they must be affected by armed conflict or by occupation; and third, they must not benefit from more favourable treatments under the Convention or the Protocol.[36] The Commentary describes the difficulties that arose at the Diplomatic Conference in discussions regarding the application of Article 75 to a state's own nationals.[37] The original draft of the Article had contained a reference to a state's own nationals, but this reference disappeared by the final text.[38] The Commentary concludes that '[a]dmittedly, it would certainly have been very useful to mention explicitly that nationals are included, but no negative conclusions should be drawn from the absence of such mention'.[39]

According to the ICRC, the protections granted under Article 75 apply to the nationals of a state, thereby including members of non-opposing forces. Thus, when the ICRC Study refers to the fundamental guarantees as applying to persons *hors de combat*, it is likely doing so in the generic sense of the individual being unable to fight due to being sick, wounded or incarcerated, rather than in the sense that the individual is in the power of an adverse party in the sense of being an opposing party to the conflict. There is therefore a strong argument to be made that the fundamental guarantees under IHL, violations of which are war crimes,[40] apply to all persons who are in the power of a party to the conflict during IACs who do not qualify for more favourable treatment under the Conventions, including non-opposing military personnel who have been detained.

Turning to NIACs: is there anything within IHL to suggest that it extends protection to members of non-opposing forces?[41] Again, there is a strong argument

35 For example, the Trial Chamber refers to the victim, Kayiolo, as 'an *hors de combat* member of the AFRC'. *RUF* case, para. 1451. It also states that: 'The Chamber is satisfied that Kanu was *hors de combat* at the time of his death', ibid., para. 1455. This is also the sense that the phrase is used in Common Article 3, which protects '[p]ersons taking no active part in the hostilities, including members of armed forces who have laid down their arms and those placed "hors de combat" by sickness, wounds, detention, or any other cause'. Also see Kleffner, *supra* FN 11, p. 294.

36 ICRC Commentary to Protocol I, para. 3009.

37 Ibid., para. 3017.

38 Ibid., para. 3018. As Kleffner argues: 'That controversy alone appears to be a good reason for the Trial Chamber to have delved into the matter somewhat more in depth.' Kleffner, *supra* FN 11, p. 296.

39 ICRC Commentary to Protocol I, para. 3020.

40 *Prosecutor v Duško Tadić*, ICTY, IT-94-1-AR72, Decision on the Defence Motion for Interlocutory Appeal on Jurisdiction, 2 October 1995, para. 94.

41 Kleffner, *supra* FN 11, pp. 297–300.

to be made that there is. First, Common Article 3 of the Geneva Conventions applies to 'persons taking no active part in hostilities, including members of the armed forces who have laid down their arms and those placed *hors de combat* by sickness, wounds, detention, or any other cause'. The article continues that such persons be treated humanely 'without any adverse distinction founded on race, colour, religion or faith, sex, birth or wealth, or any other similar criteria'. Several acts are prohibited under Common Article 3, including murder of all kinds, mutilation, cruel treatment and torture, and of these the article provides that 'the ... acts are and shall remain prohibited at any time and in any place whatsoever'. In its Commentary the ICRC states of this phrase that: 'No possible loophole is left; there can be no excuse, no attenuating circumstances.'[42] Thus, arguably the protection of Common Article 3 applies to all and is dependent upon the conduct of an individual – that they were taking no active part in hostilities at the time – rather than upon their status or affiliation.[43]

Several provisions of Protocol II also seemingly protect members of non-opposing forces. Article 2(1) states that the Protocol applies:

> Without any adverse distinction founded on race, colour, sex, language, religion or belief, political or other opinion, national or other social origin, wealth, birth or other status, or by any other similar criteria to all persons affected by an armed conflict as defined in Article 1.

Article 4(1) of Protocol II, which lists fundamental guarantees, applies to '*all persons* who do not take a direct part or who have ceased to take part in hostilities'. Article 4 prohibits, among other things, violence to the life, health and physical or mental well-being of persons.[44] In addition, Article 6, concerning penal prosecutions, applies to 'the prosecution and punishment of offences related to the armed conflict',[45] without specifying that the accused belong to an opposing side. Thus, neither Common Article 3 nor Protocol II stipulate or infer that they protect only those who belong to the opposing side.

To summarise, although IHL was originally conceived to regulate the interplay between opposing parties during armed conflict, it nevertheless imposes obligations on a party to a conflict to protect its own members. It requires parties to protect members of non-opposing forces who are wounded, sick, shipwrecked and detained in both IACs and NIACs.[46] Violations of these fundamental IHL provisions constitute war crimes. The Trial Chamber in the *RUF* case was too ready to accept the traditional view that war crimes cannot be committed by members of a military force against members of a non-opposing force, without making further enquiry into the matter.

42 ICRC Commentary to Geneva Convention III, p. 39.
43 Sivakumaran, *supra* FN 27, p. 248.
44 Article 4(2), Protocol II.
45 Ibid., Article 6(1).
46 Kleffner, *supra* FN 11, p. 300.

Indeed, there is one group of war crimes which actively requires that the perpetrator and the victim be members of the same military force, namely the war crimes of conscripting, enlisting and using children under 15 to participate actively in hostilities. In the *RUF* case, the accused were charged with these war crimes, and the Trial Chamber did not consider it to be a difficulty that the alleged victims had been members of the same armed force as the accused. Nor has this been considered to be an issue in any other case concerning the war crimes of the recruitment and use of child soldiers that have arisen before an ICT.

5.3 The ICC and the *Ntaganda* case

The issue of whether members of non-opposing forces can be victims of war crimes has also arisen before the ICC in the case of *Ntaganda*. The case concerns child soldiers as victims of crimes of sexual violence and sexual slavery under Article 8(2)(e)(vi) of the ICC Statute. At the confirmation of charges stage, the Prosecution, referring to Common Article 3 and Article 4 of Protocol II, argued that:

> Child soldiers are afforded general protections against sexual violence under the fundamental guarantees applicable to persons affected by non-international armed conflict. They also have special protections because of their vulnerability as children.[47]

The Defence responded that the protection of Article 4 of Protocol II applies only to children captured by the opposing side: crimes committed against members of non-opposing forces do not fall under the ambit of IHL. IHL is not intended to protect combatants from crimes committed by combatants within the same group; such crimes fall under national law and human rights law.[48]

When making its decision, the Pre-Trial Chamber noted the terms of Common Article 3 that 'persons taking no active part in the hostilities … shall in all circumstances be treated humanely'. It also referred to the relevant parts of Articles 4 (1) and (2) of Protocol II to the effect that 'all persons who do not take a direct part or who have ceased to take a part in hostilities … shall in all circumstances be treated humanely'; and that the acts of outrages upon personal dignity, including rape, enforced prostitution and any form of indecent assault are prohibited under the provision.[49] The Chamber found that in order to determine whether child soldiers under the age of 15 years were entitled to protection against acts of rape

47 *Prosecutor v Bosco Ntaganda*, ICC-01/04-02/06, Document Containing the Charges, 10 January 2014 (*Ntaganda*, Document Containing the Charges), para. 107.

48 *Ntaganda*, Confirmation of Charges, Open Session, ICC-01/04-02/06-T-10-Red-ENG, p. 27.

49 See *Ntaganda*, Document Containing the Charges, para. 107; and *Prosecutor v Bosco Ntaganda*, ICC-01/04-02/06, Decision on the Confirmation of Charges, 9 June 2014 (*Ntaganda* Decision), para. 77.

and sexual slavery by other members of the group, it must assess whether these persons were APH/DPH at the time they were victims of acts of rape and/or sexual slavery.[50] It concluded that the children in question could not be considered to be APH/DPH at the time they were subject to acts of a sexual nature, and it accordingly confirmed the charges.[51]

The defence proceeded to challenge the Pre-Trial Chamber's decision. One of their main arguments was that according to Common Article 3, war crimes may not be committed by members of an armed force against fellow members of the same armed force.[52] The prosecution responded that Article 8(2)(e)(vi) of the Statute does not limit criminal liability for rape and sexual slavery on the basis of the status or the activities of the victims. Even if Common Article 3 applies to victims of a crime under Article 8(2)(e)(vi), the alleged victims were not actively participating in hostilities in any event, and there is no requirement under Common Article 3 that victim and perpetrator have different affiliations.[53]

In view of the fact that the conflict in the case may require re-characterisation as an IAC, the Trial Chamber chose to consider whether rape and sexual slavery against a perpetrator's own forces constitute war crimes under both Articles 8(2)(b)(xxii) and 8(2)(e)(vi) of the ICC Statute. In response to the Defence's arguments that the victim of a war crime in a NIAC must be a protected person within the meaning of Common Article 3,[54] the Chamber found that no particular victim status is explicitly mentioned for the crimes of sexual slavery and rape listed in the relevant provisions of the Statute. There is no requirement that victims of crimes in part 8(2)(b) of the Statute be protected persons under the Geneva Conventions in the sense of that required for grave breaches of the Geneva Conventions; nor is there a requirement that victims of crimes in part 8(2)(e) be limited to those protected by Common Article 3.[55] The Chamber also noted that its case law had not required any status requirements to be proven when analysing rape as a war crime under Article 8. It concluded that the statutory framework of the ICC does not require victims of the crimes in Articles 8(2)(b)(xxii) and 8(2)(vi) to have been protected persons in the (limited) sense of grave breaches or of Common Article 3.[56]

The Chamber then considered the established framework of international law.[57] It noted that while most of the express prohibitions of rape and sexual slavery

50 *Ntaganda* Decision, para. 77.

51 'The sexual character of these crimes which involve elements of force/coercion or the exercise of rights of ownership, logically preclude active participation in hostilities at the same time.' Ibid., para. 79. For a discussion of this decision, see Joanna Nicholson, 'Is Targeting Naked Child Soldiers a War Crime?', 16 *International Criminal Law Review* (2016) 131–154.

52 *Prosecutor v Bosco Ntaganda*, ICC-01/04-02/06, Second Decision on the Defence's challenge to the jurisdiction of the Court in respect of Counts 6 and 9, 4 January 2017 (*Ntaganda* Second Decision), para. 27.

53 Ibid., paras 29–30.

54 Ibid., para. 37.

55 Ibid., paras 38–44.

56 Ibid., para. 44.

57 Ibid., paras 45 and 46.

under IHL appear in contexts protecting civilians and persons *hors de combat* in the power of a party to the conflict, these explicit prohibitions do not exhaustively define or limit the scope of the protection against such conduct.[58] It referred to the Martens clause which states that in situations not covered by specific agreements 'civilians and combatants remain under the protection and authority of the principles of international law derived from established custom, from the principles of humanity and from the dictates of public conscience'.[59] Furthermore, the fundamental guarantees provided for in Article 75, Protocol I refer to acts that 'are and shall remain prohibited at any time and in any place whatsoever', and as such apply to and protect all persons in the power of a party to the conflict.[60] In addition, the Chamber found that limiting the scope of protection would be against the rationale of IHL.

While IHL allows for combatants to DPH and allows for the targeting of members of opposing forces, as well as civilians who are DPH, the Chamber noted that there is never justification for engaging in sexual violence against any person, irrespective of whether the person may be liable to be targeted and killed under IHL.[61] Rape and sexual slavery are peremptory norms, with the result that such conduct is prohibited at all times, in times of peace and times of war, and against all persons, regardless of status. The Chamber concluded that protection against violence under IHL is not limited to members of opposing forces who are *hors de combat* or to civilians not DPH.[62]

Interestingly, unlike the Decision on the Confirmation of Charges, where the emphasis was upon the fact that the alleged victims had been child soldiers, the Trial Chamber in the *Ntaganda* Second Decision considered the matter in the context of members of non-opposing forces as a whole. In so doing, the Chamber neatly side-stepped the somewhat contentious issue of when child soldiers are members of an armed force and when they can be said to be DPH/APH.[63] It also avoided discussing whether members of non-opposing forces can be protected persons under Geneva Conventions I and II and whether they fall under the protection of Common Article 3. The Trial Chamber was very clear that its decision applied only to the crimes of Articles 8(2)(b)(xxii) and 8(2)(e)(vi) of the ICC Statute,[64] leaving open the question of whether other war crimes in parts 8(2)(b) and 8(2)(e) of the Statute could also apply to members of non-opposing forces.

On this issue, some of the provisions of parts 8(2)(b) and 8(2)(e) of the Statute are clear as to the status of the victims they protect, for example those which require that the victims be civilians.[65] Others most likely apply to members of

58 Ibid., para. 47.
59 Ibid., para. 47, referring to *United Nations Report of the International Law Commission on the Work of its Forty-sixth Session*, 1994, GA OR A/49/10, p. 317.
60 Ibid., para. 47.
61 Ibid., para. 49.
62 Ibid., para. 53.
63 Ibid., para. 53; and see Nicholson, *supra* FN 51.
64 Ibid., para. 54.
65 For example, Article 8(2)(b)(i), ICC Statute.

opposing forces only. Article 8(2)(b)(vi), for example, lists 'killing or wounding a combatant who, having laid down his arms or having no longer means of defence, has surrendered at his discretion', as being a serious violation of the laws and customs applicable in an IAC. Cottier notes that the wording of the Article follows that of Article 23(c) of the Hague Regulations and that 'the term "enemy" has been replaced by "combatant" (meaning "adversary combatant")'.[66] The use of the term 'surrendered' also suggests that the provision applies only to members of opposing forces.[67] The same can be said of Article 8(2)(b)(xi), concerning the crime of perfidy, which is expressed as the act of '[k]illing or wounding treacherously individuals belonging to the hostile nation or army'. However, the same reasoning that the Trial Chamber applied in the *Ntaganda* Second Decision to the crimes of rape and sexual slavery could equally apply to Article 8(2)(b)(xxi), concerning outrages upon personal dignity, in particular inhuman and degrading treatment. This crime is also a peremptory norm under international law and has no status requirement in the provision.

The Trial Chamber in the *Ntaganda* Second Decision has left unanswered the question of whether members of non-opposing forces can be victims of crimes under parts 8(2)(a) (grave breaches of the Geneva Conventions) and 8(2)(c) (violations of Common Article 3) of the ICC Statute. It has been argued in this chapter that Geneva Conventions I and II apply to members of non-opposing forces, as does Common Article 3, but it remains to be seen what the ICC will decide in the future. Assuming this view is correct, in IACs, crimes against members of non-opposing forces who are wounded, sick or shipwrecked, and who fall under the protection of Geneva Conventions I or II, could be prosecuted under Article 8(2)(a) as grave breaches of those Geneva Conventions. In the situation where members of non-opposing forces are detained, it is to be hoped that the ICC will follow *Prlić*'s lead in finding that such persons are 'protected persons' under Geneva Convention IV. This will depend upon whether the victims in question fulfil the requirement of having fallen into the hands of a party to the conflict of which they were not nationals.

If the court does not follow *Prlić*, its jurisdiction over war crimes against detained members of non-opposing forces in IACs will be limited to sexual offences under Article 8(2)(b)(xxii) and (perhaps) outrages upon personal dignity under Article 8(2)(b)(xxi). In NIACs, on the other hand, if the court were to confirm, as has been advocated in this chapter, that Common Article 3 protects members of non-opposing forces, it would have a much wider jurisdiction, which would include violations of Common Article 3 against detained members of non-opposing forces. Thus, in an unusual turn of affairs, the ICC Statute would give the ICC prosecutor wider scope for prosecuting this kind of case in NIACs than in IACs. This potential gap between the court's jurisdiction in IACs and NIACs is a

66 Michael Cottier, 'War Crimes', in Otto Triffterer, *Commentary on the Rome Statute of the International Criminal Court* (C.H. Beck, Hart, Nomos, 2008), p. 344.

67 The same can be said of Article 8(2)(e)(ix), killing or wounding treacherously a combatant adversary.

cause for concern. The circumstances when atrocities are committed against non-opposing forces can occur in situations where the victims showed remarkable bravery, for example, when a detained member of a non-opposing force is killed for refusing to obey an order to commit criminal acts.[68] Certainly, such crimes involving members of non-opposing forces may be prosecuted domestically, but this is not always a realistic possibility. It is important that the ICC have jurisdiction over these offences in both kinds of conflict.

5.4 Conclusion

The traditional view, as promoted in the *RUF* case, that crimes committed against members of non-opposing forces cannot constitute war crimes does not stand up to closer scrutiny. While some provisions of IHL clearly only protect military personnel on the opposing side, other provisions are equally clear that they apply to all, regardless of which side in a conflict an individual fights for. Serious breaches of these IHL provisions constitute war crimes. The *Ntaganda* case shows that there is increasing recognition of this. While this development is to be welcomed, the *Ntaganda* Second Decision is of a very narrow scope, in that it only concerns crimes of sexual violence and sexual slavery under the ICC Statute. The court neglected to take the opportunity to consider whether members of non-opposing forces are protected under other provisions of its Statute, or indeed whether they are protected under other provisions of IHL. It is to be hoped that in any future cases, courts will delve more deeply into the law when considering whether Common Article 3 and other IHL provisions protect members of non-opposing forces.

68 For example, see http://news.sky.com/skynews/Home/Libya-Soldiers-Were-Burned-Alive-By-Their-Own-Forces-For-Refusing-To-Fignt-Protesters/Article/201102415941510?f=rss and www.independent.co.uk/news/world/africa/body-bags-reveal-fate-of-soldiers-who-refused-to-fire-on-their-own-people-2228512.html.

6 Child soldiers

The phenomenon of the child soldier is not new; throughout history children have participated in armed conflicts in some capacity. In the past, children were often prevented from taking a direct role in warfare for physical reasons: weapons were heavy and cumbersome, limiting who could use them; instead, they were used in other roles, as squires or drummer boys, for example.[1] Today, the availability of lightweight, easy-to-use weapons means that children are physically capable of bearing arms at a much younger age than before.[2] Children have other qualities that make them attractive to armed forces: their size and agility make them useful for performing tasks other than combat, such as espionage, planting bombs and carrying military communications,[3] and their youth can make them easier to manipulate and more fearless than adults.[4] In recent decades, the 'scourge' of child soldiering[5] has been brought firmly onto the international agenda. Global civil society has responded to the problem in different ways. Several treaties contain provisions regarding the recruitment and use of child soldiers to participate actively in hostilities and influential soft law agreements have been created.[6] The UN has also taken a robust approach to the issue of child soldiers.[7]

1 Matthew Happold, *Child Soldiers in International Law* (Juris Publishing, Manchester University Press, 2005), pp. 4–5.
2 Child Soldiers International, 'The Arms Trade Treaty and its Implication for Preventing Child Soldiers – A Preliminary Assessment', May 2013. Available at: www.child-soldiers.org/research_report_reader.php?id=658
3 Happold, *supra* FN 1, p. 5.
4 *Prosecutor v Alex Tamba Brima, Brima Bazzy Kamara and Santigie Borbor Kanu* SCSL-04-16-T, Trial Judgment, 20 June 2007 (*AFRC* case TC), para. 362.
5 Mark A. Drumbl, *Reimagining Child Soldiers in International Law and Policy* (Oxford University Press, 2012), p. 35.
6 *Cape Town Principles and Best Practices*, 27–30 April 1997. Available at: www.unicef.org/emerg/files/Cape_Town_Principles(1).pdf (the 'Cape Town Principles'); *Paris Commitments to Protect Children from Unlawful Recruitment or Use by Armed Forces*, February 2007; The Paris Principles – Principles and Guidelines on Children Associated with Armed Forces or Armed Groups, February 2007. Available at: /www.unicef.org/emerg/files/ParisPrinciples310107English.pdf (the 'Paris Principles').
7 For a list of Security Council Resolutions and Presidential Statements on children and armed conflict, see annex to Ambassador Jean-March de La Sablière, *Security Council Engagement on the Protection of Children in Armed Conflict: Progress Achieved and the*

ICTs, too, are playing their part by considering cases involving the recruitment and 'use' of child soldiers. Criminal provisions prohibiting the conscription, enlistment and use of children under 15 to participate actively in hostilities are included in the SCSL and ICC Statutes, and cases involving these charges have featured prominently before both courts.[8] This chapter begins by considering how war crimes concerning the conscription, enlistment and use of children under the age of 15 years to participate actively in hostilities have evolved in ICL, before moving on to consider the issues that have arisen when these crimes have been prosecuted before the SCSL and the ICC.

6.1 International criminal law and child soldiers

Although the 1949 Geneva Conventions grant special protection to children during armed conflict,[9] they do not address the matter of child soldiers. While children had participated in the Second World War, this was not viewed as a problem that needed to be resolved in its aftermath. As Happold explains:

> Where children had participated in hostilities it had been as irregulars – partisans or resisters. Such participation was consequently seen by the Allied powers as voluntary and heroic or (at best) an unfortunate necessity. It was seen as something exceptional and not, consequently, requiring legal regulation; being unlikely to be repeated.[10]

It was not until the Additional Protocols to the Geneva Conventions were drafted that provisions regulating the recruitment and use of children under 15 to participate actively in hostilities were incorporated into an international treaty.[11] Since then, similar provisions have been included in other international instruments, notably the Convention on the Rights of the Child and its Optional Protocol.[12]

In the context of ICL, Article 4(c) of the SCSL Statute provides that '[c]onscripting or enlisting children under the age of 15 years into armed forces

Way Forward. Available at: http://childrenandarmedconflict.un.org/publications/Delasabliererreport_en.pdf.

8 Article 4(c), SCSL Statute and Articles 8(2)(b)(xxvi) and 8(2)(e)(vii), ICC Statute.

9 For example, Article 50, Geneva Convention IV and see Articles 14, 23, 24, 38(5), 51 and 68, Geneva Convention IV. Previously children were protected indirectly through Article 46, Hague Regulations 1907, which protects 'Family honour and rights'.

10 Happold, *supra* FN 1, p. 55.

11 Articles 77 and 78, Protocol I and Article 4(3), Protocol II.

12 Article 38, Convention on the Rights of the Child, 1989 and Articles 1–4, Optional Protocol on the Convention on the Rights of the Child on the Involvement of Children in Armed Conflict, 2000. Also see the ILO Convention 182, Concerning the Prohibition and Immediate Action for the Elimination of the Worst Forms of Child Labour, adopted by the International Labour Conference of the International Labour Organization in 1999, see 38 International Legal Materials 1207 (1999). Regulation has also taken place at a regional level, see Article 22, African Charter on the Rights and Welfare of the Child.

or groups or using them to participate actively in hostilities' constitutes a serious violation of IHL over which the SCSL has jurisdiction. The ICC Statute contains two provisions: Article 8(2)(b)(xxvi) provides that '[c]onscripting or enlisting children under the age of fifteen years into the national armed forces or using them to participate actively in hostilities' constitutes a serious violation of the laws and customs applicable in IACs; while Article 8(2)(e)(vii) states that '[c]onscripting or enlisting children under the age of fifteen years into armed forces or groups or using them to participate actively in hostilities' constitutes a serious violation of the laws and customs applicable in NIACs.

One initial question faced by both courts was to determine how many offences were included within the relevant provisions of their respective statutes. Do the three conducts of conscription, enlistment and 'use' constitute three different crimes, or are they different elements of the same crime? This would have important consequences when deciding whether or not to charge cumulatively[13] and when it came to sentencing. There are differing views on this matter.

The view that there is only one crime stems from the conducts being listed together within the same provision. Thus, in the *Norman* Decision, the majority opinion of the Appeals Chamber of the SCSL repeatedly used the term 'child recruitment'[14] as a shorthand way of covering conscripting, enlisting and 'use'.[15] In the *AFRC* case, too, the Trial Chamber opined that there is one crime, stating 'the actus reus of *the* crime can be satisfied by "conscripting" or "enlisting" children under the age of 15, or by "using" them to participate actively in hostilities'.[16] Some scholars agree that there is one crime, comprising three different conducts. Ambos, for example, argues of the *Lubanga* Trial Chamber's finding that there are three different offences, that:

13 For example, in the *CDF* case from the SCSL, one of the accused, Kondewa, was charged with enlisting children under 15 or using children under 15 to participate actively in hostilities. The Trial Chamber found him guilty of the crime of enlistment of children in respect of one child, and reasoned that it did not need to consider evidence as to whether he was also guilty of the crime of use as it had been charged as an alternative (*Prosecutor v Moinina Fofana and Allieu Kondewa*, SCSL-04-14-T, Trial Judgment, 2 August 2007 (*CDF* case, TC), paras 971–972). Consequently, on appeal, the Appeals Chamber was unable to consider any evidence or pronounce a verdict on the alternative 'use' charge. *Prosecutor v Moinina Fofana and Allieu Kondewa*, SCSL-04-14-A, Appeal Judgment, 28 May 2008 (*CDF* case, AC), paras 133–134.

14 See, for example, *Prosecutor v Sam Hinga Norman*, SCSL-2004-14-AR72(E), Appeal Decision on Preliminary Motion Based on Lack of Jurisdiction (Child Recruitment), 31 May 2004 (*Norman* Decision), paras 17, 20, 24, 39, 43 and 44.

15 *Norman* Decision, para. 53. The Appeals Chamber was concerned with one particular point, whether the enlistment of children under 15 was a crime at the time of the conduct in question, meaning that the decision should be read narrowly; see Sandesh Sivakumaran, 'War Crimes before the Special Court for Sierra Leone', 8(4) *Journal of International Criminal Justice* 1009–1034 (2010), p. 1012.

16 *AFRC* case TC, para. 733, emphasis added. Also see *CDF* case AC, para. 139, and Sivakumaran, ibid., p. 1011.

> The Chamber confuses the concept of an offence (consisting of different objective and subjective elements, including verbs describing the required conduct) with the concept of a particular conduct as one element or (objective) requirement of any offence ... the alternative structure of the offence, unambiguously reflected in the disjunctive wording ('or'), makes crystal clear that the realization of one of these conducts suffices for the realization of the offence ... each conduct stands on its own, independent from the others.[17]

A second view is that there are two different offences within the respective articles: one of child recruitment, whether by enlistment or conscription; and the other, the use of children under 15 to participate actively in hostilities. Several international treaty provisions refer simply to recruitment and 'use',[18] and there is support for this view in the jurisprudence of the SCSL and the ICC, and among some scholars.[19] The term 'recruiting' was used in the run-up to the Rome Conference,[20] but ultimately it was found to be too all-embracing and was replaced by 'enlisting' and 'conscripting' in the final ICC Statute.[21] The two-offence view has a certain intuitiveness in that an accused can at most commit two of the conducts against one child: first, as regards the means by which the child was recruited, and second, by using them to participate actively in hostilities.

A third view holds that the provisions contain three crimes. This was the view of Justice Robertson in his Dissenting Opinion in *Norman*, when he stated:

> This crime of child recruitment, as it was finally formulated in 4(c) of the Statute, may be committed in three quite different ways:

17 Kai Ambos, 'The First Judgment of the International Criminal Court (*Prosecutor v Lubanga*): A Comprehensive Analysis of the Legal Issues', 12(2) *International Criminal Law Review* 115–153 (2012), p. 133.

18 Article 77(2), Protocol I, Article 4(3)(c), Protocol II, Article 38, Convention on the Rights of the Child and Article 4 of its Optional Protocol on the Involvement of Children in Armed Conflict, 2000.

19 *CDF* case TC, para. 197; *Prosecutor v Thomas Lubanga Dyilo*, Pre-Trial Chamber I, Decision on the Confirmation of Charges, ICC-01/04-01/06, 29 January 2007 (*Lubanga* Decision), para. 246; and see Sivakumaran, *supra* FN 15, pp. 1011–1012; Alison Smith, 'Child Recruitment and the Special Court for Sierra Leone', 2 *Journal of International Criminal Justice* 1141–1153 (2004), p. 1147; and Sylvain Vité, 'Between Consolidation and Innovation: The International Criminal Court's Trial Chamber Judgment in the *Lubanga* Case', in T.D. Gill *et al* (eds), *Yearbook of International Humanitarian Law 2012* (T.M.C. Asser Press, 2014), p. 76.

20 United Nations Diplomatic Conference of Plenipotentiaries on the Establishment of an International Criminal Court, Draft Statute for the International Criminal Court, A/CONF.183/2/Add.1 14 April 1998, Article 5(t), proposed four different options, including 'forcing children under the age of fifteen to take a direct part in hostilities' and 'recruiting children under the age of fifteen years into armed forces or groups or using them to participate actively in hostilities'.

21 Charles Garraway, 'Article 8(2)(b)(xxvi) – Using, Conscripting or Enlisting Children', in Roy S. Lee (ed.), *The International Criminal Court: Elements of Crimes and Rules of Procedure and Evidence* (Transnational Publishers Inc., 2001), p. 205.

a by *conscripting* children (which implies compulsion, albeit in some cases through force of law),
b by *enlisting* them (which merely means accepting and enrolling them when they volunteer), or
c by *using* them to participate actively in hostilities (i.e. taking the more serious step, having conscripted or enlisted them, of putting their lives directly at risk in combat).

These are, in effect, three different crimes.[22]

It was also the view taken in the *Lubanga* Trial Judgment, which held: '[b]earing in mind the use of the word "or" in Article 8(2)(e)(vii), in the Chamber's view the three alternatives (*viz.* conscription, enlistment and use) are separate offences.'[23] This determination was not challenged on appeal, and the Appeals Chamber held that, without prejudice to any further consideration of the issue, it would proceed on the basis that they were separate crimes.[24] Thus, at present at least, the ICC views the conducts as different crimes.

How to solve this conundrum? The answer can perhaps be found by considering the elements of the different conducts as, despite the conducts being listed within the same provision, and despite the ICC's Elements of Crimes listing conscription, enlistment and 'use' as having identical elements,[25] the SCSL and the ICC have enumerated different elements for each.[26] As the elements for the three conducts differ, each conduct arguably constitutes a crime in its own right. Similarities can be drawn with Article 8(2)(c)(i) of the ICC Statute, which gives the court jurisdiction over '[v]iolence to life and person, in particular murder of all kinds, mutilation, cruel treatment and torture'. Although the conducts of murder, mutilation, cruel treatment and torture are contained in the same provision, they are listed in the Elements of Crimes as being separate offences, each with its own elements.[27] There is therefore a strong argument to be made that the acts of conscription, enlistment and use of children under the age of 15 to participate actively in hostilities are crimes in their own right.

In practice, both the SCSL and the ICC have had difficulties in distinguishing between the different war crimes. The following section considers how these courts have distinguished conscription from enlistment, before examining how

22 *Norman*, para. 5, emphasis added.
23 *Prosecutor v Thomas Lubanga Dyilo*, Trial Chamber I, Judgment pursuant to Article 74 of the Statute, ICC-01/04-01/06, 14 March 2012 (*Lubanga* TC), para. 609.
24 *Prosecutor v Thomas Lubanga Dyilo*, Appeals Chamber ICC-01/04-01/06, 1 December 2014 (*Lubanga* AC), para. 38.
25 The Elements of Crimes are to 'assist' the Court in the interpretations of Articles 6, 7 and 8, see Article 9(1), ICC Statute.
26 See subsequent discussion.
27 For a discussion of whether violence to life and person constitutes a crime in its own right. See *Prosecutor v Mitar Vasiljević*, ICTY, IT-98-32-T, Trial Judgment, 29 November 2002, paras 193–203.

actions concerning the recruitment of children under 15 have been untangled from their use to participate actively in hostilities.

6.2 Distinguishing conscription from enlistment

Both the SCSL and the ICC have held that it is the element of compulsion which distinguishes the crime of conscription from that of enlistment.[28] The Trial Chamber of the ICC has defined conscription as 'to enlist compulsorily' and enlistment as 'to enrol on the list of a military body'.[29]

In *Lubanga*, the Appeals Chamber held that the element of compulsion required for conscription can be established by demonstrating that an individual under the age of 15 joined an armed force or group due to 'a legal obligation, brute force, threat of force, or psychological pressure amounting to coercion'.[30] This must be established on a case-by-case basis, 'taking into account whether the force, threat of force or psychological pressure applied was of such a degree and so persuasive, that individuals can be said to have been forced to join the armed force or group'.[31] In his appeal, Lubanga argued that the element of compulsion can be established only if it is specifically demonstrated that the person was recruited into the armed force or group against his or her will.[32] This argument was rejected by the Appeals Chamber, which held that lack of consent or the requirement that the act is against the conscripted individual's will generally does not form an element of the crime of conscription.[33]

Enlistment requires some form of consent on the part of the child, their consent being no defence to the crime.[34] Some have queried whether children can ever truly consent to joining an armed group; as the Trial Chamber in the *CDF* case observed, '[a]ttributing voluntary enlistment in the armed forces to a child under the age of 15 years, particularly in a conflict setting where human rights abuses are rife, is … of questionable merit'.[35] Others argue that there are cases where children can genuinely consent to joining an armed group. Drumbl, for example, notes that in domestic law, children are often deemed competent to make decisions concerning themselves; for example, a child's consent can be a necessary requirement for medical treatment: if children are capable of deciding on these matters, why should they be deemed incapable of consenting to join an armed group?[36] However,

28 *Lubanga* AC, paras 311–312; and see *Norman*, para. 5; *AFRC* case TC, paras 734–735; and *Lubanga* TC, paras 607–608.
29 *Lubanga* TC, para. 608.
30 *Lubanga* AC, para. 278. Also see *Prosecutor v Issa Hassan Sesay, Morris Kallon and Augustine Gbao*, SCSL-2004-15-T, Trial Judgment, 2 March 2009 (*RUF* case TC), para. 186; and *Norman* Decision, para. 5.
31 *Lubanga* AC, para. 282.
32 Ibid., para. 301.
33 *Lubanga* AC, para. 301.
34 It can be used in mitigation of the sentence, see *Lubanga* TC, para. 617, *AFRC* case TC, para. 735, and *CDF* case AC, para. 140.
35 *CDF* case TC, para. 192.
36 Drumbl, *supra* FN 5, p. 15. Also see Ambos, *supra* FN 17, pp. 135–136.

there are also examples from domestic law where a child's consent is no defence to a crime: in many legal systems sexual intercourse with a child below a certain age is a crime, regardless of that child's consent. Sometimes the law protects children due to their youth and regardless of their consent, as with the war crime of enlistment.

McBride suggests that the approach that consent is no defence to the crime of enlistment may reduce the need to distinguish between the crimes of enlistment and conscription.[37] Arguably, however, the need to do so is still very real. First, they are different crimes and should be considered separately.[38] Second, the difference between 'worst-case scenarios' of conscription – for example, a child who is forcibly abducted from their family – and 'best-case scenarios' of enlistment – for example, where an older child volunteers because they want to 'do their bit' – are worlds apart. In both instances, the recruitment of the child constitutes a war crime, but the circumstances surrounding the recruitment can, and should, make a difference when it comes to sentencing.[39] Thus, whether the child in question was forced or consented to join the armed group remains relevant.

6.3 Distinguishing enlistment and conscription from 'use'

Both the SCSL and the ICC have had difficulty in distinguishing between the offences of enlistment or conscription (for the sake of brevity, in this section the crimes of enlistment and conscription will on occasion be referred to collectively as 'recruitment'), and 'use'. Some judgments have tied the recruitment of the child to their subsequent use to participate actively in hostilities. In the *AFRC* case, for example, the Trial Chamber held:

> 'Conscription' implies compulsion, in some instances through the force of law … the Trial Chamber adopts an interpretation of 'conscription' which encompasses acts of coercion, such as abductions and forced recruitment, by an armed group against children, *committed for the purpose of using them to participate actively in hostilities.*[40]

37 Julie McBride, *The War Crime of Child Soldier Recruitment* (Asser Press, 2014), p. 130.

38 This was confirmed by the *Lubanga* Appeals Chamber, which found that the Trial Chamber should set out with clarity which factual findings are the basis for the subjective and legal elements of each crime. *Lubanga* AC, para. 313.

39 In *Lubanga* the accused received a 13-year term of imprisonment for the crime of conscription and a 12-year term for enlistment, *Prosecutor v Lubanga*, Decision on Sentence pursuant to Article 76 of the Statute, ICC-01/04-01/06, 10 July 2012 (*Lubanga* Sentencing Decision), para. 98.

40 *AFRC* case TC, para. 734, emphasis added. The AFRC case was the first case to consider charges under international criminal law relating to child soldiers. Unfortunately, the charge was widely drafted and perhaps as a consequence of this, the court's guidance as to how to define the different elements was not as satisfactory as it could have been. For a critique of the pleadings in the Indictment, see Nolween Guibert and Tilman Blumenstock, 'The First Judgment of the Special Court for Sierra Leone: A

In the *CDF* case, the Appeals Chamber added a specific *mens rea* requirement for the crime of enlistment, namely that there was knowledge on the part of the perpetrator that the child 'may be trained for combat'.[41] This additional requirement unnecessarily blurs the distinction between recruitment and APH.[42] As Sivakumaran explains, Article 4(c) of the SCSL Statute prohibits conscription and enlistment in all their forms, not only certain sub-sets thereof such as conscription or enlistment with the purpose of active participation.[43] Requiring proof that the recruitment was carried out for the purposes of using the children to participate actively in hostilities unduly restricts the crimes. There are many roles in military organisations that do not amount to participating actively in hostilities: mechanics, engineers or cooks, for example, have been recruited into the organisation to the same degree as their colleagues who hold combat roles. A child may be recruited into an armed group, but the tasks they are ultimately assigned do not necessarily amount to participating actively in hostilities.

That the recruitment of children is independent of their 'use' was acknowledged in the *RUF* case, which concerned the crime of conscription in the form of abduction.[44] When determining whether the children in question had been conscripted into the armed group, the Trial Chamber stated that:

> We observe that either the abduction of persons for specific use within an organization or the forced military training of persons is independently sufficient to constitute conscription, as both practices amount to compelling a person to join an armed group.[45]

Children who had been abducted and forced to carry out military training at RUF camps were found to have been conscripted.[46] However, not all the abducted children had undergone military training,[47] and in respect of that group of children, the Trial Chamber concluded that:

> Although not all the children abducted were eventually subjected to military training, the Chamber has found that the children who were not trained were used for other purposes within the RUF. We therefore find that notwithstanding their ultimate use, these abductees were compulsorily enlisted as members of the RUF or AFRC forces and therefore conscripted.[48]

Missed Opportunity?', 6 *The Law and Practice of International Courts and Tribunals* 367 (2007), pp. 369–376, p. 380 and p. 382.

41 *CDF* case AC, para. 141. Also see *Norman* Decision, Justice Robertson, para. 46 and *RUF* case TC, para. 192.

42 Sivakumaran, *supra* FN 15, pp. 1015–1017.

43 Ibid., p. 1015.

44 Abduction is viewed as a particularly egregious form of 'conscription', see *AFRC* case TC, para. 1276.

45 *RUF* case TC, para. 1695.

46 Ibid., para. 1700.

47 Ibid., paras 1696 and 1700.

48 Ibid., para. 1700.

This 'important and very welcome finding of the Court'[49] means that the crime of conscription is committed as soon as the child has been abducted and compelled to join a military organisation, thereby obviating the need to show that they were engaged in military activities in order to prove the offence.

The ICC too has held that the enlistment and conscription of a child is independent of their 'use'. In *Lubanga*, the Trial Chamber stated:

> The status of a child under 15 who has been enlisted or conscripted is independent of any later period when he or she may have been 'used' to participate actively in hostilities, particularly given the variety of tasks that he or she may subsequently be required to undertake. Although it may often be the case that the purpose behind conscription and enlistment is to use children in hostilities, this is not a requirement of the Rome Statute.[50]

However, it has at times proven difficult to separate the recruitment of children from their use to participate actively in hostilities. Many organised armed groups lack a formal recruitment process, meaning that the circumstances surrounding their connection to the group must be examined in order to establish whether a child had been recruited. It is then that there is a risk of the boundaries between recruitment and 'use' becoming blurred.

The challenges of ensuring that 'use' is not conflated with enlistment are illustrated in the *CDF* case, where the SCSL was required to consider the cultural practices of Kamajor society in Sierra Leone.[51] The case, as it pertained to enlistment, relied heavily on the evidence of one witness, Witness TF2-021, a former child soldier. The witness testified that he had been abducted by rebels in 1995 when he was nine years old. In 1997, he was captured by the Civil Defence Forces (CDF) and forced to carry looted property.[52] He was then taken to the main CDF base for initiation, where he, along with 20 or so other boys, was initiated into Kamajor society by the accused, Kondewa. They were told that the initiation process would make them powerful for fighting and were given a potion to rub on their bodies before going into battle.[53] When the witness was 13 years old, he was initiated by Kondewa into the Avondo society, Kondewa's personal group of Kamajors. He received a certificate to this effect, bearing his photograph.[54]

49 Gus Waschefort, 'Justice for Child Soldiers? The RUF Trial of the Special Court for Sierra Leone', 1 *International Humanitarian Legal Studies* 189–204 (2010), p. 195.
50 *Lubanga* TC, para. 609.
51 The Kamajor are indigenous, tribal-based hunters. During the conflict in Sierra Leone much of the CDF was made up of Kamajors. In order to join Kamajor society, young male fighters have to be initiated. For discussions of the difficulties faced by ICTs when confronting cultural issues such as the initiation ceremonies of the Kamajors, see David M. Rosen, 'Who is a Child? The Legal Conundrum of Child Soldiers', 25 *Connecticut Journal of International Law* 82 (2009–2010), pp. 107–111; and McBride, *supra* FN 37, pp. 11–14.
52 *CDF* case TC, para. 674.
53 Ibid., para. 675.
54 Ibid., para. 682.

The Trial Chamber found that initiation into Kamajor society did not necessarily amount to enlistment into an armed force or group, and that the circumstances of each specific initiation must be examined in order to determine whether enlistment had occurred.[55] In this particular instance, the evidence showed that during his first initiation ceremony the witness and other initiates had been given potions and were told that they were to rub it on their bodies before going into battle to make them strong for fighting. They were given military training and were sent into battle soon afterwards. The Trial Chamber stated:

> the evidence is absolutely clear that on this occasion, the initiates had taken the first step in becoming fighters. It is beyond reasonable doubt that Kondewa, in these circumstances, when initiating the boys, was also performing an act analogous to enlisting them for active military service.[56]

The Trial Chamber found Kondewa guilty of the crime of enlisting child soldiers based on the witness's testimony.[57] However, on appeal his conviction was overturned in this regard. The Appeals Chamber noted that 'there is a paucity of jurisprudence on the question of how direct an act must be to constitute enlistment under Article 4(c)'.[58] It noted that for enlistment there must be a nexus between the act of the accused and the child joining the armed force or group, and whether such a nexus exists is a question of fact which must be determined on a case-by-case basis.[59] The Appeals Chamber stated:

> In the context of this case, in which the armed group is not a conventional military organization, 'enlistment' cannot narrowly be defined as a formal process. The Appeals Chamber regards 'enlistment' in the broad sense as including any conduct accepting the child as part of the militia. Such conduct would include making him participate in military operations.[60]

The enlistment of Witness TF2-021 was found to have occurred in 1997, when he had been forced to carry looted property, and not at the initiation ceremony held afterwards, performed by Kondewa.[61] Accordingly, the Appeals Chamber found Kondewa not guilty of the crime of enlisting.[62]

55 Ibid., para. 969.
56 *CDF* case TC, para. 970. However, also *see* CDF case, *Separate Opinion of Hon. Justice Itoe.*
57 The testimony given Witness TF2-021 has been criticised as being 'problematic in numerous regards', see Nancy Amoury Combs, *Fact-Finding Without Facts, The Uncertain Evidentiary Foundations of International Criminal Convictions* (Cambridge University Press, 2010), pp. 217–219.
58 *CDF* case AC, para. 141.
59 Ibid., para. 141.
60 Ibid., para. 144.
61 Ibid., para. 142.
62 Ibid., para. 146.

In her Partially Dissenting Opinion, Justice Winter disagreed with the Appeal Chamber's finding that forcing Witness TF2-021 to carry looted property constituted enlistment. She agreed that in certain circumstances the use of a child soldier may constitute enlistment; however, based on the particular facts of this case, this particular use did not constitute enlistment.[63] She argued that '[t]he key test to determine whether an act in question constituted enlistment is whether the act substantially furthers the process of a child's enrolment and acceptance into an armed force or group'.[64] By finding that Kondewa's initiation of the witness did not constitute enlistment, the Majority was implicitly holding that only one act could constitute enlistment. Justice Winter disagreed:

> Enlistment may in some circumstances be a process involving several acts which may substantially further the enrolment and acceptance of a child under the age of fifteen into an armed force or group. Religious initiation, military training and the signing of a certificate declaring a child fit for combat may all be acts that substantially further a child's enlistment. In other circumstances, enlistment may be a very short process and may constitute a single act, such as abducting a child and giving him/her a gun. In certain armed forces or groups there may be no clear record of a child's enlistment, but there may be several instances of the 'use' of a child.[65]

Where there were no formal or informal processes for enlisting a child into a group, the use of the child to participate actively in hostilities may amount to enlistment. However, in cases where it is shown that there is a process which contributes to the enrolment and acceptance of a child into an armed group, logic dictates that the 'use' of the child cannot constitute enlistment. The types of acts that constitute enlistment depend upon the particular facts of each case.[66] According to Justice Winter, the CDF had a clearly defined enlistment process using ritualised initiation and military training, which remained the case throughout the armed conflict.[67] Being forced to carry looted property was not an act amounting to participating actively in hostilities, and was not an activity which involved the CDF as a military organisation. Justice Winter found that as the act of looting was for private purposes, it did not constitute enlistment into an armed force or group, or the use of a child to participate actively in hostilities.[68] She concurred with the Trial Chamber that Kondewa was guilty of the crime of enlistment.[69]

What is to be made of the Appeal Chamber's approach in the *CDF* case? The Majority's view that enlistment cannot be defined as a formal process in the case of

63 Ibid., para. 9.
64 Ibid., para. 11.
65 Ibid., para. 12.
66 Ibid., para. 13.
67 Ibid., para. 14.
68 Ibid., para. 19.
69 Ibid., para. 20.

a non-conventional military organisation is a sensible one, as is their direction to define enlistment broadly 'including any conduct accepting the child as part of the militia'. However, the Majority's focus was arguably too narrow when it singled out one act of looting as being the act that constituted the enlistment of the witness. As Judge Winter argued, there was evidence of a defined enlistment process of which initiation into Kamajor society formed part, and the Majority would have done well to consider the process of enlistment as a series of several acts in that particular context, rather than condensing it to one single act.

6.4 Using children to participate actively in hostilities

During armed conflicts children can be used in myriad different roles. Some may have combat roles, but many are used for other jobs, such as collecting food, running errands, gathering information, spying and looting. Matters can be even more complex as regards girl soldiers,[70] who may be required to perform all of the tasks that boys do, as well as additional ones, such as performing domestic chores and providing sexual services.[71]

Different international treaties contain different phrasings regarding the use of children in armed conflict. Article 38 of the Convention on the Rights of the Child requires state parties to take all feasible measures to ensure children who have not attained the age of 15 do not 'take a direct part in hostilities'. Its Optional Protocol uses two different phrases: Article 1, which applies to State Parties, uses the same phrasing as Article 38 of the Convention, namely, 'take a direct part in hostilities'; whereas Article 4(1), which applies to armed groups that are distinct from the armed forces of a state, uses the phrase 'use in hostilities'. The Paris Principles, on the other hand, give a wide interpretation of 'a child associated with an armed force or armed group', defining him or her as 'any person below 18 years of age who is or who has been recruited or used by an armed force or armed group in any capacity, including but not limited to children, boys and girls, used as fighters, cooks, porters, messengers, spies or for sexual purposes'.

In IHL treaties, too, different phrases are used. Article 77 of Protocol I requires parties to the conflict to take all feasible measures to ensure that children under 15 'do not take a direct part in hostilities'. When considering the meaning of the phrase 'direct' part in hostilities, as contained in Article 77(2), the ICRC Commentary to Protocol I notes:

> The text refers to taking a 'direct' part in hostilities ... Can this lead to the conclusion that indirect acts of participation are not covered? Examples would

70 Noëlle Quénivet, 'Girl Soldiers and Participation in Hostilities', 16 *African Journal of International and Comparative Law* 219 (2008).

71 Save the Children, *Forgotten Casualties of War: Girls in Armed Conflict* 11 (2005). Available at: www.peacewomen.org/assets/file/Resources/NGO/HR_Forgotten Girls_SC_2005.pdf.

> include, in particular, gathering and transmission of military information, transportation of arms and munitions, provision of supplies etc. The intention of the drafters of the article was clearly to keep children under fifteen outside armed conflict, and consequently they should not be required to perform such services; if it does happen that children under fifteen spontaneously or on request perform such acts, precautions should at least be taken.[72]

The ICRC Commentary therefore advocates a wide interpretation of the phrase 'direct part in hostilities' in relation to child soldiers, and takes the view that indirect acts of participation are, generally speaking, not acceptable under Article 77(2). Article 4(3)(c) of Protocol II uses different language in that it provides that children under 15 shall not be allowed to 'take part in hostilities'.[73] The ICRC Commentary to the Protocol explains: 'A child … will not be "allowed to take part in hostilities", i.e., to participate in military operations such as gathering information, transmitting orders, transporting ammunition and foodstuffs, or acts of sabotage.'[74] To 'take part' in hostilities therefore covers a broader range of activities than direct participation in hostilities.

In ICL, both the SCSL and ICC Statutes contain identical phrasing, in that it is the act of 'using (children under fifteen) to participate actively in hostilities' which constitutes a war crime. The following section examines how the SCSL has interpreted the crime, before turning to the ICC.

6.4.1 Defining 'use' at the Special Court for Sierra Leone

The first definition of 'use to actively participate in hostilities' as it pertains to child soldiers, was given in the *AFRC* case. The Trial Chamber held that 'using' children to participate actively in the hostilities 'encompasses putting their lives directly at risk in combat'.[75] It continued:

> It is the Trial Chamber's view that the use of children to participate actively in hostilities is not limited to participation in combat. An armed force requires logistical support to maintain its operations. Any labour or support that gives effect to, or helps maintain, operations in a conflict, constitutes active participation. Hence carrying loads for the fighting faction, finding and/or acquiring food, ammunition or equipment, acting as decoys, carrying messages, making trails or finding routes, manning checkpoints or acting as human shields are some examples of active participation as much as actual fighting and combat.[76]

72 ICRC Commentary to Protocol I, para. 3187.
73 Article 4(3)(c), Protocol II.
74 ICRC Commentary to Protocol II, para. 4557.
75 *AFRC* case TC, para. 736, referring to the Dissenting Opinion of Judge Robertson, para. 5.
76 Ibid., para. 737.

This is an expansive definition of the phrase.[77] If one compares the Trial Chamber's definition of 'active participation' with the three cumulative criteria laid down in the ICRC Guidance,[78] it is evident that the Chamber's definition is broader. The ICRC Guidance includes within the definition, 'any labour or support that gives effect to, or helps maintain operations in a conflict', but excludes individual conduct that merely builds up or maintains the capacity of a party to harm its adversary, or which otherwise only indirectly causes harm.[79] The ICRC Guidance also excludes the transport of weapons and equipment from constituting DPH, unless carried out as an integral part of a specific military operation designed to cause the required threshold of harm.[80] In addition, it excludes the provision of food to the armed forces.[81] Thus, without an examination of the specific circumstances of each incident, some of the activities that the Trial Chamber in the *AFRC* case included within its definition of participating actively in hostilities fall outwith the ICRC's definition of DPH.

While this passage of the *AFRC* Trial Judgment has been referred to in other SCSL cases, they have tended to take a more nuanced approach to the matter. In *Taylor*, for example, the Trial Chamber referred to the passage, stating:

> Using children to participate actively in the hostilities encompasses putting their lives directly at risk in combat, but *may* also include participation in activities linked to combat such [as] carrying loads for the fighting faction, finding and/or acquiring food, ammunition or equipment, acting as decoys, carrying messages, making trails or finding routes, manning checkpoints or acting as human shields.[82]

77 In reaching this conclusion, the Trial Chamber relied on a footnote of the Report of the Preparatory Committee of the ICC that states: 'The words "using" and "participate" have been adopted in order to cover both direct participation in combat and also active participation in military activities linked to combat such as scouting, spying, sabotage and the use of children as decoys, couriers or at military checkpoints. It would not cover activities clearly unrelated to the hostilities such as food deliveries to an airbase or the use of domestic staff in an officer's married accommodation. However, use of children in a direct support function such as acting as bearers to take supplies to the front line, or activities at the front line itself, would be included within the terminology.' *Report of the Committee on the Establishment of an International Criminal Court*, A/CONF.183/2/Add.1, 14 April 1998, p. 21, FN 12.

78 Namely: (1) the act must be likely to adversely affect the military operations or military capacity of a party to an armed conflict or, alternatively, to inflict death, injury or destruction on persons or objects protected against direct attack, and (2) there must be a direct causal link between the act and the harm likely to result either from that act, or from a coordinated military operation of which that acts constitutes an integral part, and (3) the act must be specifically designed to directly cause the required threshold of harm in support of a party to the conflict and to the detriment of another. ICRC Guidance, p. 46.

79 ICRC Guidance, p. 53.

80 Ibid., p. 53.

81 Ibid., p. 54.

82 *Prosecutor v Charles Ghankay Taylor*, SCSL-03-01-T, Trial Judgment, 18 May 2012 (*Taylor* TC), para. 444, emphasis added.

This suggests that a more detailed analysis of the particular facts of the case is required in order to determine whether a specific act constituted participating actively in hostilities or not. In its case law, the SCSL has considered whether the following activities amount to using children under 15 to participate actively in hostilities:

(i) The use of children in combat activities

This has been found to constitute active participation.[83] In the *RUF* case, the Trial Chamber held that the use of children armed with weapons to ambush the United Nations Mission in Sierra Leone (UNAMSIL) peacekeepers, and the use of children to invade Freetown, constituted using children to participate actively in hostilities.[84] In *Taylor*, the Trial Chamber found that simply sending children to the front line was sufficient. The Trial Chamber held that even though there was no evidence as to the precise role the children played on the front line or if they were armed, 'the lives of these children were put at risk by sending them to the fighting areas, and becoming a military target',[85] and they were being used to participate actively in hostilities.[86]

(ii) The use of children in armed patrols

Children who had been used on armed patrols were found to be participating actively in hostilities, as such activities were clearly related to military operations. In the *RUF* case, the Trial Chamber explained:

> given the circumstances of guerrilla war that prevailed in Sierra Leone at that time, RUF fighters on patrol were potential targets of enemy forces and … children participating in such patrols were exposed to the risk of possible surprise attacks by adverse forces. This situation predisposed them to immediately and spontaneously engage in participating actively in armed combat if and as soon as such an eventuality occurred.[87]

The Trial Chamber laid weight upon the missions having had a military purpose, that adult fighters were present and that at least some of the participants were armed.[88]

(iii) The use of children as guards for military objects

During the war in Sierra Leone, children were used to guard military camps and diamond mines. The SCSL found that control over diamond mines was crucial for

83 *AFRC* case TC, para. 736.
84 *RUF* case TC, para. 1715.
85 *Taylor* TC, para. 1476.
86 Ibid., para. 1476.
87 *RUF* case TC, para. 1718.
88 Ibid., para. 1717.

the armed groups embroiled in the war, as the revenue from these mines was used to purchase arms, ammunition and logistics.[89] The *RUF* case held that guarding these military camps constituted participating actively in hostilities, since there was a high likelihood and realistic fear of enemy attacks.[90]

(iv) The use of children to commit crimes against civilians

The SCSL found that during the conflict in Sierra Leone, frequent and brutal acts of violence directed against civilians were a hallmark of the operations of the RUF and AFRC forces, and persons under the age of 15 years actively participated in campaigns of amputation, killing, rape and enslavement.[91] In the context of an armed conflict where violence against civilians was an integral and defining feature of the conduct of hostilities, the concept of participating actively in hostilities encompasses crimes committed against civilians.[92]

(v) The use of children to spy on enemies and to collect intelligence

The Trial Chamber in the *RUF* case found this constituted participating actively in hostilities, as the work was military in nature and directly supported the war efforts of the RUF.[93]

(vi) The use of children as bodyguards

This was found, depending on the circumstances, to be participating actively in hostilities. In the *RUF* case, the Trial Chamber held that the use of children as bodyguards to commanders constituted participating actively in hostilities, because the conduct was clearly related to the conduct of hostilities as, by virtue of their position and rank, commanders were key targets for the adversary party. Bodyguards accompanied commanders at all times, including into combat, which placed the children in a potential combat situation.[94]

(vii) The use of children to carry arms and ammunition

This was held to constitute participating actively in hostilities as the activity is related to the hostilities and directly supports the military operations of the armed group.[95]

89 Ibid., paras 1726–1727; *AFRC* case TC, para. 1267.
90 *RUF* case TC, para. 1726.
91 Ibid., para. 1720.
92 Ibid., para. 1723, and also see *Taylor* TC, paras 1490 and 1502.
93 *RUF* case TC, para. 1729.
94 Ibid., para. 1731. Also see *CDF* case TC, para. 688, and *Taylor* TC, paras 1468 and 1486.
95 *Taylor* TC, para. 1524, and *AFRC* case TC, para. 737.

(viii) The use of children to collect food

During the conflict, children were frequently used to find food. The *AFRC* Trial Chamber found this to constitute active participation.[96] In contrast, in the *RUF* case, evidence showed that the children used to participate in food missions had been unarmed, and the Trial Chamber held that in that context, participating in food-finding missions did not amount to participating actively in hostilities.[97]

In *Taylor* the Trial Chamber held that food-finding missions could constitute participating actively in hostilities where 'there is a clear link between the mission and the hostilities'.[98] This encompassed food-finding missions where children carried arms and/or committed crimes against civilians.[99] Children sent on food-finding missions armed with knives and sticks, and who beat and killed any civilians who resisted them during such missions, were being used to participate actively in hostilities.[100]

(ix) The use of children for domestic labour

The SCSL has consistently held that the use of children to perform household chores, or other such tasks, for military commanders does not constitute participating actively in hostilities.[101]

If one compares the SCSL's findings as to what activities amount to participating actively in hostilities with the three cumulative conditions for DPH laid down in the ICRC Guidance, there is little conflict between the two. The court's findings that using children for combat clearly counts as direct participation under the ICRC Guidance, as will, depending on the circumstances, the use of children in armed patrols, as military guards, as bodyguards or as spies.[102] The finding in *Taylor*, that sending children to the front line counts as participating actively in hostilities, is more controversial. This follows from the Trial Chamber's conclusion that '"[u]sing" children to participate actively in the hostilities encompasses putting their lives directly at risk in combat'.[103] As regards the use of children to commit crimes against civilians, the ICRC Guidance states that in order for an act which is not likely to cause military harm to constitute DPH, it must be likely to cause at least death, injury or destruction,[104] and that 'acts of violence directed specifically

96 *AFRC* case TC, para. 737.
97 *RUF* case TC, para. 1743.
98 *Taylor* TC, para. 1479.
99 Ibid., paras 1479 and 1509.
100 Ibid., paras 1480–1482.
101 In *Taylor*, the Trial Chamber stated: 'The Trial Chamber is not satisfied that the performance of domestic chores constitutes active participation in hostilities as these activities were not related to the hostilities and did not directly support the military operations of the armed groups.' *Taylor* TC, para. 1522. Also see *RUF* case TC, para. 1739.
102 See ICRC Guidance, pp. 46–64.
103 *Taylor* TC, para. 444.
104 ICRC Guidance, p. 49.

against civilians or civilian objects may amount to direct participation in hostilities'.[105] The court's finding in this regard therefore also accords with the ICRC Guidance. Finally, concerning food-finding missions, in *Taylor* it was held that these could constitute participating actively in hostilities, providing that a causal nexus exists between the use of the child to collect food and the armed conflict.[106] Again, providing that such a link exists, this finding complies with the ICRC Guidance.

The SCSL has tended to utilise a case-by-case approach when determining whether activities constitute participating actively in hostilities, and has been careful to explain that some of its findings were unique to the conflict in Sierra Leone.[107] This is a sensible approach. Providing a definitive list of behaviour as to what constitutes participating actively in hostilities, as in the *AFRC* case, is not necessarily wise and can prove unduly restrictive. Every situation is unique, and what may amount to 'use' in one context, may not do so under different circumstances.

6.4.2 Defining 'use' at the International Criminal Court

The concept of using children under 15 years to participate actively in hostilities is not defined in the ICC Statute or its Elements of Crimes. The meaning of the term was first considered in the *Lubanga* case in the context of Article 8(2)(e)(vii) of the Statute. In its Judgment, the Trial Chamber noted that the provision must be interpreted within the established framework of international law and IHL in particular,[108] and that the purpose of Article 8(2)(e)(vii) is to protect children from the risks that are associated with armed conflict.[109] It concluded:

> The use of the expression 'to participate actively in hostilities', as opposed to the expression 'direct participation' (as found in Additional Protocol I to the Geneva Conventions) was clearly intended to import a wide interpretation to the activities and roles that are covered by the offence of using children under the age of 15 actively to participate in hostilities.[110]

105 Ibid., p. 49.

106 Joe Tan, 'Sexual Violence against Children on the Battlefield as a Crime of Using Child Soldiers: Square Pegs in Round Holes and Missed Opportunities in Lubanga', in T.D. Gill *et al* (eds), *Yearbook of International Humanitarian Law 2012* (T.M.C. Asser Press, 2014), p. 138.

107 'The types of acts that may be characterised as hostilities, in the Chamber's view, may differ depending on the particularities of each armed conflict and the *modus operandi* of the warring factions.' *RUF* case TC, para. 1720.

108 *Lubanga* AC, para. 322. The court had recourse to the chapeau of Article 8(2)(e)(vii), the introduction to Article 8 in the Elements of Crimes and to Article 21 of its Statute.

109 *Lubanga* TC, para. 619.

110 Ibid., para. 629, and see paras 619–628.

This finding that the phrase 'to participate actively in hostilities' has a wider meaning than 'direct participation' was controversial, as until that time the phrases had been widely understood to have an identical meaning.[111]

On Appeal, the Appeals Chamber took the opportunity to clarify the court's reasoning. It explained that the term to 'participate actively in hostilities' in the context of the war crime of using children under 15, does not have to be given the same interpretation as the terms 'active' or 'direct' participation as used in the context of the principle of distinction between combatants and civilians, for example in Common Article 3.[112] The purposes of Common Article 3 and Article 8(2)(e)(vii) of the Statute are different, with the latter establishing when a civilian loses protection for taking a DPH, and the former seeking to protect individuals under the age of 15 from being used to 'participate actively in hostilities' and the concomitant risks to their lives and well-being.[113] The Appeals Chamber held that the provisions of IHL do not establish that the phrase to 'participate actively in hostilities' should be interpreted so as only to refer to forms of DPH as understood in the context of the principle of distinction, but rather it should be interpreted in a manner that bears in mind the provision's purpose.[114]

The Trial Judgment's decision that the concept of 'to participate actively in hostilities' included a larger scope of activities than those included under DPH had caused some concern. It opened up the possibility that children under 15 could potentially constitute legitimate military targets in a wider range of situations than adults.[115] The Appeal Chamber's decision should go some way to assuaging these fears and makes a workable distinction. In the context of distinction between combatants and civilians, active/direct participation has one meaning[116] that is distinct from the phrase 'to participate actively in hostilities' in the context of the use of children under 15.[117]

111 Natalie Wagner, 'A Critical Assessment of Using Children to Participate Actively in Hostilities in Lubanga', 24(2) *Criminal Law Forum* 145–203 (2013), pp. 21–37; and Vité, *supra* FN 19, pp. 77–78.

112 Lubanga AC, para. 324.

113 Ibid.

114 Ibid., paras 324–328.

115 For example see McBride *supra* FN 37, p. 118; Sivakumaran, *supra* FN 15, p. 1019; Guibert and Blumenstock, *supra* FN 40, p. 381; Vité, *supra* FN 19, p. 78; however, see Roman Graf, 'The International Criminal Court and Child Soldiers, An Appraisal of the Lubanga Judgment', 10 *Journal of International Criminal Justice* 945–969 (2012), p. 963.

116 There is precedent for a term to have one meaning in one context, and a different meaning in another, namely torture. In *Kunarac*, the ICTY held that, unlike in human rights law, the presence of a state official or of any other authority-wielding person in the torture process is not necessary for the offence to be regarded as torture under IHL. See *Prosecutor v Milorad Kunarac et al*, ICTY, IT-96-23-T, Trial Judgment, 22 February 2001 (*Kunarac* TC), paras 466–496.

117 For a discussion of whether there are different rules concerning when child soldiers can be targeted compared to adults, see Joanna Nicholson, 'Is Targeting Naked Child Soldiers a War Crime?', 16 *International Criminal Law Review* (2016) 131–154.

The *Lubanga* case also considered what test to apply when determining whether a particular conduct amounts to participating actively in hostilities for the purposes of the crime. The Trial Chamber found that the decisive factor is 'whether the support provided by the child to the combatants exposed him or her to real danger as a potential target'.[118] The Appeals Chamber disagreed with this test.[119] It noted that there is no reference to this requirement in the relevant provisions of the ICC Statute or in IHL. Rather:

> [a] plain interpretation of the relevant provisions in their context reveals that the crime of using children to participate actively in hostilities requires the existence of a link between the activity and the hostilities. Although the extent to which the child was exposed to risk due to the activity in which he or she was engaged may well be an indicator of the existence of a sufficiently close relationship between the activity of the child and the hostilities, an assessment of such risk cannot replace an assessment of the relationship itself.[120]

The Chamber concluded that in order to determine whether the crime of using children to participate actively in hostilities under Article 8(2)(e)(vii) of the Statute has occurred, it is 'necessary to analyse the link between the activity for which the child is used and the combat in which the armed force or group of the perpetrator is engaged'.[121] The Chamber noted that it was inappropriate to give further guidance on the parameters of the notion 'in view of the complex and unforeseeable scenarios presented by the rapidly changing face of warfare in the modern world'.[122] Rather, the issue should be examined on a case-by-case basis. This requirement of there being a 'link' between the hostilities and the activity is very broad; however, the Appeals Chamber states that it will be guided by the ICRC Commentary on the Additional Protocols and the Preparatory Committee's Draft Statute.

When considering what activities constitute using children to participate actively in hostilities, both the Trial and Appeal Chambers considered it beyond dispute that participation in actual combat constitutes 'use'.[123] The use of children under 15 as military guards by military chiefs and senior political officials in an active conflict zone also constituted 'use' as the activities were linked to the combat in which the armed group was engaged.[124] However, the Appeals Chamber disagreed with the Trial Chamber's finding that the formation of an armed unit

118 *Lubanga* TC, para. 628. Also see *Lubanga* TC, Separate and Dissenting Opinion of Judge Odio Benito, who argued that 'active participation' included sexual violence. This concept of a 'risk test' had been referred to in other cases, see *Norman* Decision, para. 5; *AFRC* case TC, para. 736; and *Taylor* TC, paras 1459 and 1476.

119 *Lubanga* AC, para. 332.

120 Ibid., para. 333.

121 Ibid., para. 335.

122 Ibid.

123 *Lubanga* TC, para. 915; and *Lubanga* AC, para. 336.

124 *Lubanga* TC, para. 915; and *Lubanga* AC, para. 337.

within an armed group does not of itself constitute 'use' of children to participate actively in hostilities.[125] The use of children for domestic tasks[126] was also found not to constitute 'use' for the purposes of the crime.[127]

6.5 *Mens rea* for the crimes of conscription, enlistment and 'use'

The *mens rea* for the offences of conscription, enlistment and use of children under 15 to participate actively in hostilities, is that 'the perpetrator knew or should have known that such person or persons were under the age of 15 years'.[128] However, proving that alleged child soldiers are under the age of 15 can create practical difficulties, in that documentary evidence as to age may not be available and witnesses' perceptions regarding age may be unreliable.[129]

Sometimes, the extreme youth of an individual has allowed the court to draw the conclusion that the accused knew or had reason to know that they were under 15. Thus, in the *CDF* case, the Trial Chamber found that the accused, Kondewa, knew or had reason to know that one witness was 11 years old at the time he was initiated by him into the armed group, since 'there can be no mistaking a boy of eleven years old for a boy of fifteen years or older, especially for a man such as Kondewa who regularly performed initiation ceremonies'.[130] This begs the question of where the grey area lies regarding when it becomes difficult to specify whether a child is over the age of 15 or not.[131]

In circumstances where perpetrators were unable to have actual knowledge of a child's age at the time they were abducted or trained, courts have examined surrounding factors which should have been sufficient to place them on alert. The *RUF* Trial Chamber found that perpetrators had reason to know that children under 15 were being abducted and subject to military training, in that there had been a widespread practice of abducting and training child soldiers at that time; children had been especially prized as fighters due to their agility and obedience,

125 *Lubanga* TC, para. 915; and *Lubanga* AC, para. 338.
126 *Lubanga* TC, para. 915; and *Lubanga* AC, para. 339.
127 One of the controversial aspects of the Trial Judgment concerned whether the use of child soldiers for sexual purposes amounted to participating actively in hostilities. This argument was rejected by the Trial Chamber. See *Lubanga* TC, para. 630; and *Lubanga*, Separate and Dissenting Opinion of Judge Odio Benito. For critique, see Tan, *supra* FN 106.
128 Elements of Crimes for Articles 8(2)(b)(xxvi) and 8(2)(e)(vii), and see *AFRC* case TC, para. 729. During the negotiations for the Rome Statute, some States had argued that it should be the responsibility of those who are recruiting or using to satisfy themselves that the individual was not under 15, see Knut Dörmann *et al*, *Elements of War Crimes under the Rome Statute of the International Criminal Court: Sources and Commentary* (Cambridge University Press, 2002), p. 375.
129 'The Trial Chamber is aware that an official document if authenticated or uncontested is more reliable evidence of age than a witness's perception but also acknowledges that such documentary evidence is not available in many parts of Sierra Leone.' *Taylor* TC, para. 1361.
130 *CDF* case TC, para. 970.
131 McBride, *supra* FN 37, p. 132.

and the lives of children were often spared during attacks against civilians so that they could be utilised by the armed forces. These practices were well known among RUF and AFRC fighters.[132] Cumulatively these factors put those involved on notice that the persons involved may have been under 15, and where there was doubt as to a person's age, it was incumbent on the perpetrators to ascertain it.[133]

Evidence of witnesses and video evidence has also been used to establish age.[134] In *Lubanga*, non-expert witnesses gave evidence as to the age of alleged child soldiers based upon their personal assessments of the physical appearance, physical development and overall development of each individual.[135] The Defence argued that these unverified, personal assessments were unreliable, and failed to establish beyond reasonable doubt that there were children under 15 in the armed groups.[136] In its Judgment, the Trial Chamber gave assurances that it had exercised caution when considering the evidence given by non-expert witnesses,[137] but that it was feasible for non-expert witnesses to distinguish between a child who was undoubtedly under 15 years old and one who was undoubtedly over.[138] The Prosecution also relied upon video evidence to show that some of the recruits were 'visibly' under 15. This evidence was challenged by the Defence on the grounds that it was difficult to determine from the videos whether the children were above or below the age of 15. In response, the Chamber confirmed that it would only rely on such evidence if the video clearly depicted children who were under the age of 15.[139]

Proving the age of a child is always difficult. Indeed, this would be a valid reason to raise the age for the war crimes of recruitment and 'use' of child soldiers to 18, in line with other international treaties. This would mean that in cases where the age of the children involved is unclear, the measure of error would be higher. At present, perpetrators are given the benefit of the doubt regarding children who are on the cusp of 15. Raising the age to 18 would mean that most 13- and 14-year-olds would be identified as being under the age limit, and it would be older children, 16- or 17-year-olds, who would be likely to fall through the net.

6.6 Conclusion

This chapter has argued that there are three distinct war crimes of conscription, enlistment and use of children under 15 to participate actively in hostilities within

132 *RUF* case TC, para. 1703.
133 Ibid., paras 1704 and 1745.
134 *Lubanga* TC, paras 645–758.
135 Ibid., paras 641–642.
136 Ibid., para. 642.
137 'Even allowing for a wide margin of error in assessing an individual's age, the Chamber has concluded that it is feasible for non-expert witnesses to differentiate between a child who is undoubtedly less than 15 years old and a child who is undoubtedly over 15.' *Lubanga* TC, para. 643.
138 Ibid., para. 642.
139 Ibid., para. 644. A similar approach was taken at the SCSL; see *AFRC* case TC, para. 1246, and *Taylor* TC, para. 1361.

the relevant provisions of the SCSL and ICC Statutes. This is because each of the three conducts have individual elements of crime. The distinction between the crimes of conscription and enlistment is one of compulsion. If compulsion is present, the crime is one of conscription; if the child consented to join the armed force or group, the crime is one of enlistment. Distinguishing between the manner of recruitment and the 'use' of the child has proven difficult at times. Some of the earlier cases predicated the crimes of conscription and enlistment on their use – that the children had to have been enlisted or conscripted for the purpose of being used to participate actively in hostilities. This approach blurs the distinction between the offences. Certainly, in a situation where a particular military group does not have an obvious recruitment procedure, it may be necessary to examine whether the children in question have been subject to military training, or have been used to actively participate in hostilities, in order to determine whether they have been recruited into the group. This is not an obligatory requirement, however. As with adults, children can be recruited to fulfil various roles within a military organisation and not all are recruited for the purpose of being used to participate actively in hostilities. Accordingly, children who may not have been the victims of the crime of 'use' – for example, children who have been used to collect food, to carry out domestic chores or to provide sexual services – could, nevertheless, have been victims of the crimes of enlistment or conscription. All will depend upon the facts of the particular case.

The ICC Appeals Chamber has confirmed that there is a distinction between the term 'to participate actively in hostilities' as found in the context of the war crime involving child soldiers, and the terms APH/DPH as they occur in IHL in the context of the distinction between civilians and combatants. This should allay concerns that child soldiers will lose protection in an IHL context if a wider interpretation of 'participating actively in hostilities' is applied in the context of the war crime of using child soldiers. The *Lubanga* Appeals Chamber held that in order for an act to constitute 'use' there must be a link between the activity for which the child is used and the combat in which the armed force or group of the perpetrator is engaged. This is a broad test, and it remains to be seen how it will be applied in future cases involving this fledgling crime.

7 Peacekeepers

Peacekeeping has become a well-accepted tool within the arsenal of the UN when dealing with volatile situations around the world. The notion of peacekeeping is not referred to within the UN Charter; rather, it is a concept that grew out of necessity and has evolved over time.[1] Peacekeeping is a complex activity, making it difficult to define. Every conflict or post-conflict situation is unique, and every peacekeeping mission has to respond and adapt to the needs of the particular situation in which it is engaged.[2] Peacekeeping forces are involved in some of the most dangerous, violent and unpredictable situations in the world,[3] and over the past few decades peacekeepers have increasingly become the victim of attacks.[4] Cases involving crimes against peacekeepers have been considered by the ICTY, ICTR, SCSL and ICC, reflecting perhaps the preponderance of attacks against peacekeepers in conflicts throughout the world, as well as the importance that is attached to prosecuting those responsible.[5]

Although peacekeepers are civilians, they can be drawn into the fighting. Cases involving alleged crimes committed against peacekeepers require ICTs to pay

1 'The concept of peace-keeping evolved soon after the United Nations was founded, born of necessity as a largely improvised response to the times.' United Nations, *The Blue Helmets, A Review of United Nations Peace-Keeping* (United Nations Publication, 1996), p. 3. United Nations Peacekeeping Operations, Principles and Guidelines (2008), available at: http://pbpu.unlb.org/pbps/library/capstone_doctrine_eng.pdf (Capstone Doctrine).

2 'Peacekeeping operations range from large military deployments to small observer forces, from complex integrated missions to specialist police, rule of law and other civilian operations. The flexible manner in which the Security Council has employed UN peacekeeping prevents easy definition or categorisation.' United Nations, *Department of Peacekeeping Operations and Department of Field Support, A New Partnership Agenda, Charting a New Horizon for UN Peacekeeping*, July 2009, p. 2, available at: www.un.org/en/peacekeeping/documents/newhorizon.pdf.

3 For a list of current UN operations, see www.un.org/en/peacekeeping/resources/statistics/factsheet.shtml.

4 See UN Document, *Fatalities by Year*, available at: www.un.org/en/peacekeeping/resources/statistics/fatalities.shtml.

5 For an article discussing the difficulties of prosecuting these types of cases, see Mohamed A. Bangura, 'Prosecuting the Crime of Attack on Peacekeepers: A Prosecutor's Challenge', 23(1)*Leiden Journal of International Law* 165–181 (2010).

particular attention to whether peacekeeping personnel have retained their civilian status or whether their conduct amounted to DPH, as both may affect their victimhood in ICL.

This chapter begins by briefly recounting the facts of each of the cases that have involved attacks against peacekeepers in ICL to date. It then explores the war crime of attacking peacekeepers, followed by cases involving peacekeepers as victims of other serious violations of the laws or customs of war, and finally, peacekeepers as victims of crimes against humanity.

7.1 Cases concerning peacekeepers in ICL

To date, alleged crimes against peacekeepers have been considered by the ICTR in the *Bagosora* case;[6] the SCSL in the *RUF* case;[7] the Pre-Trial Chamber of the ICC in the *Abu Garda*[8] and *Banda* Decisions;[9] and the ICTY in the *Karadžić*[10] case. In order to understand the following discussion, it might prove helpful to provide a short summary of the background to each case.

7.1.1 ICTR: Bagosora *case*

Bagosora concerned events that took place in the aftermath of the assassination of the Rwandan President Habyarimana on 6 April 1994. The president was killed when his plane was shot down as it prepared to land in Kigali. That night, peacekeepers from the United Nations Assistance Mission in Rwanda (UNAMIR) were sent to Prime Minister Uwilingiyimana's residence, with a view to escorting her to Radio Rwanda, where she was to address the nation the following morning. The escort comprised both Ghanaian and Belgian peacekeepers. In the early hours of 7 April, the prime minister's residence came under attack by the Rwandan army.[11] The peacekeepers were disarmed and taken to a Rwandan army camp. Soon after their arrival, the Belgian peacekeepers were surrounded by a crowd of Rwandan soldiers, who began beating them, ostensibly because they believed that they were involved in the assassination of the president. Four of the Belgian peacekeepers[12]

6 *Prosecutor v Bagosora et al*, ICTR-98-41-T, Trial Judgment, 18 December 2008 (*Bagosora*, TC).
7 *Prosecutor v Issa Hassan Sesay, Morris Kallon and Augustine Gbao*, SCSL-2004-15-T, Trial Judgment, 2 March 2009 (*RUF* case TC).
8 *Prosecutor v Bahar Idriss Abu Garda*, Decision on the Confirmation of Charges, ICC-02/05-02/09, 8 February 2010 (*Abu Garda* Decision).
9 *Prosecutor v Abdallah Banda Abakaer Nourain and Saleh Mohammed Jerbo Jamus*, Corrigendum of the 'Decision on the Confirmation of Charges', ICC-02/05-03/09, 7 March 2011 (*Banda* Decision).
10 *Prosecutor v Radovan Karadžić*, IT-95-5/18-T, 24 March 2016 (*Karadžić*, TC). The *Mladić* case also concerns attacks against peacekeepers, but at the time of writing the trial is still underway, see *Prosecutor v Ratko Mladić*, ICTY, Fourth Amended Indictment, IT-09-92-PT, 16 December 2011, Count 11 – Taking of Hostages.
11 *Bagosora* TC, paras 15–18.
12 The Ghanaian peacekeepers were left largely unharmed, ibid., para. 787.

were beaten to death by the mob. The remaining six Belgian peacekeepers were able to break away and barricade themselves in an office. They succeeded in disarming a Rwandan soldier, and were able to use the firearm to defend themselves for some hours. Later that day, grenades were launched at the office in which they were sheltering, killing the remaining peacekeepers.[13] The accused were charged with both murder as a crime against humanity, and violence to life and outrages upon personal dignity as violations of the laws or customs of war, as regards the attacks against the peacekeepers.

7.1.2 SCSL: RUF *case*

The part of the *RUF* case involving attacks against peacekeepers concerned events that took place in Sierra Leone from 15 April until 15 September 2000.[14] Following a peace agreement between the government of Sierra Leone and the RUF, a peacekeeping force was created: the United Nations Mission in Sierra Leone (UNAMSIL).[15] UNAMSIL's original mandate was to cooperate with the government of Sierra Leone and the RUF in implementing the peace agreement; to assist in the disarmament, demobilisation and reintegration of combatants; to monitor adherence to the ceasefire; and to facilitate in the delivery of humanitarian assistance.[16]

Members of the RUF became dissatisfied with the disarmament process.[17] An incident took place involving Gbao, one of the accused, at a UNAMSIL reception centre,[18] which culminated in RUF soldiers abducting a peacekeeper.[19] The situation escalated, with more peacekeepers being abducted from the same camp.[20] The unrest spread and similar incidents took place at other locations.[21] Over the following months, over 100 peacekeepers were abducted and threatened. Several were killed and injured.[22] Eventually, the situation was resolved and the abducted peacekeepers were released.[23]

The accused persons were charged with four different offences regarding their alleged maltreatment of the peacekeepers: first, the war crime of attacking

13 Ibid., paras 783–789, and para. 2174.

14 *Prosecutor v Issa Hassan Sesay, Morris Kallon and Augustine Gbao*, SCSL-2004-15-PT, Corrected Amended Consolidated Indictment, 2 August 2006, para. 83.

15 See *RUF* case TC, para. 1749, and see Article XVI Lomé Peace Agreement and UN Security Council Resolution 1270, 22 October 1999. UNAMSIL was composed of different units see ibid., paras 1752–1758.

16 Ibid., para. 1750, referring to UN Security Council Resolution 1270, para. 8. The mandate was extended, see ibid., para. 1751; and UN Security Council Resolution 1289. See *RUF* case TC, paras 1751–1753 regarding the disarmament process.

17 Ibid., paras 1764–1769.

18 Ibid., paras 1785–1794.

19 Ibid., paras 1793–1794.

20 Ibid., paras 1795–1822.

21 Ibid., paras 1823–1868.

22 Ibid.

23 Ibid., paras 1869–1883.

peacekeepers; second, murder as a crime against humanity;[24] third, murder as a war crime; and finally, the war crime of taking of hostages.[25]

7.1.3 ICC: Abu Garda *and* Banda *cases*

The ICC cases both concern the same incident – the attacking of a base belonging to the African Union Mission in Sudan (AMIS) in north Darfur by Justice and Equality Movement forces (JEM) and Sudan Liberation Army (SLA) forces. AMIS was deployed to north Darfur in June 2004 in order to monitor the ceasefire agreement between the government of Sudan and the SLA and JEM.[26] On 29 September 2007, a surprise attack was launched against an AMIS base, culminating in the deaths and serious injury of several peacekeepers, and the destruction and looting of property belonging to the mission.

The charges faced by the accused in both cases include the killing of 12 AMIS peacekeeping personnel and the attempted murder of eight as a war crime of violence to life under Article 8(2)(c)(i) of the ICC Statute, as well as the war crime of attacking peacekeeping personnel under Article 8(2)(e)(iii).[27]

On 8 February 2010, Pre-Trial Chamber I refused to confirm the charges against Abu Garda due to a lack of evidence that he was a perpetrator or a co-perpetrator under Article 25 of the ICC Statute.[28] In *Banda*, a Decision on the Confirmation of Charges was issued on 7 March 2011. The *Banda* Decision followed the factual findings made in the *Abu Garda* Decision, thus throughout this chapter most reference will be made to the *Abu Garda* Decision.[29]

7.1.4 ICTY: Karadžić *case*

The *Karadžić* case concerns the taking hostage of over 200 UN peacekeepers by Bosnian Serb forces in May 1995 in response to air strikes by the North Atlantic Treaty Organization (NATO) on Bosnian Serb military targets. Some were taken to locations of military significance, and some were physically mistreated.[30] Threats were made by the Bosnian Serb forces against the UN personnel that they would be killed if NATO launched further air strikes, and these threats were communicated to the UN.[31] The accused was charged with the crime of hostage-taking based on Common Article 3.

24 Article 2, SCSL Statute.
25 Articles 3(a) and 3(c), SCSL Statute, respectively.
26 *Abu Garda* Decision, para. 97.
27 They were also charged with the crime of looting under Article 8(2)(e)(v).
28 *Abu Garda* Decision, paras 234–236.
29 *Banda* Decision, paras 63–64.
30 For example, see *Karadžić* TC, paras 5863, 5900 and 5918–5919.
31 Ibid., para. 5937.

7.2 The war crime of attacking peacekeeping personnel

Both the ICC and the SCSL Statutes contain a specific war crime of attacking peacekeepers. The two provisions are identical, and provide that '[i]ntentionally directing attacks against personnel, installations, material, units or vehicles involved in a humanitarian assistance or peacekeeping mission in accordance with the Charter of the United Nations, as long as they are entitled to the protection given to civilians or civilian objects under the international law of armed conflict' is a serious violation of the laws and customs of war.[32] The origins of the crime are to be found in the 1994 Convention on the Safety of United Nations and Associated Personnel (Safety Convention),[33] and in the 1996 International Law Commission's Draft Code of Crimes against the Peace and Security of Mankind (Draft Code),[34] which included crimes against UN and associated personnel as a separate category of crime.[35]

During the negotiation period for the ICC Statute, it was envisaged that violations of the Safety Convention would form one of three treaty-based crimes to be included in the Statute.[36] It was only towards the end of the negotiations, when it became clear that treaty-based crimes were not going to be included, that attention was turned to including a specific war crimes provision concerning attacks against UN personnel.[37]

Some commentators have queried the need to include a separate provision in the ICC Statute to protect peacekeepers, as in order for peacekeeping personnel to qualify as victims under the provision, they must be entitled to civilian protection in any case, meaning the attacks could be encompassed by Articles 8(2)(b)(i) or 8(2)(e)(i) as intentionally directing attacks against the civilian population as such

32 Articles 8(2)(b)(iii) and 8(2)(e)(iii), ICC Statute and Article 4(b), SCSL Statute. This chapter discusses the crime in the context of attacks against peacekeeping personnel only; to date, no case has considered attacks against personnel of humanitarian missions. The *Abu Garda* Decision considered attacks against the objects connected with a peacekeeping mission, see *Abu Garda* Decision, paras 85–89 and 133–149.

33 The Safety Convention is partly concerned with the prosecution and punishment at a national level of those who attack the United Nations and associated personnel. See Articles 7, Safety Convention. For a discussion of the Convention see M. Christiane Bourloyannis-Vrailas, 'Crimes against United Nations and Associated Personnel', in Gabrielle Kirk McDonald and Olivia Swaak-Goldman, *Substantive and Procedural Aspects of International Criminal Law, The Experience of International and National Courts* (Kluwer Law International, 2000), Vol. I, pp. 342–350; and Ola Engdahl, *Protection of Personnel in Peace Operations, The Role of the 'Safety Convention' against the Background of General International Law* (Martinus Nijhoff Publishers, 2007), chapter 5.

34 Article 19, Draft Code.

35 Bourloyannis-Vrailas, *supra* FN 33, p. 351.

36 Michael Cottier, 'War Crimes', in Otto Triffterer, *Commentary on the Rome Statute of the International Criminal Court* (C.H. Beck, Hart, Nomos, 2008), para. 37. The other treaty-based crimes were terrorism and drug trafficking.

37 Ibid., para. 37. Once the prohibition became a war crime, its scope was extended to include humanitarian missions.

or against individual civilians not DPH.[38] Bothe, for example, suggests that there is a risk that having a separate provision for peacekeeping personnel detracts from the general protection extended to civilians.[39] Cottier, too, wonders why a separate provision is required; however, he explains that:

> Delegations felt a need to explicitly condemn and criminalize attacks against humanitarian assistance and peacekeeping missions and thereby visibly signal the exceptional seriousness of such most serious crimes of international concern.[40]

Arguably, it was necessary to include a separate war crime of attacking peacekeepers in the ICC Statute. First, as Cottier indicates, singling out peacekeepers in this way highlights the importance that the international community attaches to the prosecution of this crime.[41] Second, while it may be true that the war crimes provisions in the ICC Statute concerning attacks against civilians and civilian objects under Articles 8(2)(b)(i) and (ii) encompass the personnel and objects covered in Article 8(2)(b)(iii), in NIACs the situation is different. Articles 8(2)(d) and (e) of the Statute do not contain a provision equivalent to Article 8(2)(b)(ii) concerning attacks against civilian objects. Accordingly, without Article 8(2)(e)(iii), attacks against objects associated with peacekeeping or humanitarian assistance missions in NIACs would not constitute a war crime under the ICC Statute.

A further reason why a separate provision is necessary is that it removes any question mark as to whether peacekeepers are entitled to lay claim to civilian status.[42] That peacekeepers are entitled to civilian status may be said to be implicit in the Safety Convention. Article 2(2) of the Convention states that:

> This Convention shall not apply to a United Nations operation authorized by the Security Council as an enforcement action under Chapter VII of the Charter of the United Nations in which any of the personnel are engaged as

38 Daniel Frank, 'Article 8(2)(b)(iii) – Attacking Personnel or Objects Involved in a Humanitarian Assistance or Peacekeeping Mission', in Roy S. Lee (ed.), *The International Criminal Court: Elements of Crimes and Rules of Procedure and Evidence* (Ardsey, NY, Transnational Publishers Inc., 2001), p. 145. Also see *RUF* case TC, para. 215.

39 Michael Bothe, 'War Crimes', in Cassese *et al* (ed.), *The Rome Statute of the International Criminal Court: A Commentary* (Oxford University Press, 2002), Vol. I, p. 411.

40 Cottier, *supra* FN 36, para. 37. However, see Bourloyannis-Vrailas who argues that the crime of attacking peacekeepers should be a category of crime in its own right. Bourloyannis-Vrailas, *supra* FN 33, p. 364

41 Cottier, *supra* FN 36, para. 37.

42 See Alice Gadler, 'The Protection of Peacekeepers and International Criminal Law: Legal Challenges and Broader Protection', 11 *German Law Journal* 585 (2010), pp. 588–589; and Andrea Spagnolo, 'The Crime of Attacking Peacekeepers', in Pocar *et al*, *War Crimes and the Conduct of Hostilities, Challenges to Adjudication and Investigation* (Edward Elgar, 2013), pp. 156–157.

combatants against organized armed forces to which the law of international armed conflict applies.

That UN personnel who are involved in enforcement actions are combatants implies that those who are involved in missions which do not constitute enforcement actions are civilians. However, in the *Bagosora* case from the ICTR, discussed in more detail below, the Trial Chamber did not explicitly find that the peacekeepers in question had civilian status; rather, it implied that it viewed the peacekeepers as being persons *hors de combat*. It is not, therefore, a foregone conclusion that the ICC would view peacekeepers as constituting civilians for the purpose of Articles 8(2)(b)(i) or 8(2)(e)(i). The insertion of a specific provision in the Statute removes any doubt that may have existed on the matter.

The Elements of Crimes for the ICC Statute state that for the war crime of attacking peacekeeping personnel to be proven, it must be shown that:

1 The perpetrator directed an attack.
2 The object of the attack was personnel, installations, material, units or vehicles involved in a humanitarian assistance or peacekeeping mission in accordance with the Charter of the United Nations.
3 The perpetrator intended such personnel, installations, material, units or vehicles to be the object of the attack.
4 Such personnel, installations, material, units or vehicles were entitled to that protection given to civilians or civilian objects under the international law of armed conflict.
5 The perpetrator was aware of the factual circumstances that established that protection.

In the *RUF* case, the Trial Chamber of the SCSL largely followed the ICC's Elements of Crimes.[43] Let us now consider how the ICC and the SCSL have interpreted each of the elements.

7.2.1 The perpetrator directed an attack

When interpreting the term 'attack', both the ICC and the SCSL referred to the definition given in Article 49(1) of Protocol I, namely that of 'acts of violence against the adversary, whether in offence or in defence'.[44] Both courts have held that there is no requirement that actual damage be caused to the peacekeeping personnel for the crime to be made out.[45]

43 *RUF* case TC, para. 219. The one difference between the two lists of elements is addressed below.
44 *Abu Garda* Decision, para. 65, confirmed in *Banda* Decision, para. 61; and *RUF* case TC, para. 220.
45 *Abu Garda* Decision, para. 65; and *RUF* case TC, para. 220. Also see Knut Dörmann, *Elements of War Crimes under the Rome Statute of the International Criminal Court* (Cambridge University Press, 2003), p. 153; Cottier, *supra* FN 36, para. 57.

The term 'attack' can be interpreted narrowly or widely.[46] A narrow interpretation would be along the lines of that given by the ICRC Commentary, which defines 'attack' as found in Article 49(1) as 'combat action'.[47] This excludes some acts that are criminalised under the Safety Convention, for example kidnapping, from falling within the ambit of the war crime of attacking peacekeepers.[48] Cottier argues that, in the context of the ICC Statute, a narrow interpretation is suggested by the positioning of the relevant articles immediately after Articles 8(2)(b)(i) and 8(2)(e)(i), indicating that the drafters intended that the interpretation of 'attack' be equivalent. He notes that attacks against the person or liberty of civilians can be prosecuted under other provisions of the ICC Statute, for example as hostage-taking or unlawful confinement,[49] and argues that if the meaning of 'attack' Article 8(2)(b)(iii) does go beyond a strict Hague Law interpretation, it might be preferable to limit such an extension to specific offences such as kidnapping of humanitarian or peacekeeping personnel rather than extend the meaning to the whole range of (serious) attacks upon the person or liberty.[50]

The ICTY has consistently held that attacks involving civilians and the civilian population 'must have caused deaths and/or serious bodily injuries',[51] thereby excluding acts such as kidnapping from being included within the concept of 'attack'. In contrast, neither the ICC Statute nor the Elements of Crimes stipulates that there be evidence of a consequence; all that is required is that an attack occurred,[52] meaning that acts such as kidnapping could potentially be included as an 'attack'.[53]

The Trial Chamber in the *RUF* case gave consideration to what conduct amounts to an attack against peacekeepers.[54] It found that in view of the fact that peacekeepers are often involved in precarious situations where tensions remain high, threats in themselves are not sufficient to amount to an attack.[55] An act of violence against a peacekeeper requires 'a forceful interference which endangers

46 Thus, Cottier asks: 'Is the notion of "attacks" in this provision limited to the meaning it has in a strict Hague Law perspective of restrictions on the means and methods of warfare?' Cottier, *supra* FN 36, para. 57.

47 ICRC Commentary to Protocol I, para. 1880.

48 Article 9(1)(a), Safety Convention.

49 Cottier, *supra* FN 36, para. 57.

50 Ibid., para. 57; and see Bourloyannis-Vrailas, *supra* FN 33, p. 363.

51 *Prosecutor v Tihomir Blaškić*, ICTY, IT-95-14-T, Trial Judgment, 3 March 2000, para. 180. Also see *Prosecutor v Dario Kordić and Mario Čerkez*, ICTY, IT-95-14/2-T, Trial Judgment, 26 February 2001, para. 328; and *Prosecutor v Stanislav Galić*, ICTY, IT-98-29-T, Trial Judgment, 5 December 2003, para. 56.

52 Frank writes: 'the overall wrong of this crimes is the attack against protected persons or objects in itself, and not any actual damage.' Frank *supra* FN 38, p. 142.

53 *RUF* case TC, para. 220; and *Abu Garda* Decision, para. 65; also see Gadler, *supra* FN 42, pp. 595–596.

54 In the *Abu Garda* and *Banda* Decisions, the fact that an attack took place was not in dispute; see *Abu Garda* Decision, para. 105, *Banda* Decision, para. 63.

55 This is in contrast to Article 9(1)(c) of the Safety Convention, which criminalises threats to commit any attack of the kind prohibited under the Convention.

the person or impinges on the liberty of the peacekeeper'.[56] The Chamber found the abduction of the peacekeepers in question to constitute an act of violence, even in the absence of physical injury. The nature of the attack came from the deprivation of the peacekeepers' liberty.[57] Thus, the Trial Chamber did not limit itself to a strict Hague Law interpretation of the term.[58]

Adopting an expansive interpretation is consistent with the overall rationale of viewing crimes against peacekeepers as being of international concern. There is precedent for the notion of 'attack' being interpreted differently in different contexts, in that it has different interpretations in relation to crimes against humanity than it does in the context of war crimes.[59] However, it is unsatisfactory to have two differing interpretations of the notion within the category of war crimes itself.

It remains to be seen whether the ICC will follow suit in including the abduction of peacekeepers within the definition of 'attack' in Articles 8(2)(b)(iii) and 8 (2)(e)(iii). It would be preferable to charge crimes involving the violation of peacekeepers' liberty as the war crime of taking of hostages[60] in order to ensure that the notion of 'attack' is interpreted in the same way for both the war crime of attacks against peacekeeping personnel and attacks against other civilians.[61]

7.2.2 *The object of the attack was personnel ... involved in a humanitarian assistance or peacekeeping mission in accordance with the Charter of the United Nations*

The second element of the crime requires the court to interpret the term, a 'peacekeeping mission in accordance with the Charter of the United Nations'. This concept is not legally defined and is open to different interpretations.[62]

56 *RUF* case TC, para. 1889.

57 Ibid., para. 1897. It noted also that the peacekeepers had been physically assaulted and restrained, had been under constant guard, and had been threatened with weapons.

58 However, it may have chosen to adopt an expansive interpretation due the approach it took when interpreting the crime of the taking of hostages which resulted in the accused being found not guilty of taking the peacekeepers in question hostage. For further discussion, see below.

59 'The term "attack" in the context of a crime against humanity carries a slightly different meaning than in the laws of war. In the context of a crime against humanity, "attack" is not limited to the conduct of hostilities. It may also encompass situations of mistreatment of persons taking no active part in hostilities, such as someone in detention.' *Prosecutor v Milorad Kunarac et al*, ICTY, IT-96-23-T, Trial Judgment, 22 February 2001 (*Kunarac* TC), para. 416.

60 See Articles 8(2)(a)(viii) or 8(2)(c)(iii), ICC Statute.

61 Magdalena Pacholska, '(Il)legality of Killing Peacekeepers: The Crime of Attacking Peacekeepers in the Jurisprudence of International Criminal Tribunals', 13 *Journal of International Criminal Justice* (2015) 43–72, at p. 52.

62 The Capstone Doctrine, for example, describes peacekeeping as 'a technique designed to preserve the peace, however fragile, where fighting has been halted and to assist in implementing agreements achieved by the peacemakers'. In contrast, it describes peace enforcement as 'the application, with the authorisation of the Security Council, of a

Cottier, for example, distinguishes between peacekeeping missions, which may only use force in self-defence, and peace enforcement missions, which have a mandate, or are authorised, to use force in order to achieve their objective beyond self-defence.[63] Engdahl, on the other hand, outlines three ways of approaching the term 'peacekeeping'. The first adopts a traditional approach, whereby a peacekeeping mission is one where force is permitted only in self-defence. The second employs a more dynamic approach, and would encompass 'robust' peacekeeping missions, defined as 'involv[ing] the use of force at the tactical level with the consent of the host authorities and/or the main parties to the conflict'.[64] The third approach focuses on the personnel themselves and whether they were acting as 'combatants', as referred to in the Safety Convention, rather than looking to the mandate of the mission itself.[65] Engdahl explains that '[t]hese different approaches illustrate the weakness of this element of the crime'.[66] How then have the SCSL and the ICC defined the term?

In the *RUF* case, the Trial Chamber noted that peacekeeping missions are generally created by a resolution of the UN Security Council, based either upon Chapter VI, which allows the Security Council to take non-binding measures to settle disputes between state parties; or upon Chapter VI in conjunction with Chapter VII, which allows the Security Council to adopt binding enforcement measures that are necessary to maintain or restore international peace and security.[67] The Chamber distinguished peacekeeping missions from peace enforcement actions, which are authorised by the UN Security Council under Chapter VII of the UN Charter and do not rely on the consent of the states involved, but rather on the binding authority of the Security Council.[68] However, focusing upon which Chapter of the UN Charter a mission is founded on is not necessarily

range of coercive measures, including the use of military force'. Capstone Doctrine, *supra* FN 1, p. 18.

63 Cottier, *supra* FN 36, para. 45.

64 Capstone Doctrine, *supra* FN 1, p. 19. 'Robust' mandates authorise peacekeeping missions to '"use all necessary means" to deter forceful attempts to disrupt the political process, protect civilians under imminent threat of physical attack, and/or assist the national authorities in maintaining law and order'. Ibid., p. 34.

65 Ola Engdahl, 'Prosecution of Attacks against Peacekeepers in International Courts and Tribunals', 51/2 *Military Law and the Law of War Review* 249–284 (2012), pp. 272–273.

66 Ibid., p. 273.

67 *RUF* case TC, para. 222. See James Sloan, 'Peacekeepers under Fire: Prosecuting the RUF for Attacks against the UN Assistance Mission in Sierra Leone', 9(2) *The Law and Practice of International Courts and Tribunals* 243–293 (2010), pp. 278–279, who critiques the Trial Chamber's discussion in this regard. And see Engdahl, *supra* FN 65, p. 269.

68 *RUF* case TC, para. 230. Both Engdahl and Sloan note that when considering the definition of peacekeeping mission in the *RUF* case, the Trial Chamber referred to the Capstone Doctrine from 2008, without reflecting on whether this was appropriate, given that they were considering a mission that was established in 2000. Engdahl, *supra* FN 65, p. 270; and Sloan, ibid., pp. 283–284.

the most appropriate way to ascertain whether a particular mission qualifies as a peacekeeping mission. The Capstone Doctrine explains that:

> United Nations peacekeeping operations have traditionally been associated with Chapter VI of the Charter. However, the Security Council need not refer to a specific Chapter of the Charter when passing a resolution authorizing the deployment of a United Nations peacekeeping operation and has never invoked Chapter VI ... Linking United Nations peacekeeping with a particular Chapter of the Charter can be misleading for the purposes of operational planning, training and mandate implementation.[69]

Both the Trial Chamber of the SCSL and the Pre-Trial Chamber of the ICC found three principles to be fundamental to peacekeeping missions: (i) consent of the parties; (ii) impartiality; and (iii) the non-use of force except in self-defence.[70] However, the two Chambers used these fundamental principles in different ways. The SCSL did not concentrate unduly upon applying the principles to the facts of the case when reaching its determination that UNAMSIL was a peacekeeping mission.[71] Rather, it examined the three principles when determining whether UNAMSIL peacekeepers had been entitled to civilian protection.[72] In contrast, the Pre-Trial Chamber of the ICC did consider the three principles in the *Abu Garda* case when determining whether there were substantial grounds to believe that AMIS was a peacekeeping mission.[73] Which was the best approach will be considered shortly.

The first principle requires that the main parties had consented to the mission.[74] Both the *RUF* case and the *Abu Garda* Decision found that, at a minimum, the host state must consent to the mission and, in practice, the consent of all parties to the conflict is sought.[75] Thus, in *Abu Garda*, consent to the presence of the AMIS

69 Capstone Doctrine, *supra* FN 1, p. 14.

70 *RUF* case TC, para. 225; and *Abu Garda* Decision, paras 69–71 and para. 106. These three principles are to be found in the Capstone Doctrine, *supra* FN 1, p. 31 and in the *Report of the Panel on United Nations Peace Operations*, A/55/305, S/2000/809 (2000), available at: www.unrol.org/files/brahimi%20report%20peacekeeping.pdf ('the Brahimi Report'), p. ix and para. 48 which states 'consent of the local parties, impartiality and use of force only in self-defence should remain the bedrock principles of peacekeeping' (para. 48). However, Sloan writes that '[t]o characterize these three elements as essential is an oversimplification'. Sloan, *supra* FN 67, p. 279.

71 *RUF* TC, para. 1888; and see paras 1749–1751. Also see Sloan's critique of the Trial Chamber's findings, Sloan, *supra* FN 67, pp. 280–284.

72 *RUF* case TC, paras 1906–1911.

73 *Abu Garda* Decision, para. 119; and *Banda* Decision, para. 63.

74 *RUF* case TC, para. 226; and *Abu Garda* Decision, para. 72.

75 *Abu Garda* Decision, para. 72, making reference to the Brahimi Report, *supra* FN 70. In the *RUF* case, the Trial Chamber noted that in NIACs such consent is obtained from the warring parties not out of an obligation, but rather to ensure the effectiveness of the operation in question. *RUF* case TC, para. 226. However, see Pacholska who criticises this approach. Pacholska, *supra* FN 61, p. 49.

mission had been obtained from both the host state and the other parties involved in the conflict in Darfur.[76]

Second, the mission has to be impartial.[77] Both courts adopted the Brahimi Report's understanding of this concept, finding that 'impartiality is not to be confused with neutrality or inactivity', and that impartiality must involve 'adherence to the principles of the Charter and the objectives of a mandate'.[78] In *Abu Garda*, the Chamber had regard to the terms of the mandate of AMIS, which stated that it was an independent monitoring mission that was required to treat all parties to the conflict in an impartial manner, and the evidence indicated that this had also happened in practice.[79]

Finally, the mission must not use force other than in self-defence. In *Abu Garda*, the Chamber noted the distinction between peacekeeping missions, which can only use force in self-defence, and peace enforcement missions.[80] It had regard to the terms of the mandate and Rules of Engagement for AMIS, as well as the training that its personnel had received, noting that AMIS personnel were permitted to use force to protect civilians whom they encountered under immediate threat and who were in the immediate vicinity of its personnel.[81] The Chamber concluded that AMIS personnel were authorised to use force only in self-defence.[82]

When considering the concept of self-defence in the *RUF* case, the Trial Chamber found that force may only be used as a measure of last resort.[83] It held that the concept of self-defence for these missions has evolved to include the 'right to resist attempts by forceful means to prevent the peacekeeping operation from discharging its duties under the mandate of the Security Council'.[84] In making this statement, the Trial Chamber was referring to the Capstone Doctrine. However, the passage is slightly misquoted in the Judgment. The Capstone Doctrine actually states:

> The notion of self-defense has subsequently come to include resistance to attempts by forceful means to prevent the peacekeeping operations from discharging its duties under the mandate of the Security Council.[85]

The Capstone Doctrine does not speak of a peacekeeping mission as having a 'right to resist' to defend their mandate. Engdahl argues that '[u]sing force in defence of a mandate may … in effect blur the line between peacekeeping and peace enforcement'.[86] While Sloan writes:

76 *Abu Garda* Decision, paras 107–109.
77 Ibid., paras 73 and 110–112; and see Sloan, *supra* FN 67, pp. 281–282.
78 *Abu Garda* Decision, para. 73; and RUF TC, para. 227, referring to Brahimi Report, *supra* FN 70, para. 50.
79 *Abu Garda* Decision, paras 110–112; and *RUF* case TC, para. 227.
80 *Abu Garda* Decision, para. 74.
81 Ibid., para. 115.
82 Ibid., para. 118, and see paras 113–118. Also see *Banda* Decision, para. 63.
83 *RUF* case TC, paras 225–228.
84 Ibid., para. 228, referring to the Capstone Doctrine, *supra* FN 1, p. 34.
85 Capstone Doctrine, *supra* FN 1, p. 34.
86 Engdahl, *supra* FN 65, p. 271 and see p. 270.

> While it is indeed the case that the UN practice is such that self-defence is taken to include defence of the mandate, it is also the case that such an understanding potentially denudes the concept of 'self-defence' of much of its meaning.[87]

Any ICT assessing a situation where peacekeepers had acted in defence of their mandate would, therefore, have to be very careful to ensure that the actions of the peacekeepers fell within the narrow parameters of self-defence in ICL.

The final part of this element requires that the peacekeeping mission be established 'in accordance with the Charter of the United Nations'. In *Abu Garda*, the Pre-Trial Chamber interpreted this as including both missions established by the UN and missions that are otherwise foreseen by the UN Charter.[88] Previous to the *Abu Garda* Decision, some commentators had queried whether the provision would extend to missions acting under a regional mandate, rather than under a mandate of the UN.[89] Interpreting the element of the crime to include such missions is to be welcomed.

7.2.3 The perpetrator intended such personnel … to be the object of the attack

The offence has a specific *mens rea* requirement,[90] that the accused intended that personnel, installations, material, units or vehicles be the object of the attack. In the *Abu Garda* Decision, it was noted that the *mens rea* for the offence is similar to that for Articles 8(2)(b)(i) and 8(2)(e)(i) concerning attacks on civilians.[91] In the *RUF* case, when assessing the evidence, the Trial Chamber considered that the perpetrators knew and recognised the UNAMSIL peacekeepers, and that the peacekeepers had been specifically targeted. The fact that the attacks were committed in a brief period and in close proximity to each other showed that the RUF launched a deliberate and concerted campaign of violence against the peacekeepers.[92]

7.2.4 Such personnel … were entitled to that protection given to civilians or civilian objects under the international law of armed conflict

The fourth element of the crime requires that it be shown that the peacekeeping personnel concerned were entitled to protection as civilians under IHL. During the drafting process for the ICC Statute, it was suggested that there be further

87 Sloan, *supra* FN 67, p. 282.

88 *Abu Garda* Decision, para. 75, and see para. 76, referring to Articles 52(1) and 53(1), UN Charter. The Chamber found that AMIS had been established under the auspices of the African Union with a mandate to maintain peace and security in compliance with Chapter VII of the UN Charter. *Abu Garda* Decision, paras 120–125.

89 Bangura, *supra* FN 5, pp. 172–174.

90 *RUF* case TC, para. 232; and *Abu Garda* Decision, para. 93.

91 *Abu Garda* Decision, para. 93.

92 *Abu Garda* Decision, paras 1901–1905.

differentiation made between the personnel protected by the provision – into civilian and military humanitarian workers, and peacekeepers who were not combatants. Ultimately, it was decided that:

> The combatant status of a person would not depend on a decision of the Security Council to take a resolution on the basis of Chapter VI or VII of the Charter of the United Nations. The only relevant criteria would be the notion of 'combatant status' according to the pre-requisites of humanitarian law, as well as the actual conduct of the members of the respective mission.[93]

The approaches taken by the SCSL and the ICC will be considered in turn.

(i) RUF *case*

When interpreting this element of the crime in the *RUF* case, the Trial Chamber stated:

> It is … the Chamber's view that by force of logic, personnel of peacekeeping missions are entitled to protection as long as they are not taking a direct part in hostilities – and thus have become combatants – at the time of the alleged offence. Where peacekeepers become combatants, they can be legitimate targets for the extent of their participation in accordance with international humanitarian law.[94]

It may be that the Trial Chamber chose to use the word 'combatant' in this paragraph to mirror the use of the word in Article 2(2) of the Safety Convention. Nevertheless, the use of the term here is unfortunate. Combatants are military targets at all times unless *hors de combat*. Persons *hors de combat* do not have civilian status; their status is that of a person *hors de combat*. The use of the term by the Trial Chamber in the above passage could be interpreted as meaning that once a peacekeeper DPH, their status changes from civilian to combatant, with the result that they permanently lose their protection from attack and, therefore, their eligibility to be a victim of the war crime of attacking peacekeepers. However, the Chamber then goes on to state: 'Where peacekeepers become combatants, they can be legitimate targets *for the extent of their participation*' (emphasis added).

What the Trial Chamber seems to be trying to convey is that once peacekeepers DPH they lose their civilian protection and become legitimate targets, during which time they cannot be victims of the crime of attacking peacekeeping personnel. As soon as they cease to DPH, civilian protection is regained.[95] The use of

93 Frank, *supra* FN 38, p. 146.
94 *RUF* case TC, para. 233.
95 This accords with Article 51(3) of Protocol I, which states 'civilians shall enjoy the protection afforded by this section, unless and for such time as they take a direct part in hostilities'.

the word 'combatant' by the Trial Chamber in this instance is inaccurate and causes unnecessary confusion.

In order to establish whether UNAMSIL personnel were entitled to protection as civilians, the Trial Chamber stated that it:

> must consider the totality of the circumstances existing at the time of the alleged offence, including *inter alia*, the relevant Security Council resolutions for the operation, the specific operational mandates, the role and practices actually adopted by the peacekeeping mission during the particular conflict, their rules of engagement and operational orders, the nature of the arms and equipment used by the peacekeeping force and the parties in the conflict, the nature and frequency of such force and the conduct of the alleged victim(s) and their fellow personnel.[96]

The Chamber examined several different sources of evidence. First, it considered the terms of UNAMSIL's mandate.[97] It found that the mission was empowered by Chapter VII of the UN Charter to use force in certain exceptional and restricted circumstances, but this did not alter its fundamental nature as a peacekeeping, rather than a peace enforcement, mission.[98] Second, it looked at UNAMSIL's Operational Orders and Rules of Engagement,[99] finding that these permitted the peacekeepers to use force only in self-defence, in defence of civilians, or to ensure freedom of movement of UN personnel.[100] Third, the practice of UNAMSIL and its interaction with the RUF was scrutinised, and the mission was found to have acted in accordance with its mandate.[101] Fourth, the nature of the arms and equipment used by the peacekeeping personnel was considered. They had been lightly armed, or in the case of the military observers, unarmed, and it was noted that they would not have had the capacity to cause significant harm to the RUF should open combat have arisen.[102] Finally, the Chamber considered each individual incident in the case to see whether the peacekeeping personnel had been DPH at the time.[103] It concluded that on the occasions when peacekeepers had responded to the attacks with force, the force used had been proportionate and justified in self-defence.[104] Accordingly, the peacekeepers had not been DPH and had been entitled to protection as civilians.[105]

96 Ibid., para. 234. Also see para. 1906.
97 Ibid., paras 1907–1911.
98 Ibid., para. 1911.
99 Ibid., paras 1912–1917.
100 Ibid., para. 1917.
101 Ibid., paras 1918–1923.
102 Ibid., para. 1924.
103 Ibid., paras 1926–1936.
104 'The evidence indicates that the purpose of the use of force by UNAMSIL personnel was to defend themselves; to defend personnel under their protection (including any disarmed fighters); and to escape from the RUF attack.' Ibid., para. 1941, and see ibid., paras 1932 and 1933.
105 Ibid., para. 1937.

Was it really necessary for the Trial Chamber to undertake such a wide-ranging examination in order to determine whether the peacekeepers in question had been entitled to civilian status? Arguably, the answer to this is 'no'.

The Trial Chamber outlined three basic principles in order for a mission to constitute a peacekeeping mission (consent, impartiality, and using force only in self-defence). However, the Chamber did not investigate whether the UNAMSIL mission had in fact fulfilled these conditions when concluding that they qualified as a peacekeeping mission for the purposes of the crime.[106] Rather, they considered these matters when determining whether the peacekeeping personnel qualified for civilian status.

A more logical course of action would be to consider the terms of the mandate of a mission and their Rules of Engagement when determining whether the mission qualified as a peacekeeping mission.[107] In the event that the answer is in the negative, the mission's personnel cannot be victims of this crime; if the answer is in the affirmative, it means that the mission's personnel are *prima facie* entitled to protection as civilians. The fourth element of the crime requires the court to examine whether the peacekeepers who were attacked were entitled to protection as civilians at the time of the attack. This involves the court asking itself two questions: first, despite the fact that the mission was a peacekeeping mission, had it in fact become a party to the conflict? If the answer to this is 'yes', the mission's personnel are combatants and cannot be victims of this war crime.[108] If the answer is 'no', the peacekeeping personnel are entitled to civilian status, and the court must move on to the second question: were the personnel in question not APH/DPH at the time they were attacked? This requires the court to examine factors such as the interaction between the peacekeeping mission and the parties to the conflict, whether the peacekeepers had been armed, and what their actions were in the lead-up to, and during, the attack. This would have been a more desirable approach for the Trial Chamber to have adopted in the *RUF* case: to separate the issue of whether the mission was a peacekeeping mission from the issue of whether the peacekeeping personnel had civilian protection. Indeed, this is how the Pre-Trial Chamber of the ICC approached the matter in the *Abu Garda* Decision.

(ii) Abu Garda *Decision*

When considering whether the peacekeepers in question were entitled to civilian protection, the Pre-Trial Chamber in *Abu Garda* had regard to Article 13(3) of Protocol II, which states that civilians are protected by Part IV of the Protocol 'unless and for such time as they take a direct part in hostilities'.[109] The Pre-Trial Chamber noted that 'the same exclusion applies, under Article 2(2) of the

106 See discussion above and see ibid., para. 1988.

107 Engdahl, *supra* FN 65, p. 275.

108 Engdahl explains 'it is not impossible for peacekeepers (or possibly more accurately, members of peace operations) to become combatants'. Engdahl, *supra* FN 65, p. 277 and see p. 278.

109 *Abu Garda* Decision, paras 83 and 84.

Convention on the Safety of United Nations and Associated Personnel to personnel engaged as combatants'.[110] This statement is incorrect: the exclusion in Article 2(2) applies only to the Safety Convention, and means that UN and associated personnel who are engaged as combatants are not protected under the terms of the Convention.[111] The reference to the Safety Convention was clumsily done. That aside, the *Abu Garda* Decision is to be commended, in that it correctly regarded peacekeepers who DPH as having the status of civilians who are DPH.

The Pre-Trial Chamber considered how the concept of APH/DPH is defined,[112] concluding that:

> Personnel involved in peacekeeping missions enjoy protection from attacks unless and for such time as they take a direct part in hostilities or in combat-related activities. The Majority also finds that such protection does not cease if such persons only use armed force in exercise of their right to self-defence … any determination as to whether a person is directly participating in hostilities must be carried out on a case-by-case basis.[113]

Finally, the Pre-Trial Chamber in *Abu Garda* found that peacekeepers who are acting in self-defence are not DPH.[114] This accords with the position that a limited right to self-defence exists under IHL.[115]

Applying their legal findings to the facts of the case, the Pre-Trial Chamber found that there was no evidence that AMIS personnel DPH or used force beyond self-defence.[116] AMIS personnel had understood the terms of their mandate and that their mission was impartial.[117] They understood that they were not entitled to use force except in self-defence and to protect African Union installations, and civilians in the immediate vicinity thereof whom they found to be under imminent threat.[118] The evidence showed that AMIS had reduced activities in the area when faced with hostilities.[119] Accordingly, AMIS personnel had been entitled to civilian protection.[120]

110 Ibid., para. 78.
111 Engdahl, *supra* FN 65, p. 266.
112 *Abu Garda* Decision, paras 80–82.
113 Ibid., para. 83.
114 Also see *RUF* case TC, para. 233.
115 See discussion in Chapter 2.
116 *Abu Garda* Decision, para. 131.
117 Ibid., para. 129.
118 Ibid., para. 130.
119 Ibid., para. 131.
120 Ibid., para. 132. In the case, the Defence argued that the base had been 'used to send military orders to direct military attacks that resulted in the loss of life, so as to deprive the base of its protected status and to make that base a legitimate military objective'. *Abu Garda* Decision, para. 127, referring to ICC-02/05-02/09-T-ENG, p. 17, lines 21–24. The Defence argued that a representative from the Government of Sudan had used their presence at the base to relay information on the movement of rebel troops back to the government. The Chamber found that the representative in question had left the camp well before the attack, his departure being witnessed by members of the

In *Abu Garda* the Pre-Trial Chamber took a different approach to that taken in the *RUF* case when interpreting this element of the crime. It examined the mandate and the Rules of Engagement of the mission when deciding whether AMIS was a peacekeeping mission. As it was a peacekeeping mission, its personnel had civilian status unless and for such time as they were not DPH. The Chamber then considered whether the alleged victims in fact had been DPH at the time of the attack, concluding that they had not. It is submitted that this is the correct method to follow when determining whether this element of the crime has been met.

7.2.5 The perpetrator was aware of the factual circumstances that established that protection

The introductory comments to this section indicated that the SCSL 'largely' followed the Elements of Crimes for the ICC Statute when interpreting this crime for the purposes of the SCSL Statute. It is in relation to this element of the crime that the SCSL and the ICC differ.

The ICC Elements of Crimes requires that: 'The perpetrator was aware of the factual circumstances that established that protection.' In the *RUF* case, the Trial Chamber applied a less strict test: that the accused must have known or had reason to know that the personnel, installations, material, units or vehicles were protected.[121] The Chamber found that the knowledge need only be factual; there is no requirement to show that they had legal awareness of the protection they were entitled to under IHL.[122] When applying this to the facts of the case, the Chamber held that the conduct of the peacekeepers could not reasonably have been construed as DPH, and that:

> Even if some or all RUF fighters did subscribe to a belief that the UNAMSIL peacekeepers were taking part in hostilities, the RUF fighters had reason to know of the peacekeepers' protected status, on account of UNAMSIL's mandate as originating in the Lomé Agreement; UNAMSIL's practices in Sierra Leone and interactions with the RUF in the preceding months; the nature of UNAMSIL's arms and equipment and the use of force by peacekeepers only in self-defence.[123]

In *Abu Garda* the Pre-Trial Chamber also confirmed that there is no requirement that the perpetrator should have legal knowledge regarding the protection of the

rebel groups. It held that at the time of the attack, there were substantial grounds to believe that the objects at the compound were entitled to civilian protection. Ibid., paras 133–149.

121 *RUF* case TC, para. 235 and paras 1938–1943.

122 Ibid. For a critique of the Trial Chamber's findings in this regard, see Sloan, *supra* FN 67, pp. 290–292.

123 *RUF* case TC, para. 1942.

personnel and knowledge and that the defence of mistake of law under Article 32 of the Statute is therefore excluded.[124]

7.3 Attacks against peacekeepers as other serious violations of the laws or customs of war

Atrocities against peacekeepers can also be prosecuted as other serious violations of the laws or customs of war. In cases that concern attacks against peacekeepers during hostilities, ICTs must consider whether the peacekeeping force had become a party to the conflict, with the result that its personnel had become combatants.[125] If the peacekeeping force is found not to have been a party to the conflict, the court must look at the conduct of the personnel in question and establish that it did not amount to APH/DPH at the time of the attack. This should be considered on a case-by-case basis.[126]

In cases involving atrocities against detained peacekeepers, if the charge is one that focuses on the conduct of the victim, for example a charge founded on Common Article 3, there is no need for the court to investigate whether the peacekeeping personnel were entitled to civilian status: the fact of their detention means that they were not APH/DPH. This was the issue in the *Karadžić* case, which concerned the crime of hostage-taking as a violation of Common Article 3.[127] The Defence argued that as a consequence of the NATO airstrikes, the UN personnel had been DPH, and the peacekeeping personnel who were detained were not entitled to the protection of Common Article 3.[128] The argument was rejected by the Trial Chamber, which found that the UN and its peacekeeping forces had not been a party to the conflict, and the peacekeeping force were not combatants. At the time the UN personnel were detained, they were persons taking no APH and were protected by Common Article 3. The Chamber commented that even if the peacekeeping forces had been combatants prior to their detention, once they were detained they would have been entitled to the protection of Common Article 3 by virtue of being persons *hors de combat*.[129] Thus,

124 *Abu Garda* Decision, para. 94.

125 See for example, *Karadžić*, TC para. 5943, where the Trial Chamber found that the UN and its peacekeeping forces were not a party to the conflict and that '[w]hile the details of its operations were enlarged and strengthened over the course of the conflict in order to preserve the security of its personnel and enable the implementation of its mandate, it remained a peacekeeping force'.

126 *Abu Garda* Decision, para. 83, and *Banda* Decision, para. 102. In the *Bagosora* case the ICTR Trial Chamber confirmed that while four of the Belgian peacekeepers had obtained a weapon to defend themselves, this did not constitute DPH *Bagasora*, TC para. 2239.

127 For further consideration of the crime of taking of hostage in the context of peacekeeping personnel, see *RUF* case TC, paras 237–240, and paras 1959–1969; and *RUF* AC, paras 587–601.

128 *Prosecutor v Radovan Karadžić*, Case no IT-95-5/18-AR73.9, Appeal from Denial of Judgment for Acquittal of Hostage Taking, 25 July 2012, paras 42–52.

129 *Karadžić* TC, para. 5943. Ibid., and see *Prosecutor v Radovan Karadžić*, Case no IT-95-5/18-AR72.5, Decision on Appeal of Trial Chamber's Decision on Preliminary

once peacekeeping personnel are detained, investigations into their status or conduct prior to their detention are unnecessary, as the fact of their detention means that they are not DPH for the purposes of Common Article 3.

7.4 Peacekeepers as victims of crimes against humanity

As peacekeepers are civilians, they form part of the civilian population and attacks against them can amount to crimes against humanity. Thus, in the *Bagosora* case, the accused was charged with murder as a crime against humanity for killing the Belgian peacekeepers and the attacks were held to have formed part of a widespread or systematic attack against the civilian population.[130] However, the Trial Chamber considered the status of the peacekeepers only briefly,[131] finding that 'considering their status as United Nations peacekeepers and that they were disarmed, the Chamber is satisfied that the victims could not be considered as combatants'.[132] The Chamber's view as to the precise status of the peacekeepers is unclear. In a footnote it refers to the ICTY Appeals Chamber's decision in *Martić*, where it was held that a person *hors de combat* can be a victim of a crime against humanity, providing that all other necessary conditions are met.[133] It could therefore be inferred from this that the ICTR Trial Chamber viewed the peacekeepers as persons *hors de combat* rather than civilians,[134] suggesting that prior to their detention they were combatants. This interpretation sits awkwardly with the Chamber's statement that the peacekeepers 'could not be considered as combatants'. Alternatively, if one accepts that the Chamber regarded the peacekeepers as civilians, why did they make reference to the *Martić* Appeals Judgment at all? For clarity's sake, it would have been preferable had the Chamber made a clear determination as to the peacekeepers' status as civilians, and explained why they met the 'civilian population' requirement of the *chapeau*. The reference to the *Martić* Appeals Judgment causes unnecessary confusion.

The *RUF* case also concerned peacekeepers as victims of murder as a crime against humanity. The Trial Chamber established that the peacekeepers had civilian status and could be regarded as civilians for the purposes of the crime.[135] The

Motion to Dismiss Count 11 of the Indictment, 9 July 2009, para. 22; and *Prosecutor v Radovan Karadžić*, Case no IT-95-5/18-AR73.9, Decision on Appeal from Denial of Judgment of Acquittal for Hostage-Taking, 11 December 2012, para. 21. For a discussion of whether the peacekeepers had been victim of the crime of taking of hostages, see para. 5951.

130 *Bagosora* TC, para. 2176. The use of a weapon by some of the peacekeepers to defend themselves against the attack, did not alter this conclusion. Ibid., para. 2175.

131 Engdahl explains that the main legal issue in the case was the responsibility of Colonel Bagosora as a commander in the Rwandan army, to prevent the acts and that '[i]t is therefore not surprising that the Trial Chamber I of the ICTR dealt with the status of the Belgian peacekeepers in a very cursory manner'. Engdahl, *supra* FN 65, pp. 249–284 at p. 254.

132 *Bagosora* TC, para. 2175.

133 Ibid., para. 2175, FN 2353, referring to *Martić* AC, paras 302 and 313.

134 Engdahl, *supra* FN 65, p. 255.

135 *RUF* case TC, para. 1949.

question in the case was whether the attacks against the peacekeepers had formed part of a widespread or systematic attack against the civilian population of Sierra Leone. The Chamber found that there had been a widespread or systematic attack against the civilian population of Sierra Leone from November 1996 until January 2000. However, it had not been established that the pattern of killing, beating, raping, mutilating and enslaving of civilians had continued from February 2000 until September 2000, which was the period during which the attacks against the peacekeepers took place.[136] The Chamber confirmed that, for the purposes of the indictment, 'the "civilian population of Sierra Leone" does not import a membership requirement based on vagaries such as birth, race residence or membership of a particular group or organisation'.[137] However, it found that the attacks against the peacekeepers were distinct from the widespread or systematic attacks that had occurred against the rest of the civilian population, as their nature and purpose were different and the attacks against the UNAMSIL personnel were geographically and temporarily removed.[138] The peacekeepers constituted a distinct group of persons entitled to civilian status in Sierra Leone. Accordingly, the attacks against them were distinct from, and did not form part of, the widespread or systematic attack upon the civilian population of Sierra Leone.[139]

The prosecution countered that the UNAMSIL peacekeepers had formed a discrete civilian population in itself, and that the attacks against them during the specific period of 15 May to 15 September amounted to a widespread or systematic attack against this specific civilian population.[140] However, the Chamber rejected this argument, as it had not been pleaded by the prosecutor within the indictment.[141] The finding was not appealed.

The Trial Chamber took a strict view in this case in finding, based on the terms of the indictment, that the peacekeepers did not form part of the civilian population in Sierra Leone. The case acts as a warning that care should be taken when framing a charge of crimes against humanity involving peacekeepers as victims. Consideration should be given as to whether attacks against the peacekeepers concerned formed part of the widespread or systematic attack against the civilian population as a whole, or whether the indictment needs to be framed more concisely, perhaps describing the peacekeepers as being a distinct civilian population in themselves.

136 Ibid., para. 1948.
137 Ibid., para. 1949.
138 Ibid., para. 1952.
139 Ibid., para. 1953.
140 Ibid., para. 1954.
141 Ibid., para. 1955. The indictment stated: 'All acts and omissions charged here in as Crimes against Humanity were committed as part of a widespread or systematic attack directed against the civilian population of Sierra Leone.' *Prosecutor v Issa Hassan Sesay, Morris Kallon and Augustine Gbao*, SCSL-2004-15-PT, Corrected Amended Consolidated Indictment, 2 August 2006, para. 17.

7.5 Conclusion

Peacekeeping personnel are civilians, but due to their peculiar function within situations of conflict, in cases where it is alleged that international crimes have been committed against them, ICTs must take particular care to ensure that civilian protection has been retained.

When establishing whether the war crime of attacking peacekeepers has occurred, ICTs must determine some complex issues, including whether the mission in question constituted a peacekeeping mission and whether the peacekeepers concerned were entitled to civilian protection. It is important that ICTs adopt a structured approach to this. If it is established that the mission was a peacekeeping mission, its personnel had civilian status. The next question concerns the conduct of the alleged victims and whether their behaviour at the time they were attacked constituted APH/DPH or not.

ICTs have not always paid sufficient attention to the status and conduct of peacekeeping personnel. The *Bagosora* Judgment suggests, for example, that the peacekeepers in that case were persons *hors de combat* rather than civilians; while the Trial Judgment in the *RUF* case could be read as suggesting that once peacekeepers APH/DPH, they become combatants, meaning they lose their civilian protection entirely. Both of these judgments would have benefited from the respective courts giving more consideration to this matter. The approach taken by the ICC in the *Abu Garda* Decision is to be commended in this regard, in that the Pre-Trial Chamber began by establishing that the peacekeepers had been civilians, before turning to whether they had been DPH at the time of the attack. Courts should be more mindful of this distinction in future.

8 Crimes against humanity, genocide and fighting

Crimes against humanity and genocide were initially developed as international crimes in response to atrocities committed against civilians during the Second World War. In the intervening years, it has been established that persons *hors de combat* can also be victims of these crimes, but this journey has not been without its complications. It is these complications which will be explored in this chapter. The chapter's primary focus is upon when persons *hors de combat* can be victims of crimes against humanity. In order to comprehend the difficulties that ICTs have had in establishing this, it is necessary to understand how and why the concept of crimes against humanity was developed; this will be explored in the first section of the chapter. The chapter then investigates the drafting history of various definitions of the *chapeau* element of the crime, and examines the jurisprudence on this issue from ICTs. The next section takes a step back to ask whether persons *hors de combat* should be able to be victims of crimes against humanity at all, and analyses whether the present situation is satisfactory. Finally, the chapter considers fighting and the crime of genocide.

8.1 Developing the first definitions of crimes against humanity

The notion that there are 'laws of humanity' has been with us since time immemorial,[1] but the idea that there is such a thing as a *crime* against humanity is largely a twentieth-century conception.[2] While there were some references to the term in documents from around the time of the First World War, it was not until

1 Antonio Cassese, 'Crimes against Humanity: Comments on Some Problematical Aspects' available in Antonio Cassese, *The Human Dimension of International Law, Selected Papers* (Oxford University Press, 2008), p. 457.

2 Reference to the 'laws of humanity' can be found in treaties dating from the nineteenth century, although the legal significance of the phrase is debatable, see St Petersburg Declaration 1868 and the Hague Declarations of 1899 and 1907. Also see, Egon Schwelb, 'Crimes against Humanity', 23 *The British Yearbook of International Law* 178 (1946), p. 180; William Schabas, *Unimaginable Atrocities: Justice Politics and Rights at the War Crimes Tribunals* (Oxford University Press, 2012), pp. 51–53; and Lindsay Moir, 'Crimes against Humanity in Historical Perspective', 3 *New Zealand Yearbook of International Law* 101 (2006), pp. 102–107.

the Second World War period that a cohesive concept of crimes against humanity began to develop.[3]

In the wake of the Second World War, the Allies faced a problem. They wanted to prosecute the Nazis for the atrocities they had committed during the war, but the horrific crimes perpetrated against the German population did not fall within the well-established category of war crimes.[4] The Nazis had committed atrocities against their own people, and 'crimes committed by Germans against Germans, however reprehensible, are in a different category from war crimes and cannot be dealt with under the same procedure'.[5] It became clear to those responsible for drafting the London Charter that a further category of crimes was needed to encompass acts where the perpetrator and the victim belonged to the same side of the conflict. They turned to the notion of crimes against humanity.[6]

The first definition of the crime is to be found in Article 6(c) of the London Charter, which defines crimes against humanity as constituting acts of:

> murder, extermination, enslavement, deportation, and other inhumane acts committed against any civilian population, before or during the war, or persecutions on political, racial or religious grounds in execution of or in connection with any crime within the jurisdiction of the Tribunal, whether or not in violation of the domestic law of the country where perpetrated.

This was followed by a second definition of the crime in Control Council Law No 10, which set out a uniform legal basis for the prosecution of suspected war criminals in Germany by the Allied powers. Article II(1)(c) defined crimes against humanity as:

> Atrocities and offenses, including but not limited to murder, extermination, enslavement, deportation, imprisonment, torture, rape, or other inhumane acts committed against any civilian population, or persecutions on political, racial or religious grounds whether or not in violation of the domestic laws of the country where perpetrated.

3 See Mohamed Elewa Badar, 'From the Nuremberg Charter to the Rome Statute: Defining the Elements of Crimes against Humanity', 5 *San Diego International Law Journal* 73 (2004), pp. 77–79; and David Matas, 'Prosecuting Crimes against Humanity: The Lessons of World War I', 13 *Fordham International Law Journal* 86 (1989–1990), pp. 89–90.

4 M. Cherif Bassiouni, *Crimes against Humanity: Historical Evolution and Contemporary Application* (Cambridge University Press, 2011), p. 724.

5 Schwelb, *supra* FN 2, p. 186, quoting Richard Law, then Minister of State in the House of Commons at Hansard, House of Commons, 31 January 1945.

6 For a discussion of the principle of legality in the London Charter and in post-Second World War cases, see Bassiouni, *supra* FN 4, pp. 301–342; and Antonio Cassese, 'Crimes against Humanity', in Cassese *et al*, *The Rome Statute of the International Criminal Court: A Commentary*, Vol. I (Oxford University Press, 2002), pp. 354–355.

Although the two definitions of crimes against humanity differ, both require that the specific acts be committed against any 'civilian population'. It is this concept of 'civilian population' that has been the source of uncertainty as to whether those who have been involved in fighting can constitute victims of this category of crime.

Why did these early definitions of crimes against humanity restrict the notion to acts 'committed against any *civilian* population'? The notion of crimes against humanity was included in the London Charter and Control Council Law No 10 for a particular reason: to encompass crimes committed by the Nazi regime against its own civilians, which could not constitute war crimes. The concept of 'civilian population' also helped ensure that the specific acts were of a sufficient gravity and scale. The drafters would, most likely, have assumed that atrocities committed against enemy combatants took place within the context of the war itself, and would qualify as war crimes, while any cases involving perpetrators and victims who were fighting for the same side would be a matter for domestic law.[7]

Despite the civilian population requirement, some commentators were of the view that persons *hors de combat* could nevertheless be victims of some acts of crimes against humanity under the London Charter and Control Council Law No 10. They argued that the definitions of crimes against humanity contained two different classes of the crime: the first comprised 'murder, extermination, enslavement, deportation, and other inhumane acts committed against any civilian population' (so called 'murder-type' crimes against humanity); while the second included persecutions on political, racial or religious grounds (so called 'persecution-type' crimes against humanity).[8] Proponents of this view suggested that although those who fight could not be the victims of 'murder-type' crimes against humanity, since they had to be 'committed against any civilian population', they could be victims of 'persecution-type' crimes against humanity, which had no civilian population requirement.[9]

Not everyone agreed with this interpretation. Schwelb, for example, argued that such a distinction would 'not lead to satisfactory results', as it would be difficult to understand the rationale of a provision under which the number of persons afforded protection against a less serious crime (persecution) would be larger than that of potential victims protected against the graver offences of the murder type.[10] The UN War Crimes Commission, on the other hand, while agreeing that there were two different types of crimes against humanity, was of the view that both

7 Cassese explains: 'The rationale for this relatively limited scope of Article 6(c) is that *enemy* combatants were already protected by the traditional laws of warfare, while it was deemed unlikely that a belligerent might commit atrocities against *its own* servicemen or those of *allied* countries. In any event, such atrocities, if any, would come under the jurisdiction of the courts-martial of the country concerned; in other words they would fall under the province of *national* legislation.' Cassese, *supra* FN 1, p. 466.

8 *Report of the International Law Commission to the General Assembly*, U.N.GAOR, 5th Sess., Supp. No 12 UN Doc A/1316 (1950), para. 120.

9 See, for example, Cassese, *supra* FN 1, pp. 465–471.

10 Schwelb, *supra* FN 2, p. 190.

were restricted to civilian victims and did not include members of the armed forces.[11] In the handful of cases from post-Second World War jurisprudence which considered this matter, opinions were also mixed.

8.2 Post-Second World War jurisprudence

The issue of whether persons *hors de combat* could be victims of crimes against humanity arose in a number of cases before post-Second World War tribunals. In *P et al*,[12] the Supreme Court of Germany in the British Occupied Zone considered whether the killing of a group of German marines constituted a crime against humanity. The marines had been captured when trying to escape from Denmark back to Germany on the eve of German capitulation. Three were sentenced to death for desertion by a German court martial and were duly executed. The court found the members of the court martial to be guilty of crimes against humanity, because the sentence they had imposed on the marines was excessive in relation to the gravity of the supposed crime and was a manifestation of the Nazi's brutal regime. In relation to the wording of Article II(1)(c) of Control Council Law No 10, the Supreme Court observed 'whoever notes the expressly emphasised illustrative character of the instances and classes of instances mentioned there, cannot come to the conclusion that action between soldiers may not constitute crimes against humanity'.[13]

The issue arose before the same court in the case of *H*, concerning the actions of a German judge who had presided over cases against two officers in the German navy. One German officer had been accused of criticising Hitler, whilst the other had been accused of procuring foreign identity cards for himself and his wife. The judge sentenced both to death. The Supreme Court of Germany in the British Occupied Zone convicted the judge of crimes against humanity, finding that the excessive sentence imposed upon the German officers had been part of the system of Nazi brutality.[14] Finally, in the *RuSHA* case[15] from the US Military Tribunal,

11 *History of the United Nations War Crimes Commission and the Development of the Laws of War* (London, HMSO, 1948), p. 193.

12 *P and Others*, 7 December 1948, Entscheidungen des Obersten Gerichtshofes für die Britische Zone in Strafsachen, St S 111/48 cited in Cassese, *supra* FN 1, pp. 468–469. Also see H. Singh, 'Critique of the Mrkšić Trial Chamber (ICTY) Judgment: A Re-evaluation on whether soldiers hors de combat are entitled to recognition as victims of crimes against humanity', 8 *The Law and Practice of International Courts and Tribunals* 247–296 (2009), pp. 257–258.

13 *P and Others*, ibid., pp. 228–229, quoted in Cassese, *supra* FN 1, p. 469.

14 *H.*, 18 October 1949; Entscheidungen des Obersten Gerichtshofes für die Britische Zone in Strafsachen; St S 309/49, cited in Cassese, *supra* FN 1, p. 469; and Singh, *supra* FN 12, pp. 258–259.

15 *United States of America v Ulrich Greifelt et al*, 10 March 1948, available in Trials of War Criminals Before the Nuremberg Military Tribunals under Control Council Law No 10, Vol. V Washington DC, US GPO, 1950, Count 1, available at www.loc.gov/rr/frd/Military_Law/pdf/NT_Indictments.pdf#page=162. Also see Singh, *supra* FN 12, p. 259.

POWs were found to have been victims of crimes against humanity. None of these cases carried out any in-depth analysis as to whether the alleged victims had formed part of the civilian population for the purposes of crimes against humanity.[16]

A stricter view was taken in the case of *Pilz*, from the Dutch Special Court of Cassation,[17] which considered whether a soldier of the occupying German army, who was Dutch by birth, could have been a victim of crimes against humanity. A German army doctor was accused of ordering, or allowing, a subordinate to shoot and wound the soldier, and thereafter refusing to give him medical assistance, causing him to die. The court held that the offence did not constitute a crime against humanity, as the victim was not part of the civilian population of an occupied territory, nor could the acts with which he was charged be seen as forming part of a system of persecution on political, racial or religious grounds.[18]

Of the cases from the post-Second World War period that considered the question of whether persons *hors de combat* could qualify as victims of crimes against humanity, most contained no in-depth analysis as to whether the military victims had been members of the civilian population, and the one case that did, *Pilz*, concluded they did not.

8.3 Crimes against humanity and the civilian population requirement

There is no single definition of crimes against humanity,[19] and different definitions of the crime vary in small, yet significant, ways.[20] One such variation is as to whether an act is required to be committed against a 'civilian population' in order for it to constitute a crime against humanity. This section explores the International Law Commission's (ILC) approach; the approach taken in the ICTY, ICTR and SCSL Statutes; and finally, the approach taken in the ICC Statute.

8.3.1 The International Law Commission's approach

The ILC was created by the United Nations General Assembly following the Second World War.[21] One of its first duties was to formulate a set of principles of

16 Ibid., pp. 151–152.

17 *Pilz*, Nederlandse Jurisprudentie, 1950, No 681 at 1210–211; and *International Law Reports*, 1950, pp. 391–392; and see Cassese, *supra* FN 1, p. 466.

18 As quoted in Cassese, *supra* FN 1, p. 466 at FN 27.

19 Bassiouni lists 12 different international definitions of crimes against humanity, see Cherif M. Bassiouni, 'Crimes against Humanity: The Case for a Specialized Convention', 9 *Washington University Global Studies Law Review* 575 (2010) at FN 44.

20 See Beth Van Schaak, 'The Definition of Crimes against Humanity: Resolving the Incoherence', 37 *Columbian Journal of Transnational Law* 787 (1998–1999); and Göran Sluiter, '"Chapeau Elements" of Crimes against Humanity in the Jurisprudence of the UN Ad Hoc Tribunals', in Leila Nadya Sadat (ed.), *Forging a Convention for Crimes against Humanity* (Cambridge University Press, 2011).

21 G.A. Res. 174 (II) UN GAOR, 2d Sess., 123rd plen. mtg. at 105 UN Doc. A/519 (1947).

international law arising from the London Charter and the Judgment of the Nuremberg tribunal. It was then tasked with creating a Draft Code of Offences against the Peace and Security of Mankind (the Draft Code).[22] The Nuremberg Principles were completed in 1950.[23] They defined crimes against humanity as:

> Murder, extermination, enslavement, deportation and other inhuman acts done against any civilian population, or persecutions on political, racial or religious grounds, when such acts are done or such persecutions are carried on in execution of or in connexion with any crime against peace or any war crime.

This definition accords with that found in Article 6(c) of the London Charter, in so far as it requires that acts be committed against a 'civilian population' and makes a distinction between 'murder-type' and 'persecution-type' crimes against humanity. When considering the phrase 'civilian population' in its accompanying Report, the ILC did not discuss whether persons *hors de combat* could be victims of this class of crimes. Rather, the focus was upon whether acts committed by a perpetrator against their own population were included within the definition.[24]

The ILC prepared the first Draft Code in 1951. This was shortly followed by a revised Code, which was submitted to the General Assembly in 1954 (1954 Draft).[25] The 1954 Draft does not refer to 'crimes against humanity' as such. Article 2(11) defines one offence against the peace and security of mankind as constituting:

> Inhuman acts such as murder, extermination, enslavement, deportation or persecutions, committed against any civilian population on social, political, racial, religious or cultural grounds by the authorities of a State or by private individuals acting at the instigation or with the toleration of such authorities.

The Commentary to the 1954 Draft observes: 'This paragraph corresponds substantially to article 6, paragraph (c), of the Charter of the Nurnberg Tribunal, which defines "crimes against humanity".'[26] However, unlike the definition of crimes against humanity in Article 6(c) of the London Charter, the 1954 Draft's

22 G.A. Res. 177 (II) UN GAOR, 2d Sess., 123rd plen. mtg. at 111 UN Doc. A/519 (1947).

23 *Principles of International Law Recognized in the Charter of the Nürnberg Tribunal and the Judgment of the Tribunal*, 1950.

24 *Report of the International Law Commission*, UN GAOR, 5th Sess., Supp. No 12, UN Doc. A/1316 (1950), para. 124.

25 *Report of the International Law Commission to the General Assembly, Draft Code of Offences against the Peace and Security of Mankind*; UN GAOR, 9th Sess., Supp. No 9, Ch. 3, Article 2., sec. 11, UN Doc. A/2691 (1954).

26 Draft Code of Offences against the Peace and Security of Mankind with commentaries, 1954, available in *Yearbook of the International Law Commission*, 1951, Vol. II documents of the third session including the report of the Commission to the General Assembly at p. 136 ('Commentary to the 1954 Draft').

definition of 'inhuman act' does not distinguish between 'murder'- and 'persecution'-type 'inhuman acts' – all of the inhuman acts contained in Article 2(11) have to be 'committed against any civilian population'.[27] Notably, when outlining the differences between the two provisions, the accompanying Commentary to the 1954 Draft makes no reference to this difference. However, if one had subscribed to the view that there were two types of crimes against humanity, only one of which could be committed against persons *hors de combat*,[28] this change is significant, as it has the effect of completely precluding such individuals from being victims of the crime. The significance of this seems to have been passed unnoticed by the ILC. Perhaps this is understandable, however. The issue of whether persons *hors de combat* could be victims of crimes against humanity had arisen in very few cases in the post-war jurisprudence and was unlikely to have ranked highly on the ILC's agenda.

Work on the Draft Code was suspended until the 1980s,[29] with a new version of the Code being adopted by the ILC in 1991 ('1991 Draft').[30] As with the 1954 Draft, the 1991 Draft does not contain a specific crime entitled 'crime against humanity'. Article 21 of the 1991 Draft came closest to it. Under the heading of 'Systematic or mass violations of human rights', it states:

> An individual who commits or orders the commission of any of the following violations of human rights:
>
> - Murder
> - Torture
> - establishing or maintaining over persons a status of slavery, servitude or forced labour
> - persecution on social, political, racial, religious or cultural grounds, in a systematic manner or on a mass scale; or
> - deportation or forcible transfer of population shall, on conviction thereof, be sentenced [to …][31]

The provision contains no requirement that the acts be committed against a 'civilian population', and no indication is given in the accompanying Summary of the Records as to why this is so. The 1991 Draft's definition is of limited

27 Phyllis Hwang, 'Defining Crimes against Humanity in the Rome Statute of the International Criminal Court', 22 *Fordham International Law Journal* 457 (1998–1999), pp. 464–465.

28 See *Pilz*.

29 See G.A. Res., 106, UN GAOR, 36th sess. (1981).

30 Draft Code of Crimes against the Peace and Security of Mankind, in *Yearbook of the International Law Commission 1991*, Volume 1, Summary records of the meetings of the 43rd session 29 April–19 July 1991, A/CN.4/SER.A/1991, pp. 218–223.

31 Available in *Yearbook of the International Law Commission 1991*, Volume 1, Summary records of the meetings of the 43rd session 29 April–19 July 1991, A/CN.4/SER.A/1991, pp. 222–223.

significance, however, as it does not claim to be a definition of crimes against humanity, and the Summary of the Records does not indicate that it is based on the notion of crimes against humanity.[32]

Work on the Draft Code continued, with a further version being adopted by the ILC in 1996 ('1996 Draft').[33] This time, a specific crime of crimes against humanity was included. Article 18 of the 1996 Draft states (in part):

> A crime against humanity means any of the following acts, when committed in a systematic manner or on a large scale and instigated or directed by a Government or by any organization or group …

The 1996 Draft does not require that the specified acts be committed against a 'civilian population'.[34] Once again, the absence of the term is not commented upon within the accompanying Commentary. This is somewhat surprising given the fact that the civilian population requirement had formed a key element of the post-Second World War definitions of the crime. It has been suggested that one reason for this omission could be that the jurisprudence at that time was opting for an expansive definition of the term 'civilian population'.[35] However, no reference is made to this jurisprudence within the Commentary accompanying the 1996 Draft, and the reason for the omission of the term remains a mystery.

Of the three different draft definitions of crimes against humanity, or crimes against humanity-type crimes, that were included within the different versions of the Draft Code, only one – the 1954 Draft – contained the requirement that the acts be committed against a 'civilian population'. Most notably, there is no such stipulation in the final 1996 Draft, which was to play a seminal role in the drafting of the ICC Statute.[36] What is most intriguing is that there is no discussion within the accompanying Commentaries as to why this is so, and what consequences could flow from omitting the civilian population element from the *chapeau* of the crime.

32 Ibid., pp. 218–223.

33 Draft Code of Crimes against the Peace and Security of Mankind, UN GAOR 48th Sess., at 6–7 UN Doc. A/CN.4/L.532, 8 July 1996. Available in *Yearbook of the International Law Commission, 1996*, Vol. II, Part Two.

34 Dinstein comments that 'the most striking aspect of Article 18 is that it quite inexplicably omits the requirement that the prohibited acts be committed against a civilian population'. See Yoram Dinstein, 'Crimes against Humanity after *Tadić*', 13 *Leiden Journal of International Law* 373–393 (2000), p. 379. Also see Hwang, *supra* FN 27, p. 468; and Jean Allain and John R.W.D. Jones, 'A Patchwork of Norms: A Commentary on the 1996 Draft Code of Crimes against the Peace and Security of Mankind', 8(1) *European Journal of International Law* 100–117 (1997), p. 112.

35 Singh, *supra* FN 12, p. 279, and Allain and Jones, *supra* FN 34, pp. 112–113, referring to the *Barbie: Fédération Nationale des Déportés et Internés Résistants et Patriotes and Others v Barbie*, Court of Cassation (Criminal Chamber), 20 December 1985, reported in 78 ILR 125 ('*Barbie*') and *Touvier*, Court of Cassation (Criminal Chamber), 27 November 1992, reported at 100 ILR 338 ('*Touvier*'), discussed below.

36 William A. Schabas, *An Introduction to the International Criminal Court* (Cambridge University Press, 2011), p. 11.

8.3.2 ICTY, ICTR and SCSL Statutes

Despite the Statutes of the ICTY and the ICTR having been drafted shortly after one another, and despite both emanating from the same source, namely the UN Security Council, there are some significant differences in the way that their definitions of crimes against humanity have been drafted.[37] Be that as it may, both require that there be an attack against a 'civilian population', although Article 5 of the ICTY Statute requires it to be 'directed against any civilian population', while Article 3 of the ICTR Statute simply requires that it be 'against any civilian population'. Article 2 of the SCSL Statute uses the same phrasing as the ICTR Statute in this regard.

The Final Report of the Committee of Experts for the ICTY Statute ('Final Report')[38] paid some consideration to the phrase 'civilian population'. It noted that 'civilian population', as it appears in Article 5 of the ICTY Statute,[39] 'is used in this context in contradistinction to combatants or members of armed forces',[40] and continued:

> [i]t seems obvious that article 5 applies first and foremost to civilians, meaning people who are not combatants. This, however, should not lead to any quick conclusions concerning people who at one particular point in time did bear arms.[41]

The Final Report elaborated that:

> In the former Yugoslavia, large-scale arbitrary killings were one of the hallmarks of attacks by a given group … Many of the most barbarous onslaughts on villages started with heavy artillery bombardments followed by villages being stormed by infantry in tandem, while paramilitary groups sought the inhabitants in each and every house. A head of family who under such circumstances tries to protect his family gun-in-hand does not thereby lose his status as a civilian. Maybe the same is the case for the sole policeman or local defence guard doing the same, even if they joined hands to try to prevent the cataclysm, the distinction between improvised self-defence and actual military defence may be subtle, but [is] none the less important.[42]

From the examples given in the Final Report, it is evident that the Committee of Experts was far from envisaging that all persons *hors de combat* could be victims of

37 Dinstein, *supra* FN 34.

38 *Final Report of the Commission of Experts established pursuant to Security Council Resolution 780* S/1994/674 (1992).

39 Article 5 of the ICTY Statute states: 'The International Tribunal shall have the power to prosecute persons responsible for the following crimes when committed in armed conflict, whether international or internal in character, and directed against any civilian population …'

40 Final Report, *supra* FN 38, para. 77.

41 Ibid., para. 78.

42 Ibid.

crimes against humanity. The examples given are of civilians ostensibly acting in self-defence.[43] Reading between the lines, it would appear that the Committee envisaged that atrocities committed against persons *hors de combat* would be prosecuted as war crimes.

8.3.3 ICC Statute

From an examination of the preparatory works leading up to the Rome Conference in 1998, it is plain that the content of Article 7, the article of the ICC Statute which defines crimes against humanity for the purposes of the ICC, was far from being a foregone conclusion.[44] Some drafts prepared by the Preparatory Committee proposed alternative phrasings that did not contain the phrase 'civilian population'.[45] The final draft prepared prior to the Rome Conference proposed different alternatives, which included an option that the specified acts be committed against 'any population' rather than 'any civilian population'.[46]

During the Conference itself, the principal issues of contention concerning crimes against humanity were whether they could be committed within internal armed conflicts; whether there was a requirement that the acts be widespread and systematic; and what specific crimes should be included. There was some discussion of the phrase 'civilian population': Greece, for example, favoured the first alternative of the Preparatory Committee's final draft ('any population') as being less restrictive than the second ('civilian population').[47] The Republic of Korea suggested that the reference to 'civilian' population was confusing.[48] France proffered that crimes against humanity could be committed in peace and in war against all populations.[49] Canada expressed the strongest view regarding the suggested phrase 'grounds for

43 Whether a policeman or a 'local defence guard' has civilian status will depend on the facts of the case. IHL views members of law enforcement agencies as civilians, unless they are incorporated into the armed forces, see Article 43(3), Protocol I.

44 See *Report of the Ad Hoc Committee on the Establishment of the International Criminal Court*, A/50/22 (1995), paras 78–80.

45 For example, see *Report of the Preparatory Committee on The Establishment of an International Criminal Court*, Volume 1 GAOR, 51st Session Supplement No 22, A/51/22, p. 22; *Decisions Taken by the Preparatory Committee at its sessions held from 11 to 21 February 1997*, A/AC.249/1997/L.5 12, Annex I Report of the Working Group on the Definition of Crimes, p. 4; and M. Cherif Bassiouni, *The Legislative History of the International Criminal Court: An Article-by-Article Evolution of the Statute* (Transnational Publishers, 2005), Volume 2, pp. 46–54, containing the Zutphen Draft, the draft prepared by the Working Group at the 1997 Preparatory Committee session and the draft prepared by the 1996 Preparatory Committee.

46 'A "crime against humanity" means any of the following acts when committed [as part of a widespread [and] [or] systematic commission of such acts against any population]: [as part of a widespread [and] [or] systematic attack against any [civilian] population].' Draft Statute for the International Criminal Court, A/CONF.183/2/Add1, 14 April 1998, pp. 25–26.

47 Bassiouni, Volume 3, *supra* FN 45, p. 95.

48 Ibid., p. 96.

49 Ibid., p. 97.

attack against a population', arguing that this was not part of the definition of crimes against humanity under customary international law, and that any requirement regarding grounds would unnecessarily complicate the task of prosecution and may inadvertently exclude groups that could be victims of crimes against humanity.[50] This point does not seem to have been picked up by the other delegations.

By the beginning of July, the drafts being circulated concerning the *chapeau* for crimes against humanity referred only to 'attack directed against any civilian population'.[51] It is difficult to pinpoint what happened during the interim period. Hwang notes that 'the very limited discussion of "civilian population" failed to take into account the complex analysis that the ICTY had undertaken for this term'.[52] She explains that the delegations were concerned with two principal issues, namely, the requirement of a nexus between crimes against humanity and armed conflict, and whether 'widespread' and 'systematic' should be alternative or cumulative.[53] She refers to a Canadian Proposal to the *chapeau*, dated 1 July 1998, which required an 'attack against any civilian population'.[54] Referencing her personal notes from the conference, she states that the 'introduction of the definition of "an attack against any civilian population" attracted a broad range of comments'.[55] The text that was ultimately adopted as Article 7 of the ICC Statute, requires that the acts be part of a 'widespread or systematic attack against any civilian population'. No definition of 'civilian' or 'civilian population' is provided either in the Statute itself or in the Elements of Crimes.

Robinson reports that during the negotiations held to formulate the elements of the crime the developing law on the status of combatants as victims of crimes against humanity was discussed, and the fact that all persons are 'civilian' when there is no armed conflict. Delegations agreed that the 'civilian population' test was a flexible test. However, '[m]ost delegations quickly agreed that this was too complex a subject and an evolving area of law, better left for resolution in case law'.[56] In view of the difficulties that the ICTY has had in resolving the matter, this was not necessarily the wisest conclusion.

8.3.4 The Proposed International Convention on the Prevention and Punishment of Crimes against Humanity

Mention should also be made of the Proposed International Convention on the Prevention and Punishment of Crimes against Humanity, currently being

50 Ibid., p. 103.

51 For example: ibid., p. 421, containing a copy of Bureau Discussion Paper regarding part 2, A/CONF.183/C.1/L.53 dated 6 July 1998; and ibid., p. 445, containing a copy of Recommendations of the Coordinator regarding Article 5 A/CONF.183/C.1/L.44, dated 7 July 1998.

52 Hwang, *supra* FN 27, p. 496.

53 Ibid., p. 496.

54 Ibid., p. 497.

55 Ibid., pp. 497–498.

56 Darryl Robinson, 'The Context of Crimes against Humanity', in Roy S. Lee, *The International Criminal Court: Elements of Crimes and Rules of Procedure and Evidence* (Transnational Publishers Inc., 2001), p. 78.

considered by the ILC.[57] Draft Article 3 of the proposed Convention contains the definition of crimes against humanity for the purposes of the Convention, and states (in part):

> For the purposes of the present draft articles, 'crime against humanity' means any of the following acts when committed as part of a widespread or systematic attack directed against any civilian population, with knowledge of the attack.[58]

Following the lead of the majority of previous definitions, this definition requires that the attacks be directed against any 'civilian population'. In their report, the ILC noted that 'civilian population' has a wide definition and should be interpreted broadly, but does not indicate whether or when persons *hors de combat* fall within the ambit of the notion.[59]

To summarise, all the current major definitions of crimes against humanity require that the specific acts be committed against a 'civilian population'. From the preparatory material that is available it appears that the drafters devoted minimal discussion to the matter of whether persons *hors de combat* could be a victim of these crimes. Rather, it has been left to the courts to determine whether persons *hors de combat* fall within the notion of 'civilian population' for the purposes of crimes against humanity. The following section discusses jurisprudence from ICTs that has considered this matter.

8.4 Interpreting the 'civilian population' requirement

Before examining case law from ICTs concerning the interpretation of the civilian population requirement, mention must be made of two cases from the French Court of Cassation, which have proven influential at an international level.[60] Both cases have been cited frequently in the jurisprudence of the *ad hoc* tribunals concerning the matter of who can be victims of crimes against humanity. The first is that of *Barbie*. Klaus Barbie was the former head of the Gestapo in Lyons. He faced charges which included allegations of crimes against humanity against members of the French Resistance movement. The lower court held that

57 Proposed International Convention on the Prevention and Punishment of Crimes against Humanity drafted by the Washington University School of Law Whitney R. Harris World Law Institute Crimes against Humanity Initiative, August 2010 ('Proposed Convention'). Available at http://law.wustl.edu/harris/cah/docs/EnglishTreatyFinal.pdf.

58 Ibid., Article 3(1).

59 Report of the International Law Commission, 67th session, 4 May–5 June and 6 July 7 August 2015, A70/10, available at http://legal.un.org/ilc/reports/2015/, pp. 63–65. Also see Sean D. Murphy, *Special Rapporteur, First Report on Crimes against Humanity*, 17 February 2015, A/CN.4/680, paras 133–136.

60 Other domestic courts have considered whether persons *hors de combat* can be victims of crimes against humanity. See Singh, *supra* FN 12, pp. 275–277.

crimes committed against members of the Resistance could not qualify as crimes against humanity.[61] This verdict was overturned by the Court of Cassation, which held:

> Neither the driving force which motivated the victims, nor their possible membership of the Resistance, excludes the possibility that the accused acted with the element of intent necessary for the commission of crimes against humanity.[62]

The court concluded that membership in the Resistance movement did not disbar an alleged victim from being a victim of crimes against humanity. This was confirmed in the case of *Touvier*, where the Court of Cassation stated:

> Jews and members of the Resistance persecuted in a systematic manner in the name of a State practising a policy of ideological supremacy, the former by reason of their membership of a racial or religious community, the latter by reason of their opposition to that policy, can equally be the victims of crimes against humanity.[63]

Viewing this from an IHL perspective, some Resistance fighters would have had the status of civilians, *albeit* civilians who were DPH. Finding that they could be victims of crimes against humanity was, therefore, far from finding that all persons *hors de combat* could be victims of the crime. The following section explores how this issue has been dealt with in the jurisprudence of the ICTY, ICTR, ICC, and SCSL in turn.

8.4.1 The ICTY

Of all the ICTs, it has been the ICTY which has devoted the most time and effort, and had the greatest difficulty, in determining whether persons *hors de combat* can be victims of crimes against humanity. The cases can be divided into three phases: the early cases, which took a conservative approach; the middle cases, which took different approaches; and finally, the cases of *Martić* and *Mrškić*, which appear to have resolved the issue.

61 The lower court stated '[t]he prosecution is barred by statutory limitation to the extent that it related to unlawful imprisonment without judgment, torture, deportation and death of combatants who were members of the Resistance, or persons whom Barbie supposed to be members of the Resistance, even if they were Jewish. Even if such acts were committed in violation of human dignity and the laws of war, they could only constitute war crimes.' *Barbie*, p. 139. Also see Leila Sadat Wexler, 'The Interpretation of the Nuremberg Principles by the French Court of Cassation: From Touvier to Barbie and Back Again', 32 *Columbia Journal Transnational Law* p. 289 (1994–1995).

62 Ibid., p. 140.

63 *Touvier*, p. 411.

(i) A conservative beginning

The issue of who could be a victim of crimes against humanity arose in some of the tribunal's earliest decisions. In the *Martić* Rule 61 Decision, the Trial Chamber was clearly influenced by the *Barbie* and *Touvier* cases when it held:

> Although according to the terms of Article 5 of the Statute of this Tribunal combatants in the traditional sense cannot be victims of a crime against humanity, this does not apply to individuals who, at one point in time, carried out acts of resistance.[64]

The matter was considered again in *Tadić*, where the Trial Chamber explained the challenges in interpreting the phrase 'civilian population' to be as follows:

> that the prohibited act must be committed against a 'civilian' population itself raises two aspects: what must the character of the targeted population be and how is it to be determined whether an individual victim qualifies as a civilian such that acts taken against the person constitute crimes against humanity?[65]

With regard to the first aspect, it held that the targeted population must be of a predominantly civilian nature, and that the presence of those actively involved in the conflict does not prevent the characterisation of a population as civilian.[66] The second aspect was harder for the Trial Chamber to determine.[67] It considered Common Article 3 of the Geneva Conventions,[68] together with the definition of 'civilian' found in Article 50(1) of Protocol I, noting that these provisions form part of IHL, and can only be applied by analogy.[69] It then referred to other sources, including the UN War Crimes Commission report, the *Barbie* and *Touvier* cases, and the Secretary-General's Report, to conclude that a wide definition of the term 'civilian population' was justified. It concluded that 'those actively involved in a resistance movement can qualify as victims of crimes against humanity'.[70]

Notably, the *Tadić* Trial Chamber refers to members of a resistance movement who are 'actively involved', whereas the *Martić* Rule 61 Decision refers to 'individuals who, at one point in time, carried out acts of resistance'. The Trial Chamber in *Tadić* therefore appears to be going a step further by including

64 *Prosecutor v Milan Martić*, ICTY, IT-95-11-T, Rule 61 Hearing Decision, 8 March 1996 (*Martić* Rule 61 Decision), para. 29.
65 *Prosecutor v Duško Tadić*, ICTY, IT-94-1-T, Trial Judgment, 7 May 1997 (*Tadić* TC), para. 636.
66 Ibid., para. 638.
67 Ibid., para. 639.
68 Namely, 'persons taking no active part in the hostilities, including members of armed forces who have laid down their arms and those placed *hors de combat* by sickness, wounds, detention, or any other cause'.
69 *Tadić* TC, para. 639.
70 Ibid., para. 643.

members of resistance movements who were not *hors de combat* and who had not laid down their arms as potential victims of crimes against humanity. Such an interpretation could conflict with IHL – 'active' members of resistance movements may, depending on the circumstances, be viewed as having a continuous combat function,[71] and therefore be liable to attack at any time unless *hors de combat*. If the *Tadić* case were followed, actions such as killing them, or making them flee, which would be lawful under IHL, could be viewed as constituting the crimes against humanity of murder or forcible displacement under ICL.[72] Adopting such an approach would be incompatible with IHL.[73] In any event, in *Tadić* the facts of the case did not concern persons *hors de combat*, and the Trial Chamber did not further explore the consequences of their finding in this regard.

Both the *Martić* Rule 61 Decision and the *Tadić* Trial Chamber Judgment apply a restricted definition of the notion of 'civilian population', including only members of resistance movements and not other persons *hors de combat*. However, the distinction hinted at in *Tadić*, between the collective aspect of the term 'civilian population' and the status of individual victims of the crime, was to prove important in subsequent cases.

(ii) The ICTY gets in a muddle

Over the following years, a succession of cases at the ICTY considered the issue of whether persons *hors de combat* could be victims of crimes against humanity, resulting in some rather confusing jurisprudence.

In December 1999, the Trial Chamber in *Jelisić* held that, following the letter and spirit of Article 5, the term 'civilian population' should be interpreted broadly, and that the 'reference to a civilian population would seek to place the emphasis more on the collective aspect of the crime than on the status of the victims'.[74] The Chamber concluded that all persons placed *hors de combat* when the crime was perpetrated were included within the notion of 'civilian population' in Article 5 of the Statute.[75] This judgment therefore went beyond the precedent set in both the *Martić* Rule 61 Decision and in *Tadić*.

The *Jelisić* Trial Chamber's finding in this regard seems to have gone largely unnoticed. It was not referred to when the issue was considered a month or so later by the Trial Chamber in the case of *Kupreškić*. This is somewhat surprising, as in *Kupreškić*, the Trial Chamber paid particular consideration to the issue of whether persons *hors de combat* could be victims of crimes against humanity. The

71 See Chapter 1.

72 Discussed in more detail below.

73 Payam Akhavan, 'Reconciling Crimes Against Humanity with the Laws of War, Human Rights, Armed Conflict and the Limits of Progressive Jurisprudence', 6 *Journal of International Criminal Justice* 21–37 (2008), and see discussion below.

74 *Prosecutor v Goran Jelisić*, ICTY, IT-95-10-T, Trial Judgment, 14 December 1999 (*Jelsić* TC), para. 54.

75 Ibid., para. 54.

Chamber made reference to the possible distinction between 'murder-type' and 'persecution-type' crimes against humanity, when it stated:

> one fails to see why only civilians and not also combatants should be protected by these rules (in particular by the rule prohibiting persecution), given that these rules may be held to possess a broader humanitarian scope and purpose than those prohibiting war crimes.[76]

Faced with the limitations within Article 5, that the attack be directed against a 'civilian population', the Chamber found that 'a broad interpretation should ... be placed on the word "civilians", the more so because the limitation in Article 5 constitutes a departure from customary international law'.[77] It is not entirely clear what the Trial Chamber meant by its comment that 'the limitation in Article 5 constitutes a departure from customary international law'. The Chamber seems to be suggesting that the requirement that the attacks be against a 'civilian population' is not part of customary law, although no evidence is cited to show why this is the case. Although the Chamber stated that it was going to interpret the term broadly, it did not follow the lead of the Trial Chamber in *Jelisić*, by including persons *hors de combat* within the definition of 'civilian population'. Rather, it followed *Tadić* in holding that those actively involved in a resistance movement can qualify as victims of crimes against humanity.[78]

In March 2000 came the *Blaškić* case. Here, the Trial Chamber was of the view that:

> the contention that acts of violence perpetrated systematically or on a widespread basis against a population must not be characterised as a crime against humanity on the sole ground that the victims were soldiers and regardless of the fact that they were not combatants when the crimes were perpetrated is not in conformity with either the letter or spirit of Article 5 of the Statute ... the specificity of a crime against humanity results not from the status of the victim, but the scale and organisation in which it must be committed.[79]

The Chamber continued:

> Crimes against humanity therefore do not mean only acts committed against civilians in the strict sense of the term, but include also crimes against two categories of people: those who were members of a resistance movement and former combatants – regardless of whether they wore uniform or not – but who were no longer taking part in hostilities when the crimes were

76 *Prosecutor v Zoran Kupreškić et al*, ICTY, IT-95-16-T, Trial Judgment, 14 January 2000 (*Kupreškić* TC), para. 547.

77 Ibid.

78 Ibid., para. 549.

79 *Prosecutor v Tihomir Blaškić*, ICTY, IT-95-14-T, Trial Judgment, 3 March 2000 (*Blaškić* TC), para. 208.

> perpetrated because they had either left the army or were no longer bearing arms or, ultimately, had been placed *hors de combat*, in particular, due to their wounds or their being detained. It also follows that the specific situation of the victim at the moment the crimes were committed, rather than his status, must be taken into account in determining his standing as a civilian. Finally, it can be concluded that the presence of soldiers within an intentionally targeted civilian population does not alter the civilian nature of that population.[80]

The Trial Chamber found that persons *hors de combat* could be victims of crimes against humanity. Reading the passage above, it is not entirely clear whether the Trial Chamber includes persons *hors de combat* within the definition of 'civilians' or within the definition of 'civilian population'. As shall become clear in the following cases, this distinction has caused difficulties at the ICTY.

The *Blaškić* Trial Judgment was appealed. On Appeal, the Appeals Chamber held that:

> both the status of the victim as a civilian and the scale on which it [the crime] is committed or the level of organisation involved characterise a crime against humanity.[81]

The Appeals Chamber considered Article 50 of Protocol I and Article 4A of Geneva Convention III to find that, read together, these establish that members of the armed forces, members of militias or volunteer corps forming part of such armed forces, and members of organised resistance groups who comply with the four conditions laid down in Articles 4A(2), cannot claim civilian status.[82] The Trial Chamber's finding that the specific situation of the victim at the time the crimes were committed must be taken into account in determining their standing as a civilian, was found to be 'misleading'.[83] The Appeals Chamber held that, on the contrary, an alleged victim's specific situation at the time the crimes were committed may not be determinative of their civilian or non-civilian status.[84] If an alleged victim is a member of an armed organisation, the fact that they are not armed or in combat at the time the crimes were committed does not accord them civilian status.[85] The Appeals Chamber agreed with the Trial Chamber that the presence of soldiers within a civilian population does not deprive it of its civilian nature. In order to determine whether the presence of combatants deprives a population of its civilian character, the number of soldiers, as well as whether they are on leave, must be examined.[86] The Appeals Chamber concluded that the Trial Chamber 'erred in part' in its characterisation of 'civilian

80 Ibid., para. 214.
81 *Prosecutor v Tihomir Blaškić*, ICTY, IT-95-14-A, Appeals Judgment, 29 July 2004 (*Blaškić* AC), para. 107.
82 Ibid., para. 113.
83 Ibid., para. 114.
84 Ibid.
85 Ibid.
86 Ibid., para. 115.

population' and 'civilian',[87] but it did not state clearly whether it overruled the Trial Chamber's finding that persons *hors de combat* could be victims of crimes against humanity.

A few months later, the matter arose again in the *Kordić and Čerkez* Appeal Judgment. For the first time, some of the alleged victims in the case were persons *hors de combat.*[88] The Appeals Chamber stated that the:

> soldiers were killed after their arrest, after being placed *hors de combat.* These persons, wilfully killed by Croat forces, were without doubt ...'civilians' in the sense of Article 5 of the Statute ... There is no doubt that these acts were also part of the widespread attack conducted at that time against the civilian Muslim population.[89]

Thus, contrary to the *Blaskić* Appeal Judgment, the Appeals Chamber in *Kordić and Čerkez* found that persons *hors de combat* were 'civilian' for the purposes of crimes against humanity.

The case of *Naletilić and Martinović* also involved persons *hors de combat* in that the alleged victims were POWs. In contrast to *Kordić and Čerkez*, rather than ask whether they constituted 'civilians' for the purposes of crimes against humanity, the Trial Chamber looked at the notion of 'civilian population', and found that 'the definition of civilian population includes individuals who may at one time have performed acts of resistance and persons *hors de combat*'.[90] It concluded that the POWs had been victims of crimes against humanity.[91]

Galić is another case which highlights the civilian/civilian population confusion at the ICTY. The Trial Chamber held that individuals who at one time performed acts of resistance, as well as persons who were *hors de combat* when the crime was committed, are 'civilian' for the purposes of crimes against humanity.[92] On Appeal, the Defence challenged this expansive interpretation.[93] The Appeals Chamber stated that the Trial Chamber's assessment did not intend to give a definition of an individual civilian, but rather it had been intended to reiterate well-established jurisprudence regarding the *chapeau* element of 'civilian population', which holds that the presence of members of soldiers within a population does not necessarily deprive it of its civilian character.[94] It relied on the *Blaskić* Appeals Chamber decision to argue that persons *hors de combat* are not civilian.

87 Ibid., para. 116.
88 *Prosecutor v Dario Kordić and Mario Čerkez*, ICTY, IT-95-14/2-A, Appeal Judgment, 17 December 2004 (*Kordić and Čerkez* AC), para. 421.
89 Ibid., para. 421.
90 *Prosecutor v Mladen Naletilić and Vinko Martinović*, ICTY, IT-98-34-T, Trial Judgment, 31 March 2003 (*Naletilić and Martinović* TC), para. 235, referring to *Tadić* TC, paras 638–639.
91 See, for example, *Naletilić and Martinović* TC, paras 392.
92 *Prosecutor v Stanislav Galić*, ICTY, IT-98-29-T, Trial Judgment, 5 December 2003 (*Galić* TC), para. 143.
93 *Prosecutor v Stanislav Galić*, ICTY, IT-98-29-A, Appeal Judgment, 30 November 2006 (*Galić* AC), para. 144.
94 Ibid., para. 144.

Also warranting mention is the case of *Blagojević and Jokić*, where, again, the Trial Chamber concentrated on defining the term 'civilian'. It held that:

> The term 'civilian' refers to persons not taking part in hostilities, including members of armed forces who have laid down their arms and those placed *hors de combat* by sickness, wounds, detention or any other cause.[95]

The Trial Chamber cited the Appeals Judgment in *Blaskić* as authority for this statement.[96] However, this is not, in fact, what the Appeals Chamber in *Blaskić* found: it held that members of the armed forces or organised armed groups cannot claim civilian status. Interestingly, Bassiouni quotes the above passage of *Blagojević and Jokić* with approval when discussing the definition of 'civilian population'.[97] He cites the passage as authority for the finding that persons *hors de combat* form part of the civilian population under customary international law.[98] Bassiouni's reference to this case is unfortunate for three reasons: first, in this passage, the Trial Chamber are not defining the term 'civilian population', they are defining the term 'civilian'; second, it is disputed that persons *hors de combat* are 'civilian' for the purposes of crimes against humanity; and finally, the supposed authority on which the Trial Chamber relies – the *Blaskić* Appeals Judgment – is not an authority for the position that the Trial Chamber is taking.[99] Bassiouni's reliance on this case is therefore misplaced.

The case law from this period is muddled. One source of confusion lies in the difference between the notion of 'civilian' and that of 'civilian population'. Some judgments have endeavoured to include persons *hors de combat* within the notion of 'civilian',[100] other judgments have included them within the notion of civilian population,[101] while others suggest that they can be part of neither.

95 *Prosecutor v Ljube Boškoski and Johan Tarčulovski*, ICTY, IT-04-82-T, Trial Judgment, 10 July 2008 (*Boškoski and Tarčulovski* TC), para. 544.

96 Ibid., referring to *Blaskić* AC, paras 113–114.

97 Bassiouni, *supra* FN 4, p. 193.

98 In his book, Bassiouni makes no mention of the difficulties which the ICTY has had in determining whether fighters who are *hors de combat* can be victims of crimes against humanity. Bassiouni, *supra* FN 4.

99 Later in his book, when discussing how civilian population has been defined before the ICTY and the ICTR, Bassiouni states that '[c]ivilian population has consistently been defined as "people who are not taking any active part in the hostilities, including members of the armed forces who laid down their arms and those persons placed *hors de combat* by sickness, wounds, detention or any other cause"'. He refers purely to the jurisprudence of the ICTR as authority for this statement. As we shall see, his statement is true as regards the ICTR, but, as this analysis shows, it has not been the case at the ICTY. Bassiouni, *supra* FN 4, pp. 196–197.

100 *Blaškić* TC, para. 214; *Blaškić* AC, para. 114; *Galić* TC, para. 143; and *Galić* AC, para. 144. Also see *Kupreškić* TC, para. 547; and *Blagojević and Jokić* TC, para. 544.

101 *Naletilić and Martinović* TC, para. 235.

(iii) A resolution of the issue: the Martić *and* Mrškić *cases*

Matters finally came to a head in two cases: *Martić* and *Mrškić*. In *Martić*, the Trial Chamber agreed with the *Blaskić* Appeals Chamber that persons *hors de combat* do not fall within the definition of 'civilian'.[102] The Chamber found that classifying all persons who were not actively participating in combat at the time of the crime as civilians would impermissibly blur the necessary distinction between combatants and civilians. Victims of crimes against humanity had to be shown to have been civilians in accordance with Article 50(1) of Protocol I.[103]

Following hot on its heels came the *Mrškić* case, which concerned atrocities committed against POWs. The Trial Chamber began by noting that the jurisprudence of the Tribunal had not yet been called upon to pronounce on the question of whether the notion of crimes against humanity is intended to apply to crimes listed in Article 5 when the individual victims of such crimes are not civilians.[104] It reviewed the relevant jurisprudence to find that it supported a definition of 'civilian' based on Article 50 of Protocol I, as opposed to one based on Common Article 3, as advocated for by the Prosecution.[105] It agreed with the Trial Chamber's finding in *Martić* that persons *hors de combat* cannot be included as civilians under Article 5 of the ICTY Statute, stating:

> It has been argued that the distinction between civilians and combatants in Article 5 is obsolete and that it would be contrary to the whole spirit of modern international human rights law and humanitarian law to limit to civilians (especially in times of peace) the international protection of individuals against horrendous and large-scale atrocities. The point has been made that, if crimes against humanity may be committed in times of peace as well (*i.e.* outside armed conflicts) it no longer makes sense to require that such crimes can be perpetrated against civilians alone. Why, the argument goes, should members of military forces be excluded, since they would not be protected by international humanitarian law?
>
> It is important to observe that failing to consider atrocities against fighters *hors de combat* as crimes against humanity does not mean that these acts will go unpunished. If committed in the context of an armed conflict, they are likely to qualify as war crimes, as will be the situation in the typical case before the ICTY. If committed in peacetime, they will be punishable under national law. There may perhaps be a 'protection gap' in those situations, as crimes of this nature would fall outside the jurisdiction of international criminal courts and national authorities may not always

102 *Prosecutor v Milan Martić*, ICTY, IT-95-11-T, Trial Judgment, 12 June 2007 (*Martić* TC), para. 55, referring to *Blaškić* AC, para. 114, and *Galić* AC, para. 437.

103 *Martić* TC, para. 56.

104 Ibid., para. 443. This was not, in fact, strictly true, for the matter had been considered in *Kordić* (*Kordić and Čerkez* AC, para. 421); as the Trial Chamber later noted itself, see- *Prosecutor v Mile Mrškić et al*, ICTY, IT-95-13/1-T, Trial Judgment, 27 September 2007 (*Mrškić* TC), p. 194, FN 1717. There had also been victims who were persons *hors de combat* in *Naletilić and Martinović*.

105 *Mrškić* TC, paras 449–454.

be willing to prosecute. However, it is not for this Tribunal to fill this gap through its case law.[106]

The Chamber concluded that 'there is insufficient evidence in support of the proposition that the notion of crimes against humanity has expanded, under customary international law, so as to include crimes against combatants',[107] and that 'civilian' in Article 5 does not include persons *hors de combat*.[108] The victims of crimes against humanity must be civilians, and if they are non-civilians, the more appropriate charge is war crimes.[109] Accordingly, as the victims did not constitute civilians under Article 5, the crimes committed against them could not constitute crimes against humanity.[110] Both *Martić* and *Mrškić* were appealed. The *Martić* appeal was heard first.

The Prosecution in *Martić* urged the Appeals Chamber to follow the reasoning in the *Kordić and Čerkez* Appeal Judgment, arguing that it set a binding precedent that persons *hors de combat* are civilians under Article 5.[111] The Chamber rejected this argument, pointing to the *Blaskić* and *Galić* Appeal Judgments and their definition of 'civilian' based on Article 50 of Protocol I. The Chamber found that 'civilian' had to be interpreted in accordance with the ordinary meaning of the term,[112] and agreed with the Trial Chamber's finding that the term 'civilian' in Article 5 does not include persons *hors de combat*.[113]

However, the Appeals Chamber then examined the Prosecution's second submission. This asked the Chamber to determine whether it is a condition of the *chapeau* of Article 5 of the ICTY Statute that in order to be a victim of a crime against humanity, the victim had to have had civilian status and whether persons *hors de combat* who are present within the civilian population are excluded from constituting victims of the crime.[114] The Chamber found that the *chapeau* requirement does not require that the individual criminal acts be committed only against civilians; rather it requires proof that an attack was primarily directed against a civilian population, as opposed to being against a limited and randomly selected number of individuals.[115] The civilian population requirement serves to emphasise the collective nature of the crime. The Chamber concluded that, providing that the *chapeau* requirement is fulfilled and that there has been a widespread or systematic attack against a civilian population, individual victims who are *hors de combat* can be victims of crimes against humanity.[116]

106 Ibid., paras 459 and 460.
107 Ibid., para. 460.
108 Ibid., para. 461.
109 Ibid., para. 463.
110 Ibid., para. 481.
111 *Prosecutor v Milan Martić*, ICTY, IT-95-11-A, Appeal Judgment, 8 October 2008 (*Martić* AC), para. 293.
112 Ibid., para. 297.
113 Ibid., para. 302.
114 Ibid., para. 303.
115 Ibid., para. 305, quoting *Prosecutor v Milorad Kunarac et al*, ICTY, IT-96-23 and IT-96-23/1-A, Appeal Judgment, 12 June 2002, para. 90.
116 Ibid., para. 307, and see paras 303–314.

This was found to have been customary international law at the time of the commission of the offences.[117]

Turning to the *Mrškić* Appeal, the Appeals Chamber noted that the Trial Chamber had relied on the *Blaskić* Appeal Judgment when reaching its conclusion that individual victims of crimes against humanity must be civilians.[118] It found that the pronouncements in *Blaskić* that 'the specificity of a crime against humanity results not from the status of the victim but the scale and organisation in which it must be committed',[119] and that 'both the status of the victim as a civilian and the scale on which it is committed or the level of organization involved characterize a crime against humanity',[120] related to the jurisdictional requirement of Article 5 that crimes against humanity be committed as part of a widespread or systematic attack against a civilian population.[121] The civilian status of the victims, the number of civilians and the proportion of civilians within the civilian population, are important when determining whether the *chapeau* requirement of crimes against humanity has been fulfilled.[122] The Chamber concurred with the Appeal Chamber's finding in *Martić* in holding that there is no requirement that the individual victims of crimes against humanity be civilians, providing that it is shown there has been a widespread or systematic attack against a civilian population,[123] concluding that:

> To convict an accused of crimes against humanity, it must be proven that his acts were related to a widespread or systematic attack against a civilian population and that he knew that his acts were so related. Such an assessment must be made on a case-by-case basis.[124]

However, when applying its conclusions to the facts of the case, the Appeals Chamber found that the victims had been singled out due to their being suspected of being members of the Croatian forces. The perpetrators acted on the understanding that their acts were directed against members of the Croatian armed forces, and they treated them differently from the rest of the civilian population. This precluded the inference that they intended their acts to form part of the attack against the civilian population. There was no nexus between the crimes committed against the prisoners and the widespread or systematic attack against the civilian population of Vukovar. Accordingly, the crimes committed against the POWs did not qualify as crimes against humanity; they could only be war crimes.[125]

117 Ibid., paras 311 and 313.
118 *Prosecutor v Mile Mrškić et al*, ICTY, IT-95-13/1-A, Appeal Judgment, 5 May 2009 (*Mrškić* AC), paras 27 and 28.
119 Ibid., para. 107, quoting *Blaškić* TC, para. 208.
120 Ibid., para. 107.
121 *Mrškić* AC, para. 28.
122 Ibid., para. 32, and see paras 30 and 31.
123 Ibid., para. 33.
124 Ibid., para. 41.
125 Ibid., paras 42–44.

The *Martić* and *Mrškić* Appeal Judgments confirm that persons *hors de combat* can be victims of crimes against humanity for the purposes of Article 5 of the ICTY Statute.[126] Both judgments held that persons *hors de combat* are not 'civilian' for the purposes of crimes against humanity, nor are they part of the notion of 'civilian population'. Whether a population is a 'civilian population' or not depends upon the number of civilians and the proportion of civilians within the group.[127] However, providing that the *chapeau* elements are met, and that there is a nexus between the attack against the persons *hors de combat* and the overall attack against the civilian population, persons *hors de combat* can be victims of the crime.

8.4.2 The ICTR

The difficulties that the ICTY has had in resolving this matter can be contrasted with the experience of the ICTR, which has not wrestled with the issue in the same way. The leading ICTR case is *Akayesu*,[128] where the Trial Chamber cited with approval the *Barbie*[129] and *Touvier*[130] cases and the ICTY *Martić* Rule 61 Decision,[131] to find that:

> Members of the civilian population are people who are not taking any active part in the hostilities, including members of the armed forces who laid down their arms and persons placed *hors de combat* by sickness, wounds, detention or any other cause.[132]

The Chamber noted that this definition accords with that given in Common Article 3 of the Geneva Conventions, an assimilation which it did not find to be problematic.[133] This definition of 'civilian population' has been applied consistently by the ICTR in subsequent cases,[134] and has not been the subject of dispute.[135]

126 See *Prosecutor v Jadranko Prlić et al*, ICTY, IT-04-74-T, Trial Chamber, 29 May 2013 (*Prlić* TC), para. 38.
127 *Mrškić* AC, para. 32.
128 *Prosecutor v Jean-Paul Akayesu*, ICTR-96-4-T, Trial Judgment, 2 September 1998 (*Akayesu* TC), para. 582.
129 Ibid., paras 569–570.
130 Ibid., paras 571–575.
131 Ibid., para. 575.
132 Ibid., para. 582.
133 Ibid., at FN 146.
134 See, for example, *Prosecutor v George Anderson Nderubumwe Rutaganda*, ICTR-96-3-T, Trial Judgment, 6 December 1999, para. 72; *Prosecutor v Alfred Musema*, ICTR-96-13-A, Trial Judgment, 27 January 2006, para. 207; *Prosecutor v Semanza*, ICTR-97-20T, Trial Judgment, 15 May 2003, para. 330; *Prosecutor v Paul Bisengimana*, ICTR-00-60-T, Trial Judgment, 13 April 2006, paras 48–51; *Prosecutor v Athanase Seromba*, ICTR-2001-66-I, Trial Judgment, 13 December 2006, para. 358; *Prosecutor v Jean de Dieu Kamuhanda*, ICTR-95-54A-T, Trial Judgment, 22 January 2004, para. 667; and *Prosecutor v Juvénal Kajelijeli*, ICTR-98-44A-T, Trial Judgment, 1 December 2003, paras 873–874.
135 However, see *Prosecutor v Clément Kayishema and Obed Ruzindana*, ICTR-95-1-T, Trial Judgment, 21 May 1999 (*Kayishema* TC), para. 127.

Clearly, the approach taken by the ICTR is different from that taken in the *Martić* and *Mrškić* Appeal Judgments. The ICTR has defined the term 'civilian population' as including persons *hors de combat*, whereas the *Martić* and *Mrškić* Appeal Judgments view the term 'civilian population' as comprising only civilians; however, provided that an attack against persons *hors de combat* is connected to an attack against a civilian population, they can be victims of the crime. The difference between these two approaches could be significant. Following the ICTR's approach, an attack that is purely against persons *hors de combat* can constitute a crime against humanity, as persons who are *hors de combat* form part of the 'civilian population'. However, following the ICTY's approach, an attack purely against persons *hors de combat* cannot be a crime against humanity, as there is no nexus between the attack and an attack against a civilian population. It was for this reason that the POWs in the *Mrškić* case were found by the Appeals Chamber not to have been victims of crimes against humanity.[136] Thus, attacks solely against persons *hors de combat* can amount to a crime against humanity at the ICTR, but not at the ICTY. The implications of this will be considered shortly.

8.4.3 The ICC

The ICC has yet to consider this issue in detail. In the *Bemba* Decision, the court observed that neither 'civilian' nor 'civilian population' is defined within the Statute. However, it stated that, according to the well-established principle of IHL, '[t]he civilian population … comprises all persons who are civilians as opposed to members of armed forces and other legitimate combatants'.[137] The court did not examine the issue of whether persons *hors de combat* can nevertheless constitute victims of crimes against humanity.

The *Katanga* Trial Judgment also considered the matter. When interpreting Article 7 of the ICC Statute, the Trial Chamber referred to the definition of 'civilian' given in Article 50(1) of Protocol I and to 'civilian population' as defined in Article 50(2), to find that 'civilian population' comprises all persons who are civilians.[138] It did not, therefore, adopt the ICTR's approach of including persons *hors de combat* as part of the civilian population for the purposes of the crime. The Chamber did not refer to the ICTY cases on the matter, and it did not consider

136 *Mrškić*, paras 42–44.

137 *Prosecutor v Jean-Pierre Bemba Gombo*, Decision on Confirmation of Charges, Case no ICC-01/05-01/08, Pre-Trial Chamber II, 15 June 2009, para. 78, referring to *Prosecutor v Milorad Kunarac et al*, ICTY, IT-96-23-T, Trial Judgment, 22 February 2001, para. 425. Also see Joakim Dungel, 'Defining Victims of Crimes against Humanity: Martić and the International Criminal Court', 22(4) *Leiden Journal of International Law* 727–752 (2009), pp. 741–742.

138 *Prosecutor v Germain Katanga*, Judgment pursuant to article 74 of the Statute, Case no ICC-01/04-01/07, 7 March 2014 (*Katanga* TC), para. 1102; and see *Prosecutor v Germain Katanga and Mathieu Ngudjolo Chui*, Decision on Confirmation of Charges, Case no ICC-01/04-01/07, Pre-Trial Chamber I, 30 September 2008 (*Katanga* Decision), para. 399.

whether it would adopt the *Martić* and *Mrškić* Appeal Chambers' approach to this issue. It therefore remains a possibility that it will do so in future cases.[139]

8.4.4 The SCSL

The SCSL has also had occasion to examine the matter. In the *RUF* case, the Trial Chamber concurred with the ICTY Appeals Chamber in the *Martić* case, that where a person is *hors de combat* and the victim of an act which objectively forms part of a broader attack directed against a civilian population, this act may amount to a crime against humanity.[140] The court found that the killing of a soldier who had been *hors de combat* at the time, constituted a crime against humanity.[141]

8.5 Persons *hors de combat* as victims of crimes against humanity: a critical review

The analysis above has illustrated that while the ICTY, ICTR and SCSL agree that persons *hors de combat* can be victims of crimes against humanity, their reasoning differs as to why this is so. Some cases have tried to subsume persons *hors de combat* within the definition of 'civilian'; others have tried to include them within the concept of 'civilian population'; and others have held that they are part of neither, but can nevertheless be victims of the crime, providing that the attack against them forms part of an overall attack against a civilian population. However, is it right that persons *hors de combat* be victims of crimes against humanity? If so, which of the solutions found in the case law is most satisfactory and what challenges can arise in such cases?

8.5.1 Should persons hors de combat *be able to constitute victims of crimes against humanity?*

The concept of crimes against humanity was originally developed to counter the difficulty that atrocities committed against civilians where the perpetrators and victims belonged to the same side of an armed conflict did not qualify as war crimes at the time. It was most probably expected that atrocities perpetrated against those who had been fighting would be prosecuted either as war crimes or under domestic law. This reasoning could be said to apply equally today, raising the question of whether there is a need for atrocities committed against persons *hors de combat* to be prosecuted as crimes against humanity. The following section explores, first, whether the category of war crimes sufficiently encompasses

139 The case concerned an attack on the village of Bogoro in the Democratic Republic of the Congo. The village contained a military camp. Although fighters who were *hors de combat* had been killed during the attack, the deaths had not formed part of the charges against the accused. *Katanga* TC, para. 856.

140 *Prosecutor v Issa Hassan Sesay, Morris Kallon and Augustine Gbao*, SCSL-2004-15-T, Trial Judgment, 2 March 2009 (*RUF* case TC), para. 82.

141 Ibid., para. 1448.

atrocities committed against persons *hors de combat*; second, whether crimes against humanity are graver than war crimes; and finally, the changing nature of crimes against humanity.

(i) Does the category of war crimes sufficiently encompass atrocities committed against persons hors de combat?

Many atrocities committed against persons *hors de combat* can be prosecuted as war crimes. However, there are potentially two situations where war crimes law may not apply. The first is the situation where the perpetrator and the victim fight for the same side. The argument has been made in this book that the claim that crimes committed by a perpetrator against a member of a non-opposing force cannot qualify as war crimes is questionable.[142] Nevertheless, it remains a widely held view. If correct, it would mean that in cases where atrocities are committed against members of non-opposing forces, the only possible charge in ICL would be that the act constituted a crime against humanity, providing, of course, that the *chapeau* requirements of the crime are met.[143] Certainly, the crime could be prosecuted at a national level. However, if the acts formed part of a widespread or systematic attack, it seems illogical that they should not be prosecuted as crimes against humanity simply because the victim had been involved in the fighting. There is potentially a gap in the law;[144] a crime committed by a perpetrator against a member of a non-opposing force would not, according to the traditional view at least, qualify as a war crime, and unless it constitutes a crime against humanity, the only possible avenue for prosecution would be in a domestic court under domestic law.

Second, atrocities committed during peacetime can only qualify as crimes against humanity or genocide.[145] The view taken by the delegates at the Rome Conference was that during peacetime everyone is classified as 'civilian'.[146] However, it is not a foregone conclusion that the same view would be taken by an ICT. Ambos and Wirth, for example, write: 'in times of peace, the term "civilian" must be interpreted even more broadly than in time of war, when humanitarian law provides some protection.'[147] While they argue that the term 'civilian' be

142 See discussion in Chapter 5.

143 Whether crimes against humanity can be committed against members of non-opposing forces during peacetime is currently under consideration in Cases 003 and 004 at the ECCC.

144 This was acknowledged by the Trial Chamber in the *Mrškić* case, *Mrškić* TC, para. 460.

145 Ambos and Wirth explain: 'In times of peace, the prohibition against crimes against humanity is – apart from the very narrow law of genocide – the only applicable (criminal) law to protect human rights.' Kai Ambos and Steffen Wirth, *The Current Law of Crimes against Humanity: An Analysis of UNTAET Regulation 15/2000*, Criminal Law Forum 1–90 (2002), p. 24.

146 Darryl Robinson, 'Defining "Crimes against Humanity" at the Rome Conference', 93 *American Journal of International Law* 43 (1999).

147 Ambos and Wirth, *supra* FN 145, p. 24.

interpreted more broadly, they do not go as far as the delegates in Rome in arguing that everyone qualifies as a civilian for the purposes of crimes against humanity.

The ICTR has considered the meaning of civilian in peacetime. In *Kayishema*, the Trial Chamber held that where there was no armed conflict, the term 'includes all persons *except* those who have the duty to maintain public order and have the legitimate means to exercise force'.[148] Thus, while an ICT may interpret 'civilian' broadly in peacetime,[149] they will not necessarily view, for example, members of state armed forces as being 'civilian' for the purposes of crimes against humanity. Indeed, this would seem to be the view of the Trial Chamber in *Mrškić* when it stated:

> If [atrocities against persons *hors de combat* are] committed in peacetime, they will be punishable under national law. There may perhaps be a 'protection gap' in those situations, as crimes of this nature would fall outside the jurisdiction of international criminal courts and national authorities may not always be willing to prosecute. However, it is not for this Tribunal to fill this gap through its case law.[150]

A measure of doubt therefore exists as to who would qualify as 'civilian' during peacetime.[151]

A further reason for including persons *hors de combat* as victims of the crime is due to the nature of crimes against humanity: first, because crimes against humanity are often regarded as being graver than war crimes; and second, because of the interests that crimes against humanity protect.

(ii) Are crimes against humanity graver than war crimes?

There is some debate within ICL as to whether crimes against humanity are graver than war crimes, and indeed whether there is a hierarchy of crimes in ICL at all.[152] The statutes of the different ICTs contain no express ranking: on the face of it, genocide, crimes against humanity and war crimes are viewed as being equally serious.[153] The issue of whether crimes against humanity are more serious than war crimes has tended to arise at the sentencing stage. In the *Tadić* Sentencing Decision, the

148 *Kayishema* TC, para. 127.

149 Ibid.

150 *Mrškić* TC, para. 460.

151 At the time of writing this matter is currently under consideration at the ECCC, in cases 003 and 004.

152 See Richard May and Marieke Wierda, 'Is there a Hierarchy of Crimes in International Law?' in Vohrah *et al*, *Man's Inhumanity to Man, Essays on International Law in Honour of Antonio Cassese* (Kluwer Law International, 2003), pp. 511–532; and Micaela Frulli, 'Are Crimes against Humanity More Serious than War Crimes?', 12(2) *European Journal of International Law* 329–350 (2001).

153 However, see Frulli, who argues that there are at least three provisions in the Rome Statute which show a general persuasion that crimes against humanity are more serious than war crimes, namely Article 31(1)(c) (self defence), Article 33 (superior orders) and Article 124. Frulli, ibid., pp. 339–340.

Appeals Chamber overturned the findings of the Trial Chamber[154] to find that 'there is in law no distinction between the seriousness of a crime against humanity and that of a war crime'.[155] While the ICTY has maintained the view that there is no hierarchy of crimes within its Statute, research has shown that crimes of humanity have, in practice, tended to attract a heavier penalty than war crimes at the sentencing stage.[156] In contrast, the ICTR has acknowledged a hierarchy of crimes, with genocide being regarded as the most serious, followed by crimes against humanity and, finally war crimes.[157]

Another way of gauging the seriousness of a crime is to assess the seriousness of the conduct it encompasses. The acts of murder, torture and rape as war crimes can be as heinous as their equivalents charged as a crime against humanity.[158] However, the two categories of crime can be distinguished by the different legal requirements which must be proven in order for a specific act to constitute a war crime or a crime against humanity. Although the underlying crimes may be the same for both, whether a crime constitutes a war crime or a crime against humanity depends upon the context in which the crimes were committed. For a criminal act to constitute a war crime, it must be shown that the act had a nexus to an armed conflict. Minor crimes can constitute war crimes providing that this

154 *Prosecutor v Duško Tadić*, ICTY, IT-94-1-T *bis*-R117, Sentencing Judgment, 11 November 1999, para. 28, citing *Erdemović*, where it was held that 'all things being equal, a punishable offence, if charged and proven as a crime against humanity is more serious and should ordinarily entail a heavier penalty than if it were proceeded upon on the basis that it were a war crime'. *Prosecutor v Dražen Erdemović*, ICTY, IT-96-22-A, Appeal Judgment, 7 October 1997, Joint Separate Opinion of Judge McDonald and Vohrah, para. 20.

155 *Prosecutor v Duško Tadić*, ICTY, IT-94-1-A and IT-94.1-A *bis*, Judgment in Sentencing Appeals, 26 January 2000 (*Tadić*, Appeals Chamber Sentencing Judgment), para. 69. Also see Separate Opinions of Judge Shahabuddeen and Judge Cassese; and see Payam Akhavan, *Reducing Genocide to Law: Definition, Meaning and the Ultimate Crime* (Cambridge University Press, 2012), pp. 67–81.

156 Akhavan, ibid., p. 81. Meernik and King write: 'contrary to what the judges argue in their opinions, there is something of a rank ordering of general categories of offences. Genocide is treated differently from crimes against humanity and war crimes, and crimes against humanity are punished more severely than war crimes.' James Meernik and Kimi King, 'The Sentencing Determinants of the International Criminal Tribunal for the Former Yugoslavia: An Empirical and Doctrinal Analysis', 16 *Leiden Journal of International Law* 717–750 (2003), p. 736.

157 In *Akayesu* it was stated that crimes against humanity are 'particularly shocking to the human conscious' and 'precisely on account of their extreme gravity, crimes against humanity and genocide must be punished appropriately'. *Prosecutor v Jean-Paul Akayesu*, ICTR-96-4-T, Sentencing Judgment, 2 October 1998. Also see Frulli, *supra* FN 153, pp. 345–346.

158 Judge Shahabuddeen stated: 'A war crime can be very serious … it can be as extensive and odious as a crime against humanity. Whether it was or was not so in a particular case would turn on the facts.' *Tadić*, Appeals Chamber Sentencing Judgment, Separate Opinion of Judge Shahabuddeen, p. 41, referring to *Erdemović*, Separate and Dissenting Opinion of Judge Li, paras 20–22. Also see May and Wierda, *supra* FN 153, pp. 517–518.

nexus exists, the classic example being a soldier who steals a loaf of bread.[159] In order for a crime to constitute a war crime at an international level, it must be of a certain gravity: thus, for example, Article 8 of the ICC Statute provides that the ICC has jurisdiction over war crimes, 'particularly when committed as part of a plan or policy or as part of a large-scale commission of such crimes'. As May and Wierda explain, 'this requirement does not constitute an *element* of the offence but rather reflects the fact that all crimes tried by international courts have to meet a minimum jurisdictional threshold of seriousness to qualify as international crimes'.[160] For a war crime, the perpetrator must have the *mens rea* required for the particular criminal act and must be shown to have been aware of the factual circumstances establishing the existence of an armed conflict.[161] There is no need to show that the crime was part of a larger series of crimes, or was committed for a particular purpose.[162]

In contrast, crimes against humanity have an inbuilt contextual element: in order for a crime to constitute a crime against humanity it must form part of a bigger picture, namely part of a widespread or systematic attack directed against any civilian population. Crimes against humanity have a specific *mens rea*: that the alleged perpetrator knew, or intended that, his conduct would be part of a widespread or systematic attack directed against a civilian population.[163] Frulli explains that when comparing the elements of crimes against humanity and war crimes, for crimes against humanity 'the *dolus* is different not only in nature (more specific), but also in gravity (more serious)'.[164] Accordingly, in view of the fact that crimes against humanity have this requirement of scale and have a specific *mens rea* requirement, they are, *in general*, more serious than war crimes.[165]

Excluding persons *hors de combat* from being victims of this category of crime excludes them from being eligible as victims of the more serious of the two crimes. Of course, one could argue that this is perfectly reasonable nevertheless; the concept of crimes against humanity was developed to protect civilians rather than those who are participating in the armed conflict. This leads to a third argument regarding the changing nature of crimes against humanity.

159 *Tadić* Decision, para. 94.

160 May and Wierda, *supra* FN 153, pp. 522; and see Akhavan, *supra* FN 156, pp. 72–73. Also see *Tadić*, Appeals Chamber Sentencing Judgment, Separate Opinion of Judge Cassese, para. 13.

161 See, for example, ICC Elements of Crimes.

162 May and Wierda, *supra* FN 153, p. 524.

163 *Tadić*, Appeals Chamber Sentencing Judgment, Separate Opinion of Judge Cassese, para. 14.

164 See Frulli, who notes that there is arguably a hierarchy within crimes against humanity itself – with crimes against humanity of a persecution type (which requires a discriminatory intent that is deemed to be higher than the ordinary intent required for crimes against humanity) being more serious than crimes against humanity of the murder type. Frulli, *supra* FN 153, pp. 337–338.

165 May and Wierda, *supra* FN 153, p. 526, and see pp. 514–526; and Akhavan, *supra* FN 156, p. 79. Depending on the facts of the case, some war crimes can be more serious than crimes against humanity, see May and Wierda, *supra* FN 153, pp. 523–524.

(iii) The changing nature of crimes against humanity

Originally, the concept of crimes against humanity was tied to the notion of armed conflict, but the requirement that there be a nexus between the specific act and an armed conflict has disappeared from more recent definitions of the crime. While the ICTY Statute contains a nexus requirement, no such requirement exists within the ICTR Statute or Article 7 of the ICC Statute. According to some scholars, the concept has morphed from one that is tied to the notion of armed conflict into one which is rooted in human rights.[166] Certainly, crimes against humanity criminalise substantial violations of some human rights – the right to life, or the right not to be tortured or subject to inhuman or degrading treatment or punishment, for example – but they do not criminalise violations of all kinds of human rights; for example, violations of most economic, social and cultural rights would not constitute crimes against humanity. Rather, crimes against humanity can be viewed as 'protecting humanity from certain mass atrocity crimes'.[167] The concept of crimes against humanity therefore has a different focus to that of war crimes. In *Erdemović*, Judges McDonald and Vohrah reflected that:

> It is in their very nature that crimes against humanity differ in principle from war crimes. Whilst rules proscribing war crimes address the criminal conduct of a perpetrator towards an immediate protected object, rules proscribing crimes against humanity address the perpetrator's conduct not only towards the immediate victim, but also towards the whole of humankind … Because of their heinousness and magnitude they constitute egregious attacks on human dignity, on the very notion of humaneness. They consequently affect, or should affect, each and every member of mankind, whatever his or her nationality, ethnic group and location.[168]

If one views the concept of crimes against humanity as criminalising mass atrocity crimes which attack the very notion of humaneness,[169] it seems illogical and unjust to exclude persons *hors de combat* from being victims of this category of crime.

166 'Without a link to armed conflict, crimes against humanity are tantamount to the categorical criminalization of massive human rights violations.' Akhavan, *supra* FN 156, p. 26.
167 Bassiouni, *supra* FN 4, p. 42.
168 *Erdemović*, Judges McDonald and Vohrah, para. 20. Also see *Einsatzgruppen* case, which stated of crimes against humanity, '[i]t is fundamentally different from the mere war crime in that it embraces systematic violations of fundamental human rights committed at any time against the nationals of any nation. They may occur during peace or in war. The animus of criminal intent is directed against the rights of all men, not merely the right of persons within a war zone'. *United States of America of America v Otto Ohlendorf et al*, IV Trials of War Criminals before Nuernberg Military Tribunals under Control Council Law No 10, US Govt Printing Office, Washington DC, 1951, p. 48.
169 May explains that: 'War crimes are crimes against *humaneness*, not really crimes against all of humanity.' Larry May, *War Crimes and Just War* (Cambridge University Press, 2009), p. 42.

Some may question whether persons *hors de combat* should be protected under ICL to the same extent as civilians. If we look to IHL, once a person is *hors de combat*, he or she no longer constitutes a legitimate target.[170] Common Article 3 extends the same protection to all those who are not APH/DPH, whether they be persons *hors de combat* or civilians. Under the Geneva Conventions and their Protocols, the basic, underlying protection is the same: all those who fall under their protection are to be treated humanely.[171] Both civilians and persons *hors de combat* are to be treated with humanity, and accordingly, widespread or systematic attacks that violate the basic human rights of either group should equally constitute a crime against humanity.

8.5.2 Is the current situation satisfactory?

While the ICTY, ICTR and the SCSL concur that persons *hors de combat* can be victims of crimes against humanity, they have given different reasons as to why this is so. The majority of ICTR case law[172] views persons *hors de combat* as forming part of the civilian population. The ICTY and SCSL take the view that although persons *hors de combat* are not part of the civilian population, providing that there is a nexus between the attack against them and the overall attack against the civilian population, individual victims of crimes against humanity can be persons *hors de combat*. Which of these solutions is correct?

The ICTR's view that persons *hors de combat* are part of the civilian population is contrary to both Article 50(2) of Protocol I and customary international law, which exclude such persons from the concept.[173] The ICTY's solution – that while persons *hors de combat* do not form part of the civilian population, they can be victims of crimes against humanity if the attack against them forms part of the overall attack against a civilian population – means that the notion of 'civilian population' does not have to be twisted to encompass this class of victim. Its solution is therefore preferable to that proffered by the ICTR.

However, even if one agrees that the ICTY's solution fits within the parameters of the law, one can question whether it is necessary to have the 'civilian population' requirement in the *chapeau* requirement of crimes against humanity at all. The 'civilian population' requirement was included within the major definitions of crimes against humanity to help ensure that a specific crime of, for example, murder or torture, forms part of a larger picture: it elevates an otherwise isolated criminal act into something bigger and emphasises the collective nature of the crime.[174] This is not the only part of the *chapeau* requirement that has this function; the act must also form 'part of a widespread or systematic attack'.[175] Not all

170 Article 41(1), Protocol I.
171 Article 75, Protocol I, and Article 4, Protocol II.
172 *Kayishema* TC, para. 127.
173 See Rule 5, ICRC Study.
174 Larry May, *Crimes against Humanity: A Normative Account* (Cambridge University Press, 2005), p. 121.
175 Article 7, ICC Statute.

previous definitions of the crime contained a requirement that the acts be directed against a 'civilian population': the ILC 1996 Draft had no such requirement and during the Rome Conference it was mooted that 'any population' should be used instead. The reference to 'civilian' can be traced back to the origins of the crime: that it was developed to encompass crimes committed by the Nazis against German civilians. Perhaps the use of the word 'civilian' also soothed an underlying concern that omitting the word would mean that lawful acts of war – killing and injuring those who were DPH – could constitute crimes against humanity.

The requirement that acts be directed against a 'civilian population' means that criminal acts which are committed solely against persons *hors de combat*,[176] and which do not form part of an overall attack against the civilian population, cannot qualify as crimes against humanity, as proved to be the case in *Mrškić*.[177] Certainly, the same acts against persons *hors de combat* can be prosecuted as war crimes, and indeed this is what happened in *Mrškić*, where the Appeals Chamber found the attacks against the POWs to amount to war crimes. However, in some instances the category of war crimes is insufficient to highlight the gravity of the crime that has occurred. Crimes against humanity have a symbolic nature as crimes that offend humankind. The murder or torture of civilians or persons *hors de combat* is equally offensive, and both should constitute crimes against humanity. There is, therefore, a strong argument to be made that the 'civilian population' element of the *chapeau* is unnecessary, and should be dispensed with in any future definitions of the crime.[178]

8.5.3 The importance of bearing IHL in mind

IHL permits certain behaviour to be used against those who fight, which is prohibited for use against those who have civilian protection. This means that behaviour which may be a crime against humanity if committed against a civilian may not be if committed against military personnel.[179] Two such examples are the crimes against humanity of deportation and forcible transfer.[180] In the case of *Popović*, the Trial Chamber of the ICTY considered the case of a column of able-bodied men, comprising both military and civilian members, fleeing Srebrenica. The Trial Chamber stated that:

176 The 'civilian population' requirement prevents atrocities committed solely against child soldiers from being prosecuted as crimes against humanity. Certainly, crimes against child soldiers can be prosecuted as war crimes, but permitting acts such as rape, forced marriage or forced intoxication to be prosecuted as crimes against humanity would emphasise the distaste that the international community has for these types of crimes. Sarah L. Wells, 'Crimes against Child Soldiers in Armed Conflict Situations: Application and Limits of International Humanitarian Law', 12 *Tulane Journal of International and Comparative Law* 287 (2004), pp. 299–303.

177 *Mrškić* AC, paras 42–44.

178 However, see draft Article 3, Proposed International Convention on the Prevention and Punishment of Crimes against Humanity, discussed above.

179 *Mrškić* TC, para. 458.

180 Other examples are imprisonment and forced labour. These have been discussed in the context of war crimes, see Chapter 4.

> For the legal element of forcible transfer, the issue is whether at the time (the men) did so by choice or because of force … the Trial Chamber finds that the military component of the column, unlike the civilian component, had options other than fleeing. They had the choice to stay and fight, to surrender or to retreat … the decision of the members of the ABiH and others who were active participants in the hostilities was a strategic one in a military context. While the risks of battle and the difficult conditions for prisoners of war may have motivated the decision to leave, it was in the end a choice made and cannot be categorized as a forcible transfer.[181]

While the Trial Chamber reached the correct decision in finding that the military personnel in the column were not victims of forcible transfer, it did so for the wrong reason. Forcing fighters to retreat is a legitimate military strategy under IHL. Whether the fighters had a choice to stay, or did so for military reasons is irrelevant. Unfortunately, on Appeal, because only the civilian members of the column had been found to be victims of the crime of forcible transfer, the Trial Chamber's comments were not addressed by the Appeals Chamber.[182]

The *Popović* case also concerned another incident, where a group containing ABiH fighters was forced to retreat across a river after failing to defend a town from advancing enemy troops.[183] The Trial Chamber found this to constitute the crime of forcible transfer as a crime against humanity, stating: 'Their decision to flee cannot be categorised as a strategic one taken in military terms. Simply, they fled the enclave in fear of their lives.'[184] Again, the Chamber failed to take account of the fact that forcing military personnel to flee is a legitimate strategy. Fortunately, on Appeal, the conviction for forcible transfer was overturned. The Appeals Chamber correctly found that 'forcible displacement of enemy soldiers is not prohibited under international law'.[185]

It is therefore important that ICTs ensure that they bear IHL in mind when determining whether crimes against humanity have been committed when it is alleged that some of the victims had been fighting.[186]

181 *Prosecutor v Vujadin Popović et al*, IT-05-88-T, Trial Judgment, 10 June 2010 (*Popović* TC), para. 927.

182 Indeed, the Appeals Chamber seem to approve of the Trial Chamber's finding, which is at odds with their decision regarding the river incident. *Prosecutor v Vujadin Popović et al*, IT-05-88-A, Appeal Judgment, 30 January 2015 (*Popović* AC), para. 781.

183 *Popović* TC, para. 955.

184 Ibid., para. 956. Also see Rogier Bartels, 'Discrepancies between International Humanitarian Law on the Battlefield and in the Courtroom: The Challenges of Applying International Humanitarian Law During International Criminal Trials', in Matthee *et al* (eds), *Armed Conflict and International Law: In Search of the Human Face: Liber Amicorum in Memory of Avril McDonald* (T.M.C. Asser Press, 2013), pp. 367–368.

185 *Popović* AC, para. 774.

186 Also see *Prlić* concerning the crime of imprisonment. *Prlić* TC, para. 60; and see, for example, paras 955 and 963.

8.6 Fighting and genocide

The issue of whether those who fight can be victims of genocide has not caused nearly as much of a headache for ICTs as the issue of whether they can be victims of crimes against humanity, the reason being that there is no 'civilian population' requirement in the definition of genocide.[187] This was noted by the ICTR Trial Chamber, which explained:

> under Crimes Against Humanity all of the enumerated crimes must be committed specifically against a 'civilian population' whereas to commit the crime of genocide one must commit acts to destroy 'members of a group.' The victims' civilian or military status has no bearing on proving an allegation of genocide.[188]

However, the issue is not entirely straightforward. The difficulty lies in proving that an alleged victim who had been involved in the fighting was killed with the requisite genocidal intent, rather than for a military motive. Were they killed due to being a member of a particular group, were they killed for military purposes, or were they killed for both reasons?

While 'motive is generally irrelevant in criminal law',[189] in cases of genocide the personal motives of a perpetrator, such as obtaining personal economic benefits or political advantage, do not preclude them from also having the specific intent to commit genocide.[190] In the case of *Niyitegeka*, the Appeals Chamber rejected the Defence's argument that the words 'as such' within the definition of the crime[191] should be interpreted as meaning 'solely', in other words that the requisite finding of specific intent would be predicated on showing that the perpetrator committed the acts against members of the protected group *solely* because they were members of that group.[192] The Appeals Chamber found that the words 'as such' are an important element of the crime of genocide, in that they have the effect of drawing a clear distinction between mass murder and crimes where the perpetrator targets

187 For genocide to be made out, it must be proved that the criminal acts were committed with the 'intent to destroy, in whole, or in part, a national, ethnical, racial or religious group, as such', see Article II, Convention on the Prevention and Punishment of the Crime of Genocide, 1948, and see Article 4, ICTY Statute, Article 2 ICTR Statute and Article 6 ICC Statute.

188 *Kayishema* TC, para. 631.

189 *Tadić* AC, para. 268. Motive becomes relevant at the sentencing stage by acting in mitigation, or in aggravation, of the sentence, ibid., para. 269. For a discussion of motive as it relates to genocide, see William Schabas, *Genocide in International Law: The Crime of Crimes* (Cambridge University Press, 2009), pp. 294–306.

190 *Prosecutor v Goran Jelisić*, ICTY, IT-95-10-A, Appeal Judgment, 5 July 2001, para. 49; and *Prosecutor v Clément Kayishema and Obed Ruzindana*, ICTR-95-1-A, Appeals Judgment, 1 June 2001, para. 161.

191 See *supra* FN 188.

192 *Prosecutor v Eliézer Niyitegeka*, Case no ICTR-96-14-A, Appeal Judgment, 9 July 2004, para. 51.

a specific group because of their nationality, race, ethnicity or religion. However, the phrase:

> Does not prohibit a conviction for genocide in a case in which the perpetrator was also driven by other motivations that are legally irrelevant in this context. Thus, the Trial Chamber was correct in interpreting 'as such' to mean that the proscribed acts were committed against the victims *because of* their membership in the protected group, but not *solely* because of such membership.[193]

It is therefore possible for a perpetrator to commit the crime of genocide while having motives in addition to the specific genocidal intent. Accordingly, a victim can be killed for military reasons, and yet still be a victim of genocide, providing there is evidence of specific intent.[194]

Behrens argues that in some cases other motives 'may in the particular situation have been so dominant in the mind of the perpetrator as to leave no room for specific intent'.[195] This is particularly the case where there may have been military reasons behind the alleged genocidal act. Behrens refers to motives such as military motives as 'primary motives'. He argues that primary motives can co-exist with genocidal intent and may in certain situations replace that intent.[196]

The issue of whether alleged genocidal acts had been committed for military reasons rather than with genocidal intent arose before the ICTY in the case of *Krstić*. The case concerned mass killings in Srebrenica. The Defence argued that the killing of Bosnian Muslim men was motivated solely by the desire to eliminate them as a potential military threat, rather than with the intent of committing genocide. This argument was rejected by the Trial Chamber,[197] which went to some lengths to explain why this was so.[198] On Appeal, the Appeals Chamber agreed with the approach taken by the Trial Chamber.[199] The Chamber considered the intent element of genocide and found that:

> the intent requirement of genocide is not limited to instances where the perpetrator seeks to destroy only civilians. Provided the part intended to be destroyed is substantial, and provided that the perpetrator intends to destroy

193 Ibid., para. 53.

194 Paul Kim, 'The Law of Genocide in the Jurisprudence of the ICTY and ICTR in 2004', 5 *International Criminal Law Review* 431–446 (2005), p. 439.

195 Paul Behrens, 'Genocide and the Question of Motives', 10 *Journal of International Criminal Justice* 501–523 (2012), p. 518.

196 Ibid., pp. 514–522.

197 *Prosecutor v Radislav Krstić*, ICTY, IT-98-33-T, Trial Judgment, 2 August 2001, para. 593.

198 The Chamber found that the perpetrators had not distinguished between men of military status and civilians. The Bosnian Serb forces could not have failed to know that the selective destruction of the group would have a lasting impact on the entire group. *Krstić* TC, paras 547 and 593–598. Also see Behrens, *supra* FN 196, pp. 518–519.

199 *Prosecutor v Radislav Krstić*, ICTY, IT-98-33-A, Appeal Judgment, 19 April 2004, paras 26–35.

> that part as such, there is nothing in the definition of genocide prohibiting, for example, a conviction where the perpetrator killed detained military personnel belonging to a protected group because of their membership in that group. It may be that, in practice, the perpetrator's genocidal intent will almost invariably encompass civilians, but that is not a legal requirement of the offence of genocide.[200]

The Appeals Chamber found that '[t]he killing of the military aged men was, assuredly, a physical destruction, and given the scope of the killings the Trial Chamber could legitimately draw the inference that their extermination was motivated by a genocidal intent'.[201] Thus, even if there were some military reasons behind the criminal acts, the same acts can constitute genocide providing that the specific genocidal intent is proved.

Proving genocidal intent may prove difficult in practice where the alleged victims had been fighting. These difficulties are evident in the case of *Brđanin*, where the victims of the alleged genocide had been predominantly military-aged men, causing the Trial Chamber to comment that 'this additional factor could militate further against the conclusion that the existence of genocidal intent is the only reasonable inference that may be drawn from the evidence'.[202] It found that it was unable to rely on the scope of the killings to show that genocide had occurred;[203] the fact that the victims were military-aged men weighed against the existence of a genocidal intent.

Thus, in suspected cases of genocide where some of the alleged victims had been involved in the fighting, prosecutors have to work particularly hard to show that the alleged victims were targeted with the requisite specific intent, rather than for purely military motives.

8.7 Conclusion

Analysing the development of different definitions of crimes against humanity and the jurisprudence from ICTs from the perspective of whether persons *hors de combat* are eligible victims is an interesting and revealing exercise. When drafting different definitions of the crime, the significance of the requirement that the specified acts be committed against a 'civilian' population has been subject to minimal or no discussion. The reasons behind this may be that drafters have believed that most atrocities committed against persons *hors de combat* can be prosecuted as war crimes; or because they have viewed crimes against humanity as a crime that protects civilians rather than those who have been involved in the fighting.

200 Ibid., para. 226.
201 Ibid.
202 *Prosecutor v Radoslav Brđanin*, IT-99-36-T, Trial Judgment, 1 September 2004, para. 979.
203 Ibid., at FN 2460.

It has been left to ICTs to determine whether persons *hors de combat* can be victims of this class of crimes. The ICTR, ICTY and SCSL agree that they can be, although they have taken different approaches. The argument has been made in this chapter that the ICTR's approach under which persons *hors de combat* form part of the 'civilian population' interprets the term too broadly, and that the ICTY's approach is to be preferred. It is to be hoped that the ICC will follow the ICTY's lead in this regard.

Although this clarification that persons *hors de combat* can be victims of crimes against humanity is to be welcomed, new definitions of crimes against humanity should dispense with the 'civilian population' requirement. If the purpose of crimes against humanity is to encompass grave infringements of human rights, it is no longer logical to restrict the boundaries of the crime in this way. The concept of the 'civilian' population within the major definitions of crimes against humanity is a relic of the past; the collective element of the crime is supported by the 'widespread or systematic element'. The *chapeau* requirement should acknowledge that every human being can be a victim of a crime against humanity, regardless of whether they are a civilian or a person *hors de combat*. This would allow for atrocities committed solely against persons *hors de combat* to be regarded as crimes against humanity, subject to the strict *proviso* that the laws of war are borne in mind when determining whether or not a crime against humanity has occurred.

Proving that the crime of genocide has occurred also becomes more complex when alleged victims have been involved in the fighting. The prosecutor must show that the perpetrator had a specific genocidal intent as regards the alleged genocidal acts and that these acts were not carried out for purely military motives.

Although the vast majority of victims of crimes against humanity and genocide tend to be civilians, it is important that prosecutors and judges bear in mind that those involved in fighting can also fall victim to these crimes. While such cases may prove to be more complicated than cases involving civilian victims, it is nevertheless a worthwhile undertaking. Acts of genocide or crimes against humanity are always atrocious, whatever the victims' status.

9 Conclusion

This book began with a quotation from celebrated military historian John Keegan: 'Soldiers are not as other men.'[1] The intervening chapters have shown that this sentiment applies also, to some extent at least, in the context of fighting and victimhood in ICL. This should come as no surprise: one of the core international crimes, war crimes, is based upon IHL. IHL draws a distinction between those who fight and those who do not, and this is in turn reflected when serious violations of IHL are charged as war crimes in ICL. However, it is not only in the context of war crimes that the fact that an alleged victim of a crime had been involved in the fighting becomes relevant; it also has importance in relation to the crime of genocide and crimes against humanity. This study has shown that ICTs have struggled at times with issues surrounding fighting and victimhood in ICL, and have not always fully appreciated the differences that can arise and the relevance it can have if an alleged victim of an international crime had been involved in fighting.

One thread running through the book concerns the challenges involved in determining who constitutes a victim of an international crime. For example, ICTs have not always adequately distinguished between the notions of status (as a civilian or a combatant in the generic sense) and conduct (APH/DPH). These concepts are key when ascertaining whether an individual has been the victim of a war crime, or whether they were a lawful casualty of war. The book has argued that ICTs should be more cognisant of the difference between these notions and should take a more structured approach in war crimes cases involving persons.

Another recurring theme concerned the need to use accurate language when describing the status of alleged victims. For example, some cases have used the term 'combatant' to describe an individual who could be legitimately targeted. However, combatant status has a specific meaning in IHL, and even if the term is being used in a generic sense (which should be made clear in the judgment), it still implies that the fighter in question had lost their civilian protection and was a legitimate target at all times. ICTs have on occasion used the term 'combatant' to describe persons who would more accurately be described as civilians who had only temporarily lost their protection from attack because they were

1 John Keegan, *A History of Warfare* (Pimlico Military Classics, 2004), p. xvi.

APH/DPH.[2] Rather than make awkward assessments explaining why a certain individual was a 'combatant' in unsuitable circumstances,[3] ICTs could make greater use of the notion of civilians who APH/DPH,[4] meaning that despite their civilian status the individual in question was nevertheless legitimately targeted as they were engaging in an act of APH/DPH at the time they were attacked. Another example of incorrect labelling has occurred when detained persons have been described as 'POWs', yet the court has made inadequate assessment as to whether the requirements for POW status were met.[5] ICTs should therefore be more careful in their use of language when describing the status of alleged victims and have greater awareness as to the consequences of that status in IHL.

ICTs could also be more mindful in cases involving alleged victims who were connected to irregular armed groups. Sufficient consideration has not always been given concerning when these persons lose civilian protection and could be legitimately targeted. Courts should actively consider how to determine membership in a particular armed group and whether to follow the ICRC Guidance (that only those who had a continuous combat function in the group lose their civilian protection), or whether to adopt a different approach. This is an important and somewhat controversial issue in IHL, and ICTs should give thought as to how to deal with this matter in each case.

Chapters 3 and 4 explored issues surrounding those who fight and victimhood in the context of war crimes. During hostilities, those involved in fighting are legitimate targets (unless *hors de combat*) meaning that, generally speaking, attacks against them are not war crimes. However, IHL sets limits concerning the means and methods of warfare that may be used during conflict, some of which apply to those who fight.

IHL prohibits and restricts the use of certain weapons, and the status of the victims attacked can be relevant when determining whether a war crime has occurred. In the case of prohibited weapons, the status of those who are attacked is irrelevant to the crime: the use of chemical weapons is a war crime regardless of whether they are used against civilians or fighters. However, where the use of a weapon is restricted rather than prohibited, as with incendiary weapons or landmines, that the persons attacked were fighters has an impact upon whether the use of the weapon was permitted, and consequently, whether a war crime was committed.

At present, ICTs have very limited jurisdiction over crimes involving the use of prohibited or restricted weapons. Although it is possible for perpetrators using these weapons to be prosecuted for the harm caused rather than for the act of

2 For example, see *Prosecutor v Issa Hassan Sesay, Morris Kallon and Augustine Gbao*, SCSL-2004-15-T, Trial Judgment, 2 March 2009, para. 233.

3 See *Prosecutor v Stanislav Galić*, ICTY, IT-98-29-T, Trial Judgment, 5 December 2003, paras 556–557, and chapter 2.

4 Article 51(3), Protocol I.

5 See *Prosecutor v Mile Mrškić et al*, ICTY, IT-95-13/1-T, Trial Judgment, 27 September 2007, para. 207.

using the weapons themselves, this applies only if those who are attacked were civilians.[6] In cases where prohibited weapons cause harm to fighters or to persons *hors de combat*, ICTs may find their hands tied.[7]

Once a fighter becomes *hors de combat* they are entitled to greater protection under IHL, and can consequently be a victim of many more war crimes. Jurisprudence from ICTs has clarified that persons *hors de combat* are not civilians and cannot be victims of crimes which require that the victim have civilian status.[8] However, a person *hors de combat* is not APH/DPH and can therefore be a victim of crimes where the focus is upon the victim's conduct, such as violations of Common Article 3. A person is not APH/DPH as soon as they are detained, although this has not always been appreciated by ICTs. Some courts have made investigations into a detained person's clothing and appearance when deciding whether they were APH/DPH, when the simple fact of their detention suffices.[9]

Although persons *hors de combat* can be victims of many of the same crimes as civilians, some differences do remain. The ICTY's approach (which will hopefully be followed by the ICC) that those who do not fall under the protection of Geneva Convention III are protected under Geneva Convention IV, means that when the Conventions apply, there is a reduced need to investigate whether detainees had POW status. Nevertheless, POW status remains relevant in respect of a number of important crimes, including unlawful confinement, unlawful deportation or transfer, and forced labour.

Two special groups were discussed in the book: child soldiers and peacekeepers. Child soldiers have been one of the hot topics in ICL in recent years. Much effort has gone into clarifying and interpreting the war crimes of enlistment, conscription and use of children under 15 to actively participate in hostilities. While some questionable findings have been made in a few cases, overall, the SCSL and ICC have made great inroads in illuminating these crimes.

Peacekeepers were included in this book because although they are civilians, due to their unique position in conflict situations, special attention is needed in cases involving peacekeepers to ensure that civilian protection has been retained. Chapter 7 explored how ICTs have tackled this matter. Loss of civilian protection can occur in two distinct ways: either by the whole peacekeeping force becoming a party to the conflict, meaning its personnel become combatants; or by individual peacekeepers APH/DPH, meaning that their civilian protection is regained once they stop so participating. ICTs have not always appreciated this difference, but the *Abu Garda* Decision from the ICC has taken a firm step in the right direction in this regard.

The book also discussed some issues concerning fighting and victimhood which, perhaps somewhat surprisingly, have not yet been fully resolved. The prime

6 For example, for intentionally directing an attack against the civilian population or civilians who were not APH/DPH, see Articles 8(2)(b)(i) and 8(2)(e)(i), ICC Statute.
7 An exception could be Article 8(2)(b)(ix), ICC Statute.
8 Articles 8(2)(b)(i) and 8(iv), ICC Statute.
9 See Chapter 2.

example of this is the question of whether war crimes can be committed against members of non-opposing forces. Chapter 5 argued that the traditional view that IHL does not protect members of non-opposing forces, and that such atrocities cannot therefore constitute war crimes, is mistaken. In fact, IHL treaty law does impose obligations on armed forces *vis-à-vis* their own troops in both IACs and NIACs. The *Ntaganda* Decision has made an important, but somewhat small, step in clarifying the law in this regard by confirming that members of non-opposing forces can be victims of sexual crimes under Articles 8(2)(b)(xxii) and 8(2)(e)(vi) of the ICC Statute. The case shows that this is a topical and important issue, which is crying out for in-depth analysis and clarification at the international level.

Another issue that has only been resolved relatively recently (by the ICTY at least), is whether persons *hors de combat* can be victims of crimes against humanity. This particular puzzle cuts to the bone of what makes those who fight different from those who do not. While the decision that persons *hors de combat* can be victims of these crimes is welcome, the ICTY's approach means that attacks purely against such persons do not constitute crimes against humanity. The argument has been made that the nature of this class of crime, as constituting serious violations of basic human rights, and the gravity of this class of crime, as being considered (in general) to be more serious than war crimes, means that persons *hors de combat* should be able to qualify as victims of crimes against humanity in their own right. Future definitions of the crime should dispense with the 'civilian population' requirement entirely. This would have to be interpreted in accordance with IHL, meaning that actions against fighters or persons *hors de combat* that are permitted under IHL would not constitute crimes against humanity.

During the First World War, the majority of casualties were combatants.[10] In the intervening century, the nature of warfare has changed: today it is civilians who bear the brunt of war. When atrocities occur during modern armed conflicts, it is civilian victims who are the most numerous and whose maltreatment attracts the greatest condemnation. On the occasions when these atrocities come before international prosecutors, it is understandable that the focus is upon civilian victims, and it is understandable that crimes against those involved in the fighting (with child soldiers being the exception) do not feature prominently.[11] Indeed, some may argue that the focus within ICL should purely be upon the civilian victims of atrocities rather than upon suspected military victims. The fact that a person chose to become a member of an armed force means that he 'has allowed himself to be

10 It is estimated that 5% of the casualties in the First World War were civilians. See Simon Chesterman (ed.), *Civilians in War* (Lynne Rienner Publishers, 2001), p. 2; and see Bethany Lacina and Nils Petter Gleditsch, 'Monitoring Trends in Global Combat: A New Dataset of Battle Deaths', 21 *European Journal of Population* 145–166 (2005).

11 Claire Garbett, 'The Legal Representation of the Civilian and Military Casualties of Contemporary Conflicts: Unlawful Victimisation, its Victims and their Visibility at the ICTY', 16(7) *The International Journal of Human Rights* 1059 (2012).

made into a dangerous man'[12] and has some moral culpability, at least in comparison to a civilian unwittingly caught up in a conflict.[13]

There can undoubtedly be additional challenges in prosecuting cases involving fighters and persons *hors de combat* as victims. However, the underlying thrust of this volume has been that the fact that an alleged victim of an atrocity had been involved in the fighting should, in itself, be immaterial. If prisoners in the hands of a party to the conflict are tortured and killed, or if a poisonous gas is employed, these actions are crimes regardless of whether the victims were civilians or fighters/ persons *hors de combat.* While it may be true that 'soldiers are not as other men' in the context of fighting and victimhood in ICL, they are men (and women) nonetheless. As the Scottish poet Robert Burns wrote, 'A man's a man for a' that' – a sentiment that it is hoped this book has served to emphasise.

12 Michael Walzer, *Just and Unjust Wars: A Moral Argument with Historical Illustrations* (Basic Books, 2006), p. 145.

13 For example, there is debate concerning to what extent there is a moral duty on soldiers to prioritise the lives of others, particularly enemy civilians, if it involves putting their own lives in jeopardy. See Paul Woodruff, 'Justification or Excuse: Saving Soldiers at the Expense of Civilians', *Canadian Journal of Philosophy*, Supp. Vol. VIII 159 (1982); Eyal Benvenisti, 'Human Dignity in Combat: The Duty to Spare Enemy Civilians', 39 *Israel Law Review* 81 (2006); Jeff McMahan, 'The Just Distribution of Harm between Combatants and Non Combatants', 38(4) *Philosophy and Public Affairs* 343 (2010); David Luban, 'Risk Taking and Force Protection', *Georgetown Public Law and Legal Theory Research Paper* No 11–72 (2011); and Adil Ahmad Haque, 'Killing in the Fog of War', 86 *Southern California Law Review* 63 (2012).

Bibliography

Akande, Dapo, *Can the ICC Prosecute for Use of Chemical Weapons in Syria?* Available at: www.ejiltalk.org/can-the-icc-prosecute-for-use-of-chemical-weapons-in-syria/ (last accessed 1 May 2017)

Akhavan, Payam, 'Reconciling Crimes Against Humanity with the Laws of War, Human Rights, Armed Conflict and the Limits of Progressive Jurisprudence', 6 *Journal of International Criminal Justice* 21–37(2008)

Akhavan, Payam, *Reducing Genocide to Law: Definition, Meaning and the Ultimate Crime* (Cambridge University Press, 2012)

Alamuddin, Amal, and Philippa Webb, 'Expanding Jurisdiction over War Crimes under Article 8 of the ICC Statute', 8 *Journal of International Criminal Justice* 1219–1243 (2010)

Allain, Jean, and John R.W.D. Jones, 'A Patchwork of Norms: A Commentary on the 1996 Draft Code of Crimes against the Peace and Security of Mankind', 8(1) *European Journal of International Law* 100–117(1997)

Ambos, Kai, 'The First Judgment of the International Criminal Court (*Prosecutor v Lubanga*): A Comprehensive Analysis of the Legal Issues', 12(2) *International Criminal Law Review* 115–153(2012)

Ambos, Kai, and Steffen Wirth, 'The Current Law of Crimes against Humanity: An Analysis of UNTAET Regulation 15/2000', *Criminal Law Forum* 1–90(2002)

Badar, M.E., 'From the Nuremberg Charter to the Rome Statute: Defining the Elements of Crimes against Humanity', 5 *San Diego International Law Journal* 73(2004)

Bangura, Mohamed A., 'Prosecuting the Crime of Attack on Peacekeepers: A Prosecutor's Challenge', 23(01) *Leiden Journal of International Law* 165–181(2010)

Bartels, Rogier, 'Dealing with the Principle of Proportionality in Armed Conflict in Retrospect: The Application of the Principle in International Criminal Trials', 46(2) *Israel Law Review* 271–315(2013a)

Bartels, Rogier, 'Discrepancies Between International Humanitarian Law on the Battlefield and in the Courtroom: The Challenges of Applying International Humanitarian Law During International Criminal Trials' in M. Matthee *et al*, *Armed Conflict and International Law: In Search of the Human Face, Liber Amicorum in Memory of Avril McDonald* (Asser Press, 2013b)

Bassiouni, M. Cherif, *The Legislative History of the International Criminal Court* (Transnational Publishers, 2005)

Bassiouni, M. Cherif, *International Criminal Law, Volume I: Sources, Subjects and Contents* (Martinus Nijhoff, 2008a)

Bassiouni, M. Cherif, 'The Regulation, Control and Prohibition of the Use of Certain Weapons in the Context of War', in M. Cherif Bassiouni, *International Criminal Law, Volume I: Sources, Subjects and Contents* (Martinus Nijhoff, 2008b)

Bassiouni, M. Cherif, 'Crimes against Humanity: The Case for a Specialised Convention', 9 *Washington University Global Studies Law Review* 575(2010)

Bassiouni, M. Cherif, *Crimes against Humanity: Historical Evolution and Contemporary Application* (Cambridge University Press, 2011)

Baxter, Major Richard R., 'So Called "Unprivileged Belligerency", Spies, Guerrillas and Saboteurs', 28 *British Yearbook of International Law* 323(1951)

Baxter, Major Richard R., 'The Duties of Combatants and the Conduct of Hostilities (Law of The Hague)', in *International Dimensions of Humanitarian Law* (Henry Dunant Institute, UNESCO, 1988)

Behrens, Paul, 'Genocide and the Question of Motives', 10 *Journal of International Criminal Justice* 501–523(2012)

Benvenisti, Eyal, 'Human Dignity in Combat: The Duty to Spare Enemy Civilians', 39 *Israel Law Review* 81(2006)

Bill, Brian J., 'The Rendulic "Rule": Military Necessity, Commander's Knowledge, and Methods of Warfare', 12 *Yearbook of International Law* 119(2009)

Blank, Laurie R., 'Operational Law Experts Roundtable on the Gotovina Judgment: Military Operations, Battlefield Reality and the Judgment's Impact on the Effective Implementation and Enforcement of International Humanitarian Law', *Public Law & Legal Theory Research Paper Series*, Research Paper no 12–186(2012)

Boelaert-Suominen, Sonja, 'Grave Breaches, Universal Jurisdiction and International Armed Conflict: Is Customary Law Moving Towards a Uniform Enforcement Mechanism for All Armed Conflicts?' 5 *Journal of Conflict and Security Law* 63–103(2000)

Bonomy, Iain, *Principles of Distinction and Protection at the ICTY* (Torkel Opsahl Academic EPublisher, 2013)

Boothby, William H., *Weapons and the Law of Armed Conflict* (Oxford University Press, 2009)

Boothby, William H., '"And for such time as": The Time Dimension to Direct Participation in Hostilities', 42 *New York University Journal of International Law & Policy* 741(2010)

Boothby, William H., *The Law of Targeting* (Oxford University Press, 2012)

Bothe, Michael, 'War Crimes' in Antonio Cassese *et al* (ed.) *The Rome Statute of the International Criminal Court: A Commentary*, Volume I (Oxford University Press, 2002)

Bourloyannis-Vrailas, M.-Christiane, 'Crimes against United Nations and Associated Personnel' in Gabrielle Kirk McDonald and Olivia Swaak-Goldman (eds), *Substantive and Procedural Aspects of International Criminal Law, The Experience of International and National Courts*, Volume I (Kluwer Law International, 2000)

Cassese, Antonio, 'Crimes against Humanity' in Cassese *et al*, *The Rome Statute of the International Criminal Court: A Commentary*, Volume I (Oxford University Press, 2002)

Cassese, Antonio, 'On Some Merits of the Israeli Judgment on Targeted Killings', 5(2) *Journal of International Criminal Justice* 339(2007)

Cassese, Antonio, 'Crimes against Humanity: Comments on Some Problematical Aspects' in Cassese, *The Human Dimension of International Law, Selected Papers* (Oxford University Press, 2008a)

Cassese, Antonio, *International Criminal Law* (Oxford University Press, 2008b)

Cassese, Antonio *et al*, *The Rome Statute of the International Criminal Court: A Commentary* (Oxford University Press, 2002)

Cassese, Antonio *et al*, *The Oxford Companion to International Criminal Justice* (Oxford University Press, 2009)

Chesterman, Simon (ed.), *Civilians in War* (Lynne Rienner Publishers, 2001)

Chiesa, Luis E., 'Duress Demanding Heroism and Proportionality', 41 *Vanderbilt Journal of Transnational Law* 741(2008)

Child Soldiers International, *The Arms Trade Treaty and its Implication for Preventing Child Soldiers – A Preliminary Assessment*, May 2013. Available at: www.child-soldiers.org/research_report_reader.php?id=658 (last accessed 1 May 2017)

Clark, Janine Natalya, 'Courting Controversy: The ICTY's Acquittal of Croatian Generals Gotovina and Markač', 11(2) *Journal of International Criminal Justice* 399–423(2013)

Clark, Roger S., 'Building on Article 8(2)(b)(xx) of the Rome Statute of the International Criminal Court: Weapons and Methods of Warfare', 12(3) *New Criminal Law Review* 366–389(2009)

Combs, Nancy Amoury, *Fact-Finding Without Facts: The Uncertain Evidentiary Foundations of International Criminal Convictions* (Cambridge University Press, 2010)

Corn, Geoffrey, and Chris Jenks, 'Two Sides of the Combatant Coin: Untangling Direct Participation in Hostilities from Belligerent Status in Non-international Armed Conflicts', 33 *University of Pennsylvania Journal of International Law* 313(2011)

Cottier, Michael, 'War Crimes' in Otto Triffterer, *Commentary on the Rome Statute of the International Criminal Court* (C.H. Beck, Hart, Nomos, 2008)

Coupland, Robin, and Peter Herby, 'Review of the Legality of Weapons: A New Approach – The SIrUS Project', 835(1) *International Review of the Red Cross* 583 (1999)

Crawford, Emily, *The Treatment of Combatants and Insurgents Under the Law of Armed Conflict* (Oxford University Press, 2010)

Cryer, Robert, 'Hague Law Comes Home: Prosecuting Weapons Offences at the International Criminal Court', *Acta Juridica* 238(2003)

Cryer, Robert, *Prosecuting International Crimes, Selectivity and the International Criminal Law Regime* (Cambridge University Press, 2005)

Cryer, Robert, 'Of Custom, Treaties, Scholars and the Gavel: The Influence of the International Criminal Tribunals on the ICRC Customary Law Study', 11(2) *Journal of Conflict and Security Law* 239–263(2006)

Dehn, John C., 'Permissible Perfidy? Analysing the Colombian Hostage Rescue, the Capture of Rebel Leaders and the World's Reaction', 6(4) *Journal of International Criminal Justice* 627(2008)

Del Ponte, Carla, 'Investigation and Prosecution of Large-scale Crimes at the International Level, the Experience of the ICTY', 4 *Journal of International Criminal Justice* 539(2006)

Dinstein, Yoram, 'The System of Status Groups in International Humanitarian Law' in Wolff Heintschel von Heinegg and Volker Epping (eds), *International Humanitarian Law Facing New Challenges: Symposium in the Honour of Knut Ipsen* (Springer, 2007)

Dinstein, Yoram, *The Conduct of Hostilities under the Law of International Armed Conflict* (Cambridge University Press, 2010)

Doria, José *et al*, *The Legal Regime of the International Criminal Court: Essays in Honour of Professor Igor Blishchenko: In Memoriam Professor Igor Pavlovich Blishchenko (1930–2000)* (Martinus Nijhoff, 2009)

Dörmann, Knut, 'The Legal Situation of "Unlawful/Unprivileged Combatants"', 85(849) *International Review of the Red Cross* 45–74(2003)

Dörmann, Knut *et al*, *Elements of War Crimes under the Rome Statute of the International Criminal Court: Sources and Commentary* (Cambridge University Press, 2002)

Draper, Colonel G.I.A.D., 'The Status of Combatants and the Question of Guerrilla Warfare', in Michael A. Meyer and Hilaire McCoubrey (eds), *Reflections on Law and Armed Conflicts: The Selected Works on the Laws of War by the Late Professor Colonel G.I.A.D. Draper* (Kluwer Law International, 1998)

Drumbl, Mark A., *Reimagining Child Soldiers in International Law and Policy* (Oxford University Press, 2012)

Dungel, Joakim, 'Defining Victims of Crimes against Humanity: Martić and the International Criminal Court', 22(4) *Leiden Journal of International Law* 727–752(2009)

Engdahl, Ola, *Protection of Personnel in Peace Operations, The Role of the 'Safety Convention' against the Background of General International Law* (Martinus Nijhoff, 2007)

Engdahl, Ola, 'Prosecution of Attacks against Peacekeepers in International Courts and Tribunals', 51/2 *Military Law and the Law of War Review* 249(2012)

Epps, Valerie, 'The Soldier's Obligation to Die when Ordered to Shoot Civilians or Face Death Himself', 37(4) *New England Law Review* 987(2002)

Fenrick, William J., 'The Prosecution of Unlawful Attack Cases Before the ICTY', 7 *Yearbook of International Humanitarian Law* 153–189(2004)

Fenrick, William J., 'Riding the Rhino: Attempting to Develop Usable Legal Standards for Combat Activities', 30 *Boston College International & Comparative Law Review* 111 (2007a)

Fenrick, William J., 'The Targeted Killings Judgment and the Scope of Direct Participation in Hostilities', 5(2) *Journal of International Criminal Justice* 332(2007b)

Fleck, Dieter, 'The Law of Non-International Armed Conflict' in Dieter Fleck (ed.), *The Handbook of International Humanitarian Law* (Oxford University Press, 2013)

Frank, Daniel, 'Article 8(2)(b)(iii) – Attacking Personnel or Objects Involved in a Humanitarian Assistance or Peacekeeping Mission' in Roy S. Lee (ed.), *The International Criminal Court: Elements of Crimes and Rules of Procedure and Evidence* (Transnational Publishers Inc., 2001)

Frulli, Micaela, 'Are Crimes against Humanity More Serious than War Crimes?', 12(2) *European Journal of International Law* 329–350(2001)

Gadler, Alice, 'The Protection of Peacekeepers and International Criminal Law: Legal Challenges and Broader Protection', 11 *German Law Journal* 585(2010)

Gaeta, Paola, 'Serious Violations of the Law on the Conduct of Hostilities: A Neglected Class of War Crimes?' in Fausto Pocar *et al*, *War Crimes and the Conduct of Hostilities: Challenges to Adjudication and Investigation* (Edward Elgar, 2013)

Garbett, Claire, 'The Legal Representation of the Civilian and Military Casualties of Contemporary Conflicts: Unlawful Victimisation, its Victims and their Visibility at the ICTY', 16 *The International Journal of Human Rights* 1059(2012)

Garraway, Charles, 'Article 8(2)(b)(xxvi) – Using, Conscripting or Enlisting Children', in Roy S. Lee (ed.) *The International Criminal Court: Elements of Crimes and Rules of Procedure and Evidence* (Transnational Publishers Inc., 2001a)

Garraway, Charles, 'Elements of War Crimes', in Roy S. Lee *et al*, *The International Criminal Court: Elements of Crimes and Rules of Procedure and Evidence* (Transnational Publishers Inc., 2001b)

Garraway, Charles, 'Combatants. Substance or Semantics' in Michael N. Schmitt *et al*, *International Law and Armed Conflict: Exploring the Faultlines: Essays in Honour of Yoram Dinstein* (Martinus Nijhoff, 2007)

Geiβ, Robin, 'Poison, Gas and Expanding Bullets: The Extension of the List of Prohibited Weapons at the Review Conference of the International Criminal Court in Kampala', 13 *Yearbook of International Humanitarian Law* 337–352(2011)

Goodman, Ryan, 'The Detention of Civilians in Armed Conflict', 103(1) *American Journal of International Law* 48–74(2009)

Goodman, Ryan, 'The Power to Kill or Capture Enemy Combatants', 24(3) *European Journal of International Law* 819–853(2013)

Graf, R., 'The International Criminal Court and Child Soldiers: An Appraisal of the Lubanga Judgment', 10(4) *Journal of International Criminal Justice* 945–969(2012)

Guibert, Nolween, and Tilman Blumenstock, 'The First Judgement of the Special Court for Sierra Leone: A Missed Opportunity?' 6 *The Law and Practice of International Courts and Tribunals* 367(2007)

Haines, Steven, 'Weapons, Means and Methods of Warfare' in Elizabeth Wilmshurst *et al*, *Perspectives on the ICRC Study on Customary International Humanitarian Law* (Cambridge University Press, 2007)

Happold, Matthew, *Child Soldiers in International Law* (Juris Publishing, Manchester University Press, 2005)

Haque, Adil Ahmad, 'Killing in the Fog of War', 86 *Southern California Law Review* 63(2012)

Hayashi, Nobuo, 'The Role of Judges in Identifying the Status of Combatants', 2 *Acta Societatis Martensis* 69–92(2006)

Hays Parks, W., 'Part IX of the ICRC "Direct Participation in Hostilities" Study: No Mandate, No Expertise and Legally Incorrect', 42 *New York University Journal of International Law & Politics* 769(2010)

Heller, Kevin John, *The Nuremberg Military Tribunals and the Origins of International Criminal Law* (Oxford University Press, 2011)

Heller, Kevin John, *Syria, Chemical Weapons and the Incoherence of the VCLT*. Available at: http://opiniojuris.org/2013/08/23/syria-chemical-weapons-incoherence-vclt/ (last accessed 1 May 2017)

Henckaerts, Jean-Marie, 'The Conduct of Hostilities: Target Selection, Proportionality and Precautionary Measures under International Humanitarian Law' in The Netherlands Red Cross, *Protecting Civilians in 21st-Century Warfare, Target Selection, Proportionality and Precautionary Measures in Law and Practice* (8 December 2000)

Henckaerts, Jean-Marie, 'Customary International Law – A Rejoinder to Judge Aldridge', 76 *British Yearbook of International Law* 525(2005)

Henckaerts, Jean-Marie, and Louise Doswald-Beck, *Customary International Humanitarian Law, Volume I: Rules* (Cambridge University Press, 2005)

Henderson, Ian, 'Civilian Intelligence Agencies and the Use of Armed Drones', in Michael N. Schmitt *et al* (eds), 13 *Yearbook of International Humanitarian Law* 133–173(2011)

Hwang, Phyllis, 'Defining Crimes against Humanity in the Rome Statute of the International Criminal Court', 22 *Fordham International Law Journal* 457–504(1998–1999)

International Committee of the Red Cross, *The SIrUS Project: Towards a Determination of which Weapons Cause 'Superfluous Injury or Unnecessary Suffering'* (1997). Available at: www.loc.gov/rr/frd/Military_Law/pdf/SIrUS-project.pdf (last accessed 1 May 2017)

International Committee of the Red Cross, *Interpretive Guidance on the Notion of Direct Participation in Hostilities under International Humanitarian Law*, adopted by the Assembly of the International Committee of the Red Cross, 26 February 2009. Available at: www.icrc.org/eng/assets/files/other/irrc-872-reports-documents.pdf (last accessed 1 May 2017)

International Committee of the Red Cross, *Study on Customary International Law*. Available at: www.icrc.org/customary-ihl/eng/docs/home (last accessed 1 May 2017)

International Institute of Humanitarian Law, *The Manual of Non-International Armed Conflict* (San Remo, 2006). Available at: www.iihl.org/iihl/Documents/The%20Manual%20on%20the%20Law%20of%20NIAC.pdf (last accessed 1 May 2017)

Jinks, Derek, 'The Declining Significance of POW Status', 44 *Harvard International Law Journal* 367(2004)

Jones, H., *Violence against Prisoners of War in the First World War: Britain, France and Germany, 1914–1920* (Cambridge University Press, 2011)

Kalshoven, Frits, 'Conventional Weapons in the "Reaffirmation and Development of the 1970s"', in 'Arms, armaments and international law', *Collected Courses of The Hague Academy of International Law 191* (Martinus Nijhoff, 1985)

Keegan, John, *A History of Warfare* (Pimlico Military Classics, 2004)

Kim, Paul, 'The Law of Genocide in the Jurisprudence of the ICTY and ICTR in 2004', 5 *International Criminal Law Review* 431–446(2005)

Kleffner, Jann K., 'From "Belligerents" to "Fighters" and Civilians Directly Participating in Hostilities – on the Principle of Distinction in Non-International Armed Conflicts One Hundred Years after the Second Hague Peace Conference', 54(2) *Netherlands International Law Review* 315–336(2007)

Kleffner, Jann K., 'Section IX of the ICRC Guidance on Direct Participation in Hostilities: The End of Jus in Bello Proportionality As We Know It?', 45(1) *Israel Law Review* 35–52(2012)

Kleffner, Jann K., 'Friend or Foe? On the Protective Reach of the Law of Armed Conflict: A Note on the SCSL Trial Chamber's Judgment in the Case of *Prosecutor v Sesay, Kalon and Gbao*', in M. Matthee *et al* (eds), *Armed Conflict and International Law: In Search of the Human Face, Liber Amicorum in Memory of Avril McDonald* (Asser Press, 2013)

Kramer, Alan R., 'Prisoners in the First World War', in Sibylle Scheipers (ed.), *Prisoners in War* (Oxford University Press, 2010)

Kravetz, Daniela, 'The Protection of Civilians in War: The ICTY's Galić Case', 17(3) *Leiden Journal of International Law* 521–536(2004)

Lee, Roy S. (ed.), *The International Criminal Court: Elements of Crimes and Rules of Procedure and Evidence* (Transnational Publishers Inc., 2001)

Levie, Howard S., 'Penal Sanctions for Maltreatment of Prisoners of War', 56 *American Journal of International Law* 433(1962)

Levie, Howard S., 'The Employment of Prisoners of War', 57(2) *American Journal of International Law* 318(1963)

Luban, David, 'Risk Taking and Force Protection', *Georgetown Public Law and Legal Theory Research Paper* No 11–72(2011)

McBride, Julie, *The War Crime of Child Soldier Recruitment* (Asser Press, 2014)

McDonald, Gabrielle Kirk, and Olivia Swaak-Goldman, *Substantive and Procedural Aspects of International Criminal Law, The Experience of International and National Courts*, Volume I (Kluwer Law International, 2000)

McKeogh, Colm, *Innocent Civilians: The Morality of Killing in War* (Palgrave, 2002)

McMahan, Jeff, 'The Just Distribution of Harm between Combatants and Non Combatants', 38(4) *Philosophy and Public Affairs* 343(2010)

Matas, David, 'Prosecuting Crimes against Humanity: The Lessons of World War I', 13 *Fordham International Law Journal* 86(1989–1990)

Matthee, M. *et al* (eds), *Armed Conflict and International Law: In Search of the Human Face, Liber Amicorum in Memory of Avril McDonald* (Asser Press, 2013)

May, Larry, *Crimes against Humanity: A Normative Account* (Cambridge University Press, 2005)

May, Larry, *War Crimes and Just War* (Cambridge University Press, 2007)

May, Richard, and Marieke Wierda, 'Is there a Hierarchy of Crimes in International Law?' in Lal Chand Vohrah *et al*, *Man's Inhumanity to Man, Essays on International Law in Honour of Antonio Cassese* (Kluwer Law International, 2003)

Meernik, James, and Kimi King, 'The Sentencing Determinants of the International Criminal Tribunal for the Former Yugoslavia: An Empirical and Doctrinal Analysis', 16 *Leiden Journal of International Law* 717–750(2003)

Melzer, Nils, 'The Principle of Distinction between Civilians and Combatants' in Andrew Clapham and Paola Gaeta (eds), *The Oxford Handbook of International Law in Armed Conflict* (Oxford University Press, 2014)

Moir, Lindsay, 'Crimes against Humanity in Historical Perspective', 3 *New Zealand Yearbook of International Law* 101(2006)

Moir, Lindsay, 'Conduct of Hostilities – War Crimes' in Doria *et al*, *The Legal Regime of the International Criminal Court: Essays in Honour of Professor Igor Blishchenko: In Memoriam Professor Igor Pavlovich Blishchenko (1930–2000)* (Martinus Nijhoff, 2009a)

Moir, Lindsay, 'Grave Breaches and Internal Armed Conflicts', 7 *Journal of International Criminal Justice* 763–787(2009b)

Mullins, Claud, and E.M. Pollock, *The Leipzig Trials: An Account of the War Criminals' Trials and a Study of German Mentality* (H.F. & G. Witherby, 1921)

Nettelfield, Lara J., 'From the Battlefield to the Barracks: The ICTY and the Armed Forces of Bosnia and Herzegovina', 4(1) *International Journal of Transnational Justice* 87–109(2010)

Nicholson, Joanna, 'Is Targeting Naked Child Soldiers a War Crime?', 16 *International Criminal Law Review* 131–154(2016)

Oeter, Stefan, 'Methods and Means of Combat' in Dieter Fleck, *The Handbook of International Humanitarian Law* (Oxford University Press, 2008)

Ohlin, Jens David, 'The Duty to Capture', 97 *Minnesota Law Review* 1268(2013)

Ohlin, Jens David, 'The Combatants' Privilege in Asymmetric and Covert Conflicts', 40 *Yale Journal of International Law* 337–393(2015)

Olásolo, Héctor, *Unlawful Attacks in Combat Situations: From the ICTY's Case Law to the Rome Statute* (Martinus Nijhoff, 2008)

Pacholska, Magdalena, '(Il)legality of Killing Peacekeepers: The Crime of Attacking Peacekeepers in the Jurisprudence of International Criminal Tribunals', 13 *Journal of International Criminal Justice* 43–72(2015)

Pictet, Jean S. (ed.), *Commentary I Geneva Convention for the Amelioration of the Condition if the Wounded and Sick Armed Forces in the Field* (ICRC, Geneva, 1958a)

Pictet, Jean S. (ed.), *Commentary III Geneva Convention Relative to the Treatment of Prisoners of War* (ICRC, Geneva, 1958b)

Pictet, Jean S. (ed.), *Commentary IV Geneva Convention Relative to the Protection of Civilian Persons in Time of War* (ICRC, Geneva, 1958c)

Pinzauti, Giulia, 'Protecting Prisoners of War, The Mrkšić *et al* Appeal Judgment', 8 *Journal of International Criminal Justice* 199–219(2010)

Pocar, Fausto *et al*, *War Crimes and the Conduct of Hostilities, Challenges to Adjudication and Investigation* (Edward Elgar, 2013)

Quénivet, Noëlle, 'Girl Soldiers and Participation in Hostilities', 16 *African Journal of International and Comparative Law* 219(2008)

Reydams, Luc Jan Wouters, and Cedric Ryngaert, *International Prosecutors* (Oxford Scholarship Online, 2012)

Roberts, Adam, 'Lives and Statistics: Are 90% of War Victims Civilians?' 52(3) *Survival: Global Politics and Strategy* 115(2010)

Robinson, Darryl, 'Defining "Crimes against Humanity" at the Rome Conference', 93 *American Journal of International Law* 43(1999)

Robinson, Darryl, 'The Context of Crimes against Humanity', in Lee (ed.), *The International Criminal Court, Elements of Crimes and Rules of Procedure and Evidence* (Transnational Publishers Inc., 2001)

Rogers, Anthony, *Law on the Battlefield* (Juris Publishing, 2004)

Rosen, David M., 'Who is a Child? The Legal Conundrum of Child Soldiers', 25 *Connecticut Journal of International Law* 82(2009–2010)

Sassòli, M., 'The Status of Persons held in Guantánamo under International Humanitarian Law', 2 *Journal of International Criminal Justice* 96–106(2004)

Save the Children, 'Forgotten Casualties of War: Girls in Armed Conflict' 11(2005). Available at: www.peacewomen.org/assets/file/Resources/NGO/HR_ForgottenGirls_SC_2005.pdf

Schabas, William, 'Prohibited Weapons and the Belgian Amendment: Symbolic, but of what?', 22 May 2010. Available at: http://iccreviewconference.blogspot.no/search?q=weapons (last accessed 1 May 2017)

Schabas, William, *An Introduction to the International Criminal Court* (Cambridge University Press, fourth edition, 2011)

Schabas, William, *Unimaginable Atrocities: Justice Politics and Rights at the War Crimes Tribunals* (Oxford University Press, 2012)

Schmitt, Michael N., 'Humanitarian Law and Direct Participation in Hostilities by Private Contractors or Civilian Employees', 5 *Chicago Journal of International Law* 511(2005)

Schmitt, Michael N., 'Deconstructing Direct Participation in Hostilities: The Constitutive Elements', 42 *New York University Journal of International Law & Politics* 697(2010a)

Schmitt, Michael N., 'The Interpretive Guidance on the Notion of Direct Participation in Hostilities – A Critical Analysis', 1 *Harvard National Security Journal* 5(2010b)

Schmitt, Michael N., and Jelena Pejić (eds), *International Law and Armed Conflict: Exploring the Faultlines: Essays in Honour of Yoram Dinstein* (Martinus Nijhoff, 2007)

Schwelb, Egon, 'Crimes against Humanity', 23 *The British Yearbook of International Law* 178(1946)

Sciacovelli, Annita Larissa, 'The Criminalization of the Use of Biological and Chemical Weapons' in Pocar *et al*, *War Crimes and the Conduct of Hostilities, Challenges to Adjudication and Investigation* (Edward Elgar, 2013)

Singh, H., 'Critique of the Mrkšić Trial Chamber (ICTY) Judgment: A Re-evaluation on Whether Soldiers hors de combat are Entitled to Recognition as Victims of Crimes against Humanity', 8 *The Law and Practice of International Courts and Tribunals* 247–296(2009)

Sivakumaran, Sandesh, 'War Crimes before the Special Court for Sierra Leone', 8(4) *Journal of International Criminal Justice* 1009–1034(2010)

Sivakumaran, Sandesh, *The Law of Non-International Armed Conflict* (Oxford University Press, 2014)

Sloan, James, 'Peacekeepers under Fire: Prosecuting the RUF for Attacks against the UN Assistance Mission in Sierra Leone', 9(2) *The Law and Practice of International Courts and Tribunals* 243–293(2010)

Sluiter, Göran, 'Pilz', in Cassese (ed.) *The Oxford Companion to International Criminal Justice* (Oxford University Press, 2009)

Sluiter, Göran, '"Chapeau Elements" of Crimes against Humanity in the Jurisprudence of the UN Ad Hoc Tribunals' in Leila Nadya Sadat (ed.), *Forging a Convention for Crimes against Humanity* (Cambridge University Press, 2011)

Smith, Alison, 'Child Recruitment and the Special Court for Sierra Leone', 2 *Journal of International Criminal Justice* 1141–1153(2004)

Solf, Waldemar A., 'The Status of Combatants in Non International Armed Conflicts under Domestic Law and Transnational Practice', 33 *The American University Law Review* 53–65(1983)

Solis, Gary D., 'Targeted Killing and the Law of Armed Conflict', 60 *Naval War College Review* (2007)

Spagnolo, Andrea, 'The Crime of Attacking Peacekeepers' in Pocar *et al*, *War Crimes and the Conduct of Hostilities, Challenges to Adjudication and Investigation* (Edward Elgar, 2013)

Stewart, James G., 'Rethinking Guantánamo: Unlawful Confinement as Applied in International Criminal Law', 4 *Journal of International Criminal Justice* 12–30(2006)

Tan, Joe, 'Sexual Violence against Children on the Battlefield as a Crime of Using Child Soldiers: Square Pegs in Round Holes and Missed Opportunities in Lubanga', in T.D. Gill *et al* (eds), *Yearbook of International Humanitarian Law 2012* (T.M.C. Asser Press, 2014)

Taylor, Telford, *Nuremberg and Vietnam: An American Tragedy* (Quadrangle Books, 1970)

Triffterer, Otto, *Commentary on the Rome Statute of the International Criminal Court* (C.H. Beck, Hart, Nomos, second edition, 2008)

Turns, David, 'Weapons in the ICRC Study on Customary International Humanitarian Law', 11(2) *Journal of Conflict and Security Law* 201–237(2006)

UK Ministry of Defence, *The Manual of the Law of Armed Conflict* (Oxford University Press, 2004)

United Nations, *The Blue Helmets: A Review of United Nations Peace-Keeping* (United Nations Publication, 1996)

United Nations, *United Nations Peacekeeping Operations: Principles and Guidelines* (2008). Available at: http://pbpu.unlb.org/pbps/library/capstone_doctrine_eng.pdf (last accessed 1 May 2017)

United Nations, *Department of Peacekeeping Operations and Department of Field Support, A New Partnership Agenda, Charting A New Horizon for UN Peacekeeping* (July 2009). Available at: www.un.org/en/peacekeeping/documents/newhorizon.pdf (last accessed 1 May 2017)

United Nations War Crimes Commission, *History of the United Nations War Crimes Commission and the Development of the Laws of War* (London, HMSO, 1948)

Van Schaak, Beth, 'The Definition of Crimes against Humanity: Resolving the Incoherence', 37 *Columbia Journal of Transnational Law* 787(1998–1999)

Van Schaak, Beth, 'Chemical Weapons Use Returns to Syria'. Available at: www.justsecurity.org/32309/chemical-weapons-returns-syria/ (last accessed 1 May 2017)

Verchio, Major Donna Marie, 'Just Say No! The SIrUS Project: Well-Intentioned, but Unnecessary and Superfluous', 51 *The Air Force Law Review* 183(2001)

Vité, Sylvain, 'Between Consolidation and Innovation: The International Criminal Court's Trial Chamber Judgment in the Lubanga Case' in T.D. Gill *et al*, 15 *Yearbook of International Humanitarian Law* 61–85(2014)

Vohrah, Lal Chand *et al*, *Man's Inhumanity to Man: Essays on International Law in Honour of Antonio Cassese* (Kluwer Law International, 2003)

Wagner, Natalie, 'A Critical Assessment of Using Children to Participate Actively in Hostilities in Lubanga', 24(2) *Criminal Law Forum* 145–203(2013)

Walzer, Michael, *Just and Unjust Wars – A Moral Argument with Historical Illustrations* (Basic Books, 2006)

Waschefort, Gus, 'Justice for Child Soldiers? The RUF Trial of the Special Court for Sierra Leone', 1 *International Humanitarian Legal Studies* 189–204(2010)

Watkin, Kenneth, *Warriors Without Rights? Combatants, Unprivileged Belligerents and the Struggle Over Legitimacy*, Program on Humanitarian Policy and Conflict Research, Harvard University, Occasional Paper Series, Volume 2, Winter 2005

Watkin, Kenneth, 'Opportunity Lost: Organised Armed Groups and the ICRC "Direct Participation in Hostilities" Interpretive Guidance', 42 *New York University Journal of International Law & Politics* 641(2010)

Wells, Sarah L., 'Crimes against Child Soldiers in Armed Conflict Situations: Application and Limits of International Humanitarian Law', 12 *Tulane Journal of International and Comparative Law* 287(2004)

Werle, Gerhard, *Principles of International Criminal Law* (TMC Asser Press, 2005)

Wexler, Leila Sadat, 'The Interpretation of the Nuremberg Principles by the French Court of Cassation: From Touvier to Barbie and Back Again', 32 *Columbia Journal of Transnational Law* 289(1994–1995)

Wilmshurst, Elizabeth *et al*, *Perspectives on the ICRC Study on Customary International Humanitarian Law* (Cambridge University Press, 2007)

Woodruff, Paul, 'Justification or Excuse: Saving Soldiers at the Expense of Civilians', *Canadian Journal of Philosophy*, Supp. Volume VIII, 159(1982)

Wuerzner, Carolin, 'Mission Impossible? Bringing Charges for the Crime of Attacking Civilians or Civilian Objects before International Criminal Tribunals', 90(872) *International Review of the Red Cross* 907–930(2008)

Index

For Product Safety Concerns and Information please contact our EU representative GPSR@taylorandfrancis.com
Taylor & Francis Verlag GmbH, Kaufingerstraße 24, 80331 München, Germany

www.ingramcontent.com/pod-product-compliance
Ingram Content Group UK Ltd.
Pitfield, Milton Keynes, MK11 3LW, UK
UKHW011010180926
475701UK00004B/654

* 9 7 8 0 3 6 7 8 7 7 7 7 4 *